Principles of Politics

A Rational Choice Theory Guide to Politics and Social Justice

Modern rational choice and social justice theories allow scholars to develop new understandings of the foundations and general patterns of politics and political behavior. In this book, Joe Oppenheimer enumerates and justifies the empirical and moral generalizations commonly derived from these theories. In developing these arguments, Oppenheimer gives students a foundational basis of both formal theory, and theories of social justice, and their related experimental literatures. He uses empirical findings to evaluate the validity of the claims. This basic survey of the findings of public choice theory for political scientists covers the problems of collective action, institutional structures, citizen well-being and social welfare, regime change, and political leadership. *Principles of Politics* highlights what is universal to all of politics and examines both the empirical problems of political behavior and the normative conundrums of social justice.

Joe Oppenheimer is Emeritus Professor in the Department of Government and Politics at the University of Maryland.

Principles of Politics

A Rational Choice Theory Guide to Politics and Social Justice

JOE OPPENHEIMER
University of Maryland

CAMBRIDGE
UNIVERSITY PRESS

CAMBRIDGE UNIVERSITY PRESS
Cambridge, New York, Melbourne, Madrid, Cape Town,
Singapore, São Paulo, Delhi, Mexico City

Cambridge University Press
32 Avenue of the Americas, New York, NY 10013-2473, USA

www.cambridge.org
Information on this title: www.cambridge.org/9781107601642

© Joe Oppenheimer 2012

First published 2012

Printed in the United States of America

A catalog record for this publication is available from the British Library

Library of Congress Cataloging in Publication Data
Oppenheimer, Joe A.
Principles of politics : a rational choice theory guide to politics and social justice / Joe
Oppenheimer.
   pages cm
Includes bibliographical references and indexes.
ISBN 978-1-107-01488-6
1. Political science.   2. Rational choice theory.   3. Social justice.   I. Title.
JA71.O65   2012
320.01–dc23

                                                                         2011051220

ISBN 978-1-107-01488-6 Hardback
ISBN 978-1-107-60164-2 Paperback

Abstract

People have claimed to understand the empirical and moral principles of politics for thousands of years. These assertions have never escaped contention. This book is about some of the empirical and moral generalizations arrived at with the tools that comprise what might be called the new political science. The book deals with the findings directly. It also explores how one justifies such claims. It reveals how the quality of the justification helps to determine the quality of the claims. The foundations used to develop the arguments, or justifications, are those of rational choice and social justice theories. But one usually needs more than reason to establish (or, for that matter, to disestablish) claims of knowledge about politics. Empirical findings, especially those gleaned from careful laboratory experiments, are introduced to help the reader evaluate the validity of the claims. The principles discussed improve our understanding of concepts such as social welfare, collective action, altruism, distributive justice, group interest, democratic performance, and more. The methods employed help us understand what is universal to all of politics. This volume zeros in on these universals with an eye to both the empirical problems and the normative conundrums of politics.

Contents

Propositions and Corollaries

Throughout, empirical propositions are in **bold**; corrolaries are not. Both are in SMALL CAPS. Normative propositions (in **bold**) and corollaries (not bold) are *italicized*.

AN UNORGANIZED GROUP CANNOT OPTIMALLY SATISFY ITS SHARED OR COLLECTIVE INTERESTS. *page* 27

A GROUP CAN ONLY GET MEMBERS TO CONTRIBUTE TO SOLVE ITS SHARED PROBLEMS BY PROVIDING INCENTIVES INDEPENDENT OF THE PUBLIC GOOD. *page* 27

INDIVIDUALS DON'T HAVE AN INCENTIVE TO GIVE THEIR TRUE VALUATION OF A PUBLIC GOOD. *page* 28

FOR GROUPS OF PEOPLE TO MEET THEIR SHARED NEEDS OVER TIME THEY MUST HAVE THE FREEDOM TO ORGANIZE THEMSELVES POLITICALLY. *page* 28

THE LARGER THE GROUP, THE FURTHER FROM OPTIMAL WILL BE THE AMOUNT OF A PUBLIC GOOD WHICH AN *UNORGANIZED* GROUP WILL SUPPLY ITSELF. *page* 29

THE FURTHER FROM OPTIMAL THE GROUP IS WITHOUT ORGANIZATION, THE GREATER WOULD BE THE POTENTIAL PROFIT IN ORGANIZING THE GROUP TO SATISFY THEIR COMMON INTERESTS OR TO SUPPLY THEM WITH PUBLIC GOODS. *page* 29

POLITICS IS POTENTIALLY MORE PROFITABLE FOR POLITICAL LEADERS IN LARGER GROUPS. *page* 29

POLITICAL COMPETITION WILL BE STIFFER IN LARGER GROUPS. *page* 29

IN MOST COLLECTIVE ACTION PROBLEMS THERE WILL BE A BREAKEVEN POINT, SUCH THAT IF MORE THAN THE BREAKEVEN NUMBER OF PEOPLE CAN

BE ORGANIZED TO GIVE, THEY WILL FIND IT REASONABLE TO GIVE, EVEN
THOUGH THEY HAD A DOMINANT STRATEGY TO NOT GIVE. *page* 31

POLITICAL LEADERS CAN USUALLY SUCCEED IN TURNING A COLLECTIVE
ACTION DILEMMA INTO SOMETHING OF A COLLECTIVE SUCCESS BY ORGAN-
IZING JUST A SUBGROUP OF INDIVIDUALS. *page* 31

WHEN PEOPLE CARE ABOUT THE FUTURE PAYOFFS FROM INTERACTIONS
THAT ARE REPEATED, THERE IS SUBSTANTIALLY GREATER POTENTIAL FOR
COOPERATION IN PROBLEMS OF COLLECTIVE ACTION. *page* 37

PEOPLE WHO ARE TRANSITORY MEMBERS OF GROUPS (SHORT TIMERS)
ARE LESS LIKELY TO BEHAVE COOPERATIVELY TO SOLVE COLLECTIVE
ACTION PROBLEMS. *page* 37

SOMETIMES POLITICAL LEADERS CAN SUCCEED BY TURNING A COLLEC-
TIVE ACTION DILEMMA INTO AN ASSURANCE GAME, AND THEN BY ORGAN-
IZING A SUFFICIENT SUBGROUP, GENERATING A BANDWAGON EFFECT IN
THE GROUP AS A WHOLE. *page* 44

EFFECTIVE POLITICAL LEADERS ENGINEER SITUATIONS TO EXPAND THE
RANGE OVER WHICH A CONTRIBUTION WILL MAKE A DIFFERENCE. *page* 48

EFFECTIVE POLITICAL LEADERS ENCOURAGE INDIVIDUALS TO BELIEVE
THE PROBABILITY THAT THEIR CONTRIBUTION WILL MAKE A BIG DIFFER-
ENCE IS HIGH. *page* 48

INDIVIDUALS HAVE A DISCOUNTED INTEREST IN ACQUIRING INFORMATION
ABOUT POLITICAL AFFAIRS AND WILL, IN GENERAL, REMAIN RATIONALLY
IGNORANT REGARDING POLITICS. *page* 50

THE WEALTHY WILL BE BETTER POLITICALLY INFORMED THAN THE
POOR. THEREFORE, WITHOUT MASS ORGANIZATIONS SUCH AS UNIONS OR
CLASS-BASED PARTIES, THE POOR, MORE OFTEN THAN THE WEALTHY, WILL
MISIDENTIFY THEIR POLITICAL INTERESTS. *page* 51

DEMOCRACIES ARE NOT LIKELY TO HAVE MUCH BETTER FOREIGN POL-
ICIES THAN NON-DEMOCRACIES; THE BENEFITS FROM DEMOCRACY WILL
MAINLY BE IN THEIR IMPROVED DOMESTIC POLICIES. *page* 51

POLITICAL BEHAVIOR BY CITIZENS (ALTHOUGH NOT LEADERS) CAN BE
EXPECTED TO BE SUBSTANTIALLY MORE AMORAL AND IRRESPONSIBLE
THAN THEIR ECONOMIC AND PERSONAL BEHAVIOR. *page* 52

THE GREATER THE COSTS OF ACQUIRING INFORMATION FROM COMPET-
ING SOURCES, THE LARGER WILL BE THE MORAL GAP BETWEEN POLITICAL
AND PERSONAL BEHAVIOR. *page* 52

*If common-pool resources that are vital to life are to be privatized,
then programs are required to ensure the less fortunate economic security
or access to these resources in times of shortages when prices are liable to
rise. page* 55

A SMALL GROUP OF INTENSELY MOTIVATED INDIVIDUALS IS FAR MORE LIKELY TO TAKE ACTION TO ACHIEVE A SHARED GOAL THAN IS A LARGE GROUP OF INDIVIDUALS WHO ARE EACH NOT VERY SERIOUSLY AFFECTED BY THE OUTCOME. *page 56*

TURNOUT WILL BE HIGHER IN ELECTIONS THAT APPEAR TO BE CLOSER AND WHERE THE STAKES ARE LARGER. *page 59*

TURNOUT WILL GO DOWN WHEN VOTING BECOMES MORE INCONVEN-IENT OR MORE COSTLY. *page 59*

WITH SINGLE-PEAKED PREFERENCES IN ONE DIMENSION, THE EQUILIBRIUM OUTCOME OF A MAJORITY RULE, PAIRWISE VOTE WILL BE THE MOST PREFERRED (OR IDEAL) POINT OF THE MEDIAN VOTER. *page 68*

WITH SINGLE-PEAKED PREFERENCES IN ONE DIMENSION, AND PAIRWISE MAJORITY RULE, THE MEDIAN VOTER'S MOST PREFERRED (OR IDEAL) POINT WILL BE THE CORE. *page 69*

THE ALTERNATIVE CLOSER TO THE MEDIAN WILL ALWAYS WIN IN PAIR-WISE MAJORITY RULE. *page 69*

MAJORITY RULE, WHEN ALL VOTERS HAVE SINGLE-PEAKED PREFERENCES, DELIVERS PARETIAN, OR OPTIMAL, RESULTS. *page 70*

IN SIMPLE TWO-PARTY ELECTIONS, CANDIDATES WILL HAVE A STRONG TENDENCY TO ADOPT A POSITION NEAR THAT OF THE MEDIAN VOTER. *page 71*

IN PRIMARIES THERE WILL BE A TENDENCY FOR THE COMPETITORS TO ADOPT POSITIONS NEAR THE MIDDLE OF THE DISTRIBUTION OF THEIR OWN PARTY'S VOTERS. GIVEN CONSISTENCY AND CREDIBILITY REQUIRE-MENTS, THERE MAY BE LIMITED ROOM TO MOVE AWAY FROM THAT POSI-TION TOWARD THAT OF THE MEDIAN VOTER. *page 71*

IF THERE ARE ONLY TWO PARTIES IN AN ELECTION, AND BOTH TAKE AN UNAMBIGUOUS STAND ABOUT THE ISSUES OF THE DAY, THE PARTIES MAY EACH BE REPRESENTED BY A SINGLE POINT IN SOME LARGER (MULTIDIMENSIONAL) SPACE. VOTERS CAN BE EXPECTED TO SUPPORT THE PARTY WITH THE POSITION CLOSEST TO THEM. *page 73*

WHEN THERE IS A BICAMERAL LEGISLATURE AND THE DISTRIBUTION OF VOTERS VARIES BETWEEN THE CHAMBERS OF THE LEGISLATURE, THEN WHICH CHAMBER DECIDES FIRST MAY DETERMINE WHETHER THE STATUS QUO WILL PREVAIL, AS WELL AS WHAT CAN REPLACE IT. *page 76*

INTRODUCING CHECKS AND BALANCES RESTRICTS THE RESPONSIVENESS OF THE SYSTEM TO THE NEEDS, WELFARE, AND PREFERENCES OF THE MEDIAN VOTER. *page 79*

WHEN ISSUES ARE MULTIDIMENSIONAL, MAJORITY RULE CAN LEAD TO RESULTS THAT ARE NOT PARETO OPTIMAL. *page 83*

IN GENERAL, WITH SINGLE-PEAKED PREFERENCES IN MORE THAN ONE
DIMENSION THERE IS NO POINT THAT WILL BE IN EQUILIBRIUM WITH THE
USE OF MAJORITY RULE. *page* 84

IN MULTIDIMENSIONAL SITUATIONS AND USING MAJORITY RULE, PREF-
ERENCES ARE LIKELY TO SUPPORT VOTING CYCLES. *page* 85

IN GENERAL, WITH SINGLE-PEAKED PREFERENCES IN MORE THAN ONE
DIMENSION AND THE USE OF MAJORITY RULE, THERE IS NO POINT THAT
WILL BE IN THE CORE: THE CORE WILL BE EMPTY. *page* 85

WITH A SET OF ALTERNATIVES THAT ARE IN MORE THAN ONE DIMENSION,
MAJORITY RULE CAN LEAD A GROUP TO CHOOSE OUTCOMES THAT ARE
ANYWHERE IN THE ALTERNATIVE SPACE. *page* 86

WITH MAJORITY RULE, ANY SUBOPTIMAL OUTCOME IS LIKELY TO BE
REPLACED BY ONE THAT IS CLOSER TO THE PARETO SET AND, HENCE,
PREFERRED BY ALL. *page* 86

SPECIAL MAJORITY RULES CAN HELP STABILIZE GAINS THAT GROUPS
CAN ACHIEVE IN THE MAKING OF BINDING DECISIONS WITH DEMOCRATIC
RULES. *page* 87

IN GENERAL WHEN THE PLACEMENT OF "BADS" ARE THE SUBJECT OF
COLLECTIVE DECISIONS, PLACEMENT WILL BE FAR FROM THE PHYSICAL
LOCATION OF THE PREDOMINANT CLUSTER OF VOTERS. IF THERE IS NO
SUCH CLUSTER, IT WILL STILL BE PLACED AT OR NEAR THE EDGE OF THE
POSSIBLE SPACE. *page* 89

DEMOCRATIC PROCESSES AMONG PROFESSIONAL POLITICIANS LEAD TO
OUTCOMES IN PREDICTABLE RANGES EVEN IF THEY CANNOT BE SPECIFIED
MORE EXACTLY. WITH WIDE LATITUDE OF ARRANGEMENTS THESE RANGES
TEND TO THE CENTER OF THE DISTRIBUTION OF THE VOTER'S IDEAL POINTS
AND CAN BE EXPECTED TO BE WITHIN THE UNCOVERED SET. *page* 92

WHEN WE FACE EXTERNALITIES, ONLY WHEN A PARETIAN BARGAIN IS IN
EQUILIBRIUM CAN WE EXPECT INDIVIDUAL RATIONAL BEHAVIORAL
OUTCOMES TO GENERATE OPTIMALITY. *page* 102

FACED WITH EXTERNALITIES, GOVERNMENTAL ACTION IS AS LIKELY TO
BE NECESSARY TO ACHIEVE GOOD SOCIAL OUTCOMES AS NOT. *page* 102

IN MOST PUBLIC GOOD SITUATIONS THE SUPPLIER IS A NATURAL
MONOPOLIST. *page* 103

COMPETITION AMONG WOULD-BE SUPPLIERS OF PUBLIC GOODS IS
ABOUT REPLACEMENT RATHER THAN MARKET SHARE. *page* 103

*The first requirement of any decent political system is to ensure political
succession not be contested in a manner that jeopardizes the welfare of the
general population. page* 103

NON-DEMOCRATIC GOVERNMENT BY SELF-INTERESTED RULERS CAN LEAD TO A PROSPEROUS CITIZENRY. FOR CIVILIZATION TO THRIVE, DEMOCRACY IS NOT NECESSARY BUT GOVERNMENT MUST HAVE AN INCENTIVE FOR THE POPULATION TO THRIVE. *page* 104

INCREASED COSTS OF A NON-DEMOCRATIC RULER'S COALITION INCREASES THE RULER'S RAPACIOUSNESS AND HURTS THE WELL-BEING OF THE CITIZENS. *page* 105

THE LARGER THE DEMOCRATIC (MAJORITARIAN) COALITION THAT RULES, THE MORE THEIR INCENTIVES WILL COINCIDE WITH THOSE OF THE CITIZENRY. *page* 105

BETTER OUTCOMES FOR BENEFICIARIES REQUIRE THAT THEIR INTERESTS IMPACT THE REWARD STREAM OF AGENTS. *page* 108

INSTITUTIONAL DESIGN TO INCREASE COMMITMENT TO POLICY DECISIONS IMPLIES A DECREASE IN POLITICAL RESPONSIVENESS. *page* 109

DEMOCRACY IS EASIER TO ACHIEVE FROM A POLITICAL STRUGGLE INVOLVING REGIME CHANGE WHEN CAPITAL IS MOBILE AND THE SOCIETY IS RELATIVELY EGALITARIAN. *page* 110

WHEN INDIVIDUALS HAVE RIGHTS AND WHEN THEIR BEHAVIOR IS OF GREATER IMPORTANCE TO OTHERS THAN TO THEMSELVES, AND THEIR PREFERENCES ARE IN CONFLICT, PARETO OPTIMALITY MAY BE SACRIFICED. *page* 115

WHEN THE GOVERNMENTAL BOUNDARIES DON'T MATCH THE BOUNDARIES OF THE BENEFIT GROUP FOR THE PUBLIC GOODS BEING SUPPLIED, ONE CAN EXPECT A PARETO SUBOPTIMAL OUTCOME. *page* 118

ALLOWING SUBGROUPS OF BENEFICIARIES TO SET UP A LOCAL AUTHORITY TO IMPROVE THE DELIVERY OF PUBLIC GOODS FOR THEMSELVES WILL USUALLY HAVE REDISTRIBUTIVE CONSEQUENCES THAT CONFLICT WITH NOTIONS OF FAIRNESS. *page* 119

COMPULSORY VOTING LEADS TO LESS POLARIZATION OF PLATFORMS. *page* 121

Compulsory voting leads to platforms that, as a set, better reflect the values of the population as a whole. page 121

Any acceptable conception of social well-being requires that individuals' welfare be comparable. page 129

No one, in general, is in a better position than the individual to gain direct knowledge of what is good for herself based on observation, discussion, consultation, and inward reflection. *page* 132

In a democracy the social good is inextricably wound up with the well-being of the citizenry. *page* 132

Individual welfare is given an implicit moral status in democracies: it is good. page 133

WITHOUT INTERPERSONAL COMPARISONS, WE WILL BE UNABLE TO DO MORE THAN SEEK PARETO OPTIMALITY WHEN DECIDING WHAT IS BETTER FOR THE GROUP. *page 137*

WHERE EACH VOTER IS FREE TO PROPOSE NEW ALTERNATIVES, PURELY DISTRIBUTIVE ISSUES CYCLE IF THE JUDGMENTS ARE BASED ON SIMPLE SELF-INTEREST. *page 142*

EFFECTIVE VOTE-TRADING REQUIRES AN UNDERLYING CYCLIC PREFERENCE PATTERN. *page 142*

POLITICAL OUTCOMES ARE NOT EXPLICABLE BY THE PREFERENCES OF THE VOTERS AND THE VOTING RULES ALONE. RATHER EXPLANATION REQUIRES CONSIDERATION OF THE STRATEGIES VOTERS CHOOSE, ALONG WITH THE RULES OF THE POLITICAL INSTITUTIONS THAT GOVERN THE AGENDA. *page 142*

THE CHOICE OF VOTING RULES WILL MAKE A SUBSTANTIAL DIFFERENCE IN THE QUALITY, RESPONSIVENESS, AND STABILITY OF THE OUTCOMES THAT THE GROUP CHOOSES. *page 148*

PEOPLE WANT A FLOOR OF SUPPORT SO ALL MAY BE ABLE TO MEET THEIR BASIC NEEDS. *page 157*

DEMOCRATIC GOVERNMENTS ARE IN PART LEGITIMATED BY MEETING THEIR CUSTODIAL OBLIGATIONS TO THEIR CITIZENS. *page 158*

Democratic governments have an obligation to ensure conditions are met so the basic needs of their citizenry can be satisfied. page 158

Tables

Figures

Sidebars

Definitions

Preface

Politics is the subject of this volume. We can think of politics as those activities and behaviors associated with a group reaching "collective decisions" and with individuals undertaking "collective actions." The true origin of politics may never be established. Some might believe it comes from our having fallen from grace by eating the forbidden fruit in the Garden of Eden. My perspective leads to more empirical responses. Politics arises because groups of people have to do things together to achieve shared goals such as building a bridge or, under some circumstances, even survival. There are things that we cannot achieve when we remain "unorganized." This is especially so when groups of individuals share a desire for something costly that they would accomplish as a group. Examples abound but include such things as roads, environmental protection, and law and order. In the social sciences these are known as "public goods."

To accomplish the objectives of securing public goods, leaders are selected and rewarded, taxes are collected, and political competition arises. Often, however, these are the very activities that get in the way and actually *prevent* groups from getting things done in their own interest. This volume explains why these sorts of contradictions occur: why politics is necessary, but so often dysfunctional. Indeed, politics is often so nasty that some people become anarchists and argue that politics can't possibly be justified by the welfare needs of the group members.

For most of recorded history it was held that citizens were to support the welfare of the rulers. In this book such an ethical justification of politics and its hierarchies is reversed (as it has been by most political theorists since Thomas Hobbes' *Leviathan*, 1651). Democracies are predicated on the notion that the political is justified by the welfare of the citizens. This is asserted and enshrined in the Declaration of Independence. It claims that "all men are created equal, that they are endowed by their Creator with certain unalienable rights, that among these are life, liberty and the pursuit of happiness." Then politics, or more specifically government, is asserted to be related to these rights, which include happiness: "That to secure these rights, governments are instituted among men, deriving their just powers from the consent of the governed."

One concern of this volume is to identify and explain the empirical and normative principles implied by this simple perspective on politics. By themselves, such normative principles aren't a call to action. In medicine, it is not enough to say we want people to be healthy. We must understand disease. To control flooding rivers, we must understand hydraulics. To design political institutions that support the welfare of individuals, we must understand how individuals behave and how institutions work: we must understand the patterns that are inherent in politics. So the second, and indeed, primary, aim of this book is to give the reader an understanding of, and that means an explanation for, the deep patterns of politics. To illustrate, these include the universal emergence of monopolistic governments, the omnipresent wealth of political leaders, and the difficulty of holding political leaders accountable including.

To understand the patterns of politics in a group, we build on understanding the behavior of individuals in the group.[1] Many of the modern explanations of the twists and turns that make up the purposive behavior of individuals are premised on a relatively intuitive idea: When people choose, their choices reflect their values and their constraints. Leverage over this behavior is often obtained through the logic of rational choice theory. It is perhaps counterintuitive that such a simple starting point can shine a powerful light on our understanding of the behaviors of governments, political organizations, and individuals. But the reader will discover it is so.

Indeed, the findings based on these theories are sufficiently broad to be of concern to many politically active citizens of the world. Although the main audience for this book is advanced undergraduates and graduate students of political science and political economy, hopefully the explanations are sufficiently clear to be of interest to the politically engaged citizen. Here I present the field's major substantive conclusions, with some of their important and controversial implications. I also touch

---

[1] This presumption is often called "methodological individualism."

upon some of the research frontiers and transmit a feel for the logic of the arguments. Since the theoretical arguments are often mathematical, and I do not wish the formalisms to get in the way of the substance, when they are needed, I put much of those (simplified) arguments in "sidebars" and present the arguments less technically in the main text.[2]

Not all of the foundations of this "new" political science are recent. Rational choice theory has been around for a long time (certainly since Adam Smith's eighteenth-century foray onto the philosophical stage). But until recently, mainly economists used the theory. Perhaps the nineteenth-century division of the social sciences into their modern Anglo-Saxon "departmental" identities led to this compartmentalization. Economists focused narrowly on markets, and political scientists on governments. Over the decades, the disciplines grew apart, but shortly before World War II economists arrived at theoretical conclusions that once again made the partial fusion of the fields somewhat possible.[3]

But the major expansion of the theory to cover political patterns grew out of the post-WWII effort of a few economists to cover nonmarket events. Their models ran into some difficulties and research to understand the problems helped spawn a new branch of inquiry: experimental economics. The rich crop we are currently reaping was sown by a few major characters, most of whom established a number of what are now standard subdisciplines within economics and the social sciences. The subfields include public finance (and the theory of public goods developed by Paul Samuelson, Economics Nobel laureate in 1970); game theory (begun by John von Neumann, but given a radical twist by John Nash, Economics Nobel laureate in 1994); experimental economics (begun by Vernon Smith, who was the Economics Laureate in 2002, and Charles Plott); social choice theory (invented almost whole cloth by Kenneth Arrow, who was the Economics Nobel laureate in 1972, and Duncan Black); and public choice theory (Mancur Olson, James Buchanan, who was the Economics Nobel laureate in 1986, Anthony Downs, and Gordon Tullock).

---

[2] In the Introduction I discuss why the justification of one's conclusions is important. This "method" of argument is one of the main elements in the powerful growth of claimed knowledge. How this "works" to expand knowledge is one of the main subjects of the Introduction.

[3] Some of the earliest modern forays into political studies were made by Smithies (1929) and Hotelling (1941). They noted that rational choice theory could explain aspects of political competition. They saw politicians as picking a point in political space to attract voters much as shop owners choose to place a store in a town to pick up customers. Then von Neumann (1944) developed a theory (of "games") to explain, among other things, coalition formation and strategic behavior – a topic of general concern to political scientists.

Their insights, founded on a view of choice based on selfish calculation, led to empirical anomalies. As such, researchers became concerned with how individuals' feelings toward others (loyalty, fairness, doing the right thing) might be balanced with economists' standard fare: the assumption of self-interest. Such an expansion meant that some of the conclusions needed to take into account what individuals thought to be fair, right, and just. Thus, some other major threads of the new political economy butt up against fields such as philosophy. There, theories of fairness and justice developed by John Rawls, Amartya Sen (Economics Nobel laureate in 1998), and others added immeasurably to the mix. Psychologists also got involved by considering how well rational choice theory fit into the observations they had made regarding personal choices. Notions both of bounded rationality developed by Herbert Simon (a political scientist and Economics Nobel laureate in 1978) and of prospect theory developed by Daniel Kahneman (Economics Nobel laureate, 2002) and his research partner, Amos Tversky (both psychologists) also added fundamentally to our understandings. Since many of the choices we make involve gambles and risk, we are enriched by the fundamental insights of those who worked on probability theory over the last few hundred years: individuals such as von Neumann and Thomas Bayes (the eighteenth-century English mathematician and Presbyterian minister).[4] Finally, political scientists have also worked on these threads to weave a wide tapestry covering parts of all the traditional subfields of political science (for examples, see Riker, 1962 and 1982; Boix, 2003; Fearon, 1995 and 1998; Tsebelis, 2002; Lohmann, 1994 and 2000; Weingast, 1997; Miller and Hammond, 1990; Ostrom (Economics Nobel laureate in 2009), 1990 and 1998; Shepsle and Bonchek, 1997 – many of whose contributions will be discussed in this volume).

These multiple strands lead to a completely new, theoretically coherent, empirically powerful approach to the analysis of political events. The analysis is of relevance to anyone trying to make sense of politics: journalists, campaign advisors and other political strategists, citizens, and academicians. With these theoretical developments political science has been set on a faster track: one in which the field is regularly finding new discoveries and generalities relevant to old puzzles.

---

[4] Bayes had the bright idea that people update their beliefs on the basis of evidence, and hence that the fit of one's beliefs with the "world" is likely to improve.

Overview of the Book

Claims of new knowledge (both empirical and moral) regarding politics have been made over the millennia. The new era finds not only that the pace has picked up, but also that the consensus on research methods has at least partially resolved some of the old contentious debates. Progress has been made by requiring both logical justification for one's theoretical conclusions or propositions, and careful testing of the conclusions with data from experiments and historical (or field) events and data.

The book is organized around the new conjectures and law-like propositions that have been made about politics and justified on the basis of the theories of rational choice and social justice. These assertions are collected together and tabulated in a table of propositions and corollaries. These propositions are of three sorts, and are differentiated by their type style in the text. All of them are offset in the text, with the major empirical claims in BOLD SMALL CAPS. Secondary implications or corollaries of these principles are distinguished by being shown in SMALL CAPS but not bold. The generalizations that are normative and concern traditional topics of political philosophy are distinguished by being shown in ***bold italics*** with the derivative claims being displayed in *italics* but not in bold.

Although I make an effort to distinguish between those claims that have a normative basis and those that are empirical, the membrane is not impermeable. Some of the universal claims that may appear to be normative have to do with conjectures of universal *empirical* characteristics of moral judgments. Such claims, though, with moral implications, are *not* listed as normative conjectures. So to cite an example, let us say that we are considering a definition of fairness and someone says, "to understand what is fair, you must reason impartially." That is a normative claim (there can be other suggested bases for arriving at a fair choice). But if, when reasoning impartially, all individuals come to a particular conclusion, that conclusion is not normative. It would, however, reflect conditional normative weight from the asserted relation of fairness and impartial reasoning.

The book is divided into four parts and a substantive Introduction. Although experimental findings are discussed somewhat throughout, in a few chapters a separate section discusses evidence and questions that have been raised about the central propositions in the chapter and identifies some of the research frontiers that these imply. These sections are referred to as Research Frontiers. Suggestions for further reading are included at the end of each part.

So that the reader can understand the basis for the assertions, both evidence and reasoning are discussed. More technical aspects of how the claims are justified is usually limited but sometimes sketched in sidebars. Although I discuss the quality of the justifications and claims, the reader should keep in mind (with due deference to Descartes) that reason is insufficient grounds for the establishment or, except by contradiction, the disestablishment, of claims of knowledge. Although our understanding of how to judge theories, conjectures, and knowledge is still incomplete, we humans have learned a great deal about how best to establish, and falsify, claims of knowledge.

Even if they remain incomplete, current standards of epistemology help us understand what are to count as claims of knowledge and as candidates for universal principles. These standards also yield guidelines for empirical methods, which, in conjunction with reason, are required to establish our understanding of scientific principles, whether of motion, energy, mass, economics, or politics. Scientific methods have also been useful in improving our understanding of a very wide range of human behavior and institutions: markets, altruism, other-regardingness, distributive justice, moral points of view, and the like. These methods can thus help us understand what if anything is universal in the way of behavior and principles. The reader will find the volume is oriented around the following questions: What practical questions can we now find answers for? How do we justify our conclusions?

The Introduction has two goals, both of which are fundamental: First, it establishes a common understanding for readers as to what is meant by knowledge and similar methodological matters; and second, it sets up the basic elements of the theory of rational choice. The volume then is organized in terms of the substance of politics. The book is meant to be a complete guide to neither the understanding of rational choice theory nor to politics. Rather, I introduce elements of the theory of rational choice as needed to explain major findings of regularities in politics.

Part I considers how the individual decides whether or not to engage in collective action and the implications of these findings. The implications of the theory of collective action will branch off into topics such as voter behavior and information acquisition by the citizenry of democracies, as well as some policy and institutional design issues.

But collective action is often premised on the collective, or group, coming to a decision or choice for itself. Group decision making becomes the subject of Part II and is again central to Part IV. In Part II we pick up the notion, introduced by Hotelling and Smithies (see footnote 3 of the Preface) that in democracies much political decision making is determined by political competition. We use their insights to think of the arena of political competition as a "space." So doing helps us form expectations about collective choice. Some of these implications inform us regarding institutional design. Others force us to consider problems of achieving the goals of collective choice. Presumably the goals of politics (if not politicians) include something like the satisfying of citizens' needs. The implications of spatial models for these questions are the topic of Part II. But the topic is larger than spatial models can accommodate and are raised again in Part IV of the volume.

How politics and the structures of governments both help and hinder us in the achievement of getting what we want is much of what we consider in Part III. There we consider why political "deals" and "bargains" often take the form they do and how these can predictably affect the stability of governments, political systems, and regimes.

All this analysis is related to satisfying the collective desires of citizens. It is one thing to talk of the needs of individuals, but how are we to understand collective needs and desires? We explore these questions in Part IV. Only after coming to grips with the problem of aggregating individual choices and needs can we fully explore the relation between institutional design and the possibility of satisfying those needs. Once we are in the throes of such questions as "what constitutes the needs of the people," we must consider the problem of social welfare more fully. Here we examine the more general topic of social choice and its relationship to social welfare.

Such concerns regarding what we want from government place us in the discourse of political philosophy. They require us to examine the substantive notions behind social welfare. Are there general goals of democracies? And if there are, how can specific institutional arrangements affect the achievement of social goals? These are the sorts of problems we approach with some of the major implications of the theory for democratic governance. The perspective allows us to consider whether different democratic structures generate differences in the quality of performance of democratic regimes.

Acknowledgments

My wife, Bonnie, encouraged me to undertake this project when I was going to let it go. She has been an invaluable supporter and partner. Others have also been exceptionally helpful in the design and development of this volume. Keith Dougherty gave me detailed suggestions after reading the manuscript for Cambridge. He was not alone: I had a wonderful bevy of anonymous evaluators of the manuscript. These reviewers made many useful suggestions. Some of my faculty colleagues at the University of Maryland were also very helpful in commenting on early drafts of one or more chapters. These include Karol Soltan, Piotr Swistak, Christopher Morris, and Jóhanna Birnir. The many students at the University of Maryland who helped me formulate answers to their questions were also indispensable. At least one of those must be singled out for his helpful suggestions regarding parts of the manuscript: Cyrus Aghamolla. Jackie Coolidge and Habib Gharib made numerous suggestions and corrections to improve the arguments and exposition of the manuscript. Finally, I must thank Norman Frohlich, whom I had always hoped would work as a full coauthor on this manuscript. He chose to sit this one out, although he helped draft one chapter and gave me comments on some other sections. He has been a great intellectual partner for years, and I would not have been able to reach clarity on many of these questions without him.

Introduction: Politics, Universals, Knowledge Claims, and Methods

Presumably you are reading this book to gain insight into politics. Politics means different things to different people. For some it is an electoral fight for city hall. For others it is the legislative struggle to change a law. In non-democratic countries it may be the struggle of an autocrat to maintain power, or of citizens to organize a rebellion. Still others may view it as the bureaucratic hassle of getting a business license. For our purposes these are all politics. Politics consists of behavior undertaken either to make centralized decisions for a group, or to secure interests shared by members of a group.

This book makes claims – big claims – about enduring patterns to be found in politics. Hopefully, these patterns will help you understand why certain things happen, and even how you can make some things happen. The book cannot give us a complete understanding of politics: nothing holistic. But we can explain why certain problems, certain patterns, occur over and over again. Barring a few insights, these are not things I have discovered. Rather, a substantial group of scholars has expanded the theories of rational choice to explain many aspects of politics. They, along with a skilled, and often skeptical, bunch of others have tested these conjectures. In this volume, I present generalizations about politics that are justified by a chain of reasoning. Most have also survived some serious testing. These generalizations amount to claims of knowledge regarding both empirical and normative political questions. Knowledge claims have been made by other political theorists over the millennia, never without contention. Contention continues. So before we begin our exploration of these knowledge claims, let us consider the ground rules.

You will want to know how to evaluate the assertions: how to distinguish wheat from chaff. How *does* one establish or falsify a claim of knowledge – about politics, or anything else? How do our methods of inquiry affect both the quality and the enduring survival of what we claim to know? Lest you consider these idle concerns, notice that this book is being written after the fruits of science have cured diseases, wired every home, recorded all entertainment, and made remote control warfare a thing of joysticks forever. It is also at a time when many Americans reject the scientific findings of evolution and push for the teaching of intelligent design in our schools. Such attacks on science make the task of reasserting and following justified methods to ensure the quality of our judgements a matter that is related to the actual survival of civilization as we know it.[1]

Reason alone is insufficient for deciding disputes regarding empirical truths. Reason yields insufficient grounds to adjudicate empirical claims unless it lets one demonstrate logical error, and hence show that an argument said to justify a conclusion just doesn't. For eons, philosophers felt that they could use reason to understand and identify the truth of both normative and empirical claims. So in his *History of Animals*, Aristotle claimed that women had fewer teeth than men, and he and others argued that it could be shown that slavery was just. Universal claims have been made in these ways, and such claims are still studied by weary scholars. But the disutility and lack of viability of such claims usually ensure that they are museum pieces: not useful bits of knowledge. Empirical methods, *in conjunction with reason*, have, on the other hand, helped us understand such principles as those of motion, energy, mass, evolution, and justice.

Empirical methods in the form of experimental and statistical methods, are widely understood in both the academy and the lay public, and won't be belabored by me. What is less widely appreciated outside the "sciences" is the role of logic in the processes and the accumulation of assertions of scientific knowledge. And to understand that, it is useful to have a short segue to clarify "what is knowledge."

---

[1] But do not read into this a presumption that we can establish a "method' of science and corroboration. Such a recipe for obtaining sure knowledge is beyond us. At best we can accept some aspects of methods as helpful and reject others as dysfunctional. The search for these methods is the continuing holy grail of the philosophy of science: see the volume edited by Nola and Sankey (2000), or Giere (1988) for illustrative overviews.

KNOWLEDGE

What *is* knowledge? The reader may roll her eyes at this point. Why step into such

> Definition – *Knowledge:* Justified, true belief.

a quagmire as a prelude to understanding politics? After all, isn't this just another irresolvable, difficult question? Why not let philosophers battle this one out? Surprisingly, philosophers don't battle over this; there is considerable consensus in philosophical quarters as to knowledge's basic properties.[2] And as we shall see, understanding what knowledge *is* helps us know what we are looking for as we search for knowledge about politics. It helps us comprehend why the foundations of rational choice theory have been stipulated so carefully as to have become quite complex. It will illuminate why such complexities are needed to understand what politics *is* and how it works.

Let's dive in. What does it mean to make a knowledge claim? For example, what does it mean to say, "I know my hat is on the kitchen table"? Philosophers and others who have examined this agree that if I assert that "I *know* my hat is on the kitchen table," then for it to be a true assertion, my assertion must have three properties.

First, I must *believe* that "my hat is on the kitchen table." If I don't believe it, how could I assert that I *know* it? For example, if I actually believed the hat to be in the hall closet but asserted, "I know my hat is on the kitchen table," we wouldn't say that my assertion ("I know my hat is on the kitchen table") was true, even though the factual component regarding the whereabouts of my hat may (or may not) be accurate. I must believe what I assert to know.

Second, what I believe must be *true*. Assume I do *believe* the hat *is* on the kitchen table. What if it is actually in the closet? Certainly we wouldn't want to say that "I know my hat is on the kitchen table" is true.[3] I may believe it, but I wouldn't know it.

---

[2] A quick check of this in Wikipedia or at the Stanford Encyclopedia of Philosophy, http://plato.stanford.edu/, should convince the skeptic and provide some understanding of the range of debate on the subject.

[3] Implicit in my illustration is an acceptance of a popular theory of "truth:" the correspondence theory of truth. Theories of truth are given an accessible treatment in White (1970). And the two major theories, Correspondence and Coherence, are well described in White (1967) and Prior (1970) respectively. But standard accounts can also be easily found at http://plato.stanford.edu, the major online philosophy encyclopedia. In correspondence theory, the truth of a statement ("My hat is on the table,") is dependent upon the conditions in the real world: is my hat *really* on the table? If so, then the statement is true: it corresponds with the real world. If not, *tant pis*. Although this is the "standard" theory, many of our

And finally, my belief must be *justified*. For example, imagine that I believe it is on the table but my belief stems from a message in a computer game that said, "Your hat is on the kitchen table." If this were the basis for my belief, you might object "a computer game message is not a viable justification for the empirical belief concerning the placement of your hat." Even if the hat were to end up being on the kitchen table, we wouldn't endorse that I *knew* it if the only basis I had for my claim was the message. In other words: true belief is insufficient to claim knowledge. The quality or strength of the justification is an essential element.

How then do we justify claims of knowledge? To say a claim is justified means that some argument has been put forward to justify the claim. Justification is comprised of the grounds we use to make our claim. We can get this via an argument (or deduction), as contrasted with justification via observation (or induction). Justification via an argument requires that some premises *imply* the conclusions (i.e., the thing we claim we know).

For such a justification to be valid, we would want to know two things about the premises. First, are they true? And second, does the claim follow as a valid conclusion from the premises (is the reasoning correct?). In other words, if the premises were true, the conclusion would *have to be*. In part, that is what was wrong with the assertion based on the message received from the computer game. Of course, the message could have said that my hat was on the kitchen table, but that certainly wouldn't ensure that my hat would be there! If the argument justifies the conclusion, then *if* the premises are true, the conclusion *must* be. Such a relationship between one's claim and its justification a logical one: it is the relationship of logical deduction.[4] Let us examine why these two elements are important, and yet, why both of these aspects of justification raise problems.

---

claims of knowledge are not backed by simple observations of the real world and often they go beyond what we can directly observe (think of such cases as string theory, quantum mechanics, and preferences). Partly driven by the lack of direct observation, alternative theories of truth have flourished. The major alternative is known as the "coherence" theory of truth. It insists that our knowledge claims "fit" together to make or maintain a coherent pattern or fabric. Disputes then entail as to what precisely is to be the role of the existing claims regarding the empirical world in the determination of "truth" regarding new claims (see White, 1967). But virtually all conceptions of the empirical science use some conception of the "correspondence" theory as part of their methodology. Just as tires must grip the road, the claims of science must grip reality (Nola, 2004).

[4] That would make our claim the conclusion of a valid argument. When based on true premises such an argument is referred to as "sound."

The Status of the Premises: Truth

Consider the truth of the premises. In most scientific arguments the premises include vast generalizations about, for example, motion, or cells, or carbon molecules. Such claims are both necessary and problematic: the generalizations cover many observations, but we can't be sure they hold for the entire hypothesized class. In other words, they are always questionable. Further, some generalizations are known to be only approximations of the realities that we observe. Take for example, a Newtonian model that allows us to predict a ball's velocity at the end of a roll on an inclined plane. It usually yields wrong predictions! Unaccounted-for factors are said to cause the predictions to be inaccurate. "Bridge principles," such as those dealing with air resistance and friction, are added to explain the deviation from the predicted results. More to the point, generalizations are often simplifications: fruitful in helping to develop theory but only approximations. "Firms attempt to maximize profits" is a good example from economics. In much of what follows, the major premises of rational choice theory that are employed are also mere approximations. Sometimes we might settle for such approximations as useful for the logical inferences they permit. Other times, we will find that small tinkering will generate more useful inferences and models.

Ideally, the premises in arguments are true: the conclusions of sound arguments are then knowledge. But in reality, we can rarely be sure of the truth of the premises. The conclusions, as in all science, aren't strictly knowledge, but rather only good candidates for knowledge, or "knowledge claims."[5] Although in the end, scientific progress and claims rest on judgments rather than absolutes, this is the best we can do. To understand why the methods are still powerful, we need to examine the other aspect of justification: the relation between an argument and its conclusions. Such an examination helps illuminate why this style and method of argument have led to progress in so many of the empirical sciences, including, recently, political science.

The Relationship of the Premises to the Knowledge Claim: Logical Inference

Now let's explore that second property, justified: if the premises are true, the conclusion must be. In other words, logic. Logic requires a particular

---

[5] Although Karl Popper (1959) didn't use the term, he might recognize these as conjectures that have survived repeated tests of falsification.

structure to an argument: for one, it sets down rules as to what you can conclude from any starting point. Most specifically, in a logical argument, if you start with some true point, then by following the rules, all that you can arrive at are other truths. In other words, providing you begin with truthful statements, logic preserves the truth all the way to the conclusion (see Sidebar 1).[6] Here, then, is some of the power that one gets from logic. Let's say you begin with what you believe to be truthful premises, and a logical argument leads to some "testable" conclusion.

As an example, say you are a "strong believer" in the value of the messages from the computer game. You presume that every prediction of the messages from the computer is true. This logically implies that you presume that the message that predicted that my hat was on the kitchen table was true. Now we look in the kitchen, and the hat isn't on the table. Given the power of logic, there was something wrong with at least one of the premises. Indeed both are false: the message's prediction was wrong *and by virtue of the logical link between those premises (and given the facts)* the game messages are NOT always right. Logic gave us the power to construct an *indirect* test of the premises. So logic enables one to construct these tests and allows us to see the relation between theory and test. Indeed, this simple property of logic lies behind the construction of all scientific tests: one tests a conjecture by seeing if something that it logically requires is true. If that is not true, the conjecture must be false.

Theories, in the sciences, are premises coupled to logically related conclusions (usually referred to as conjectures[7] or hypotheses). These conclusions are often appended to some other premises to allow application of the theory to an empirical problem. In this fashion, scientists may be said to expand the theory by developing a model of an empirical problem. This development of "models" is a particularly useful move: it increases the range of indirect tests of the theory.[8] If the model and its tests are properly constructed, and the test is negative, something must be wrong with one or more of the premises.

---

[6] Indeed, logic is *the* set of rules that preserves truth in argument (providing that truth is two-valued). Although mathematics is not the same as logic, there are sufficient family resemblances and ties so that this property is maintained in mathematical arguments.

[7] A conjecture would be a testable generalization.

[8] One can't develop an application of a theory to a new circumstance without the use of auxiliary hypotheses (i.e., regarding contextual changes). Then, the indirect tests are not of the theory alone, but also of these auxiliary hypotheses. (See Hempel, 1965 or Lambert and Brittan, 1970 for a good introductory account of some of these aspects of theory's role in the pursuit of knowledge.)

Sidebar 1 – On the Power of Deduction

An argument has a conclusion, or set of conclusions, that are *justified* by a set of premises. What does this mean? It means if the argument is correct, the conclusions follow from the premises. In other words, if the premises are true, the conclusions MUST be true. Or, if the conclusions prove to be false, then there was something wrong in the premises. But how do we ensure that we have such a relationship?

In the relationship that we are seeking, the deductive argument needs to be correct – or as it is called, valid. This lets us know that *if* the conclusions are false then the premises must be. For example, imagine that I am having an argument with my neighbor John. I claim his dog kept me up by barking; he denies it:

"I saw you come in with your dog last night! You brought him into your apartment – right next to mine. About 10 o'clock the dog started barking and it kept me up all night."

John responds, "My dog can't bark."

"Nonsense," I respond, "all dogs can bark."

Have I established my conclusion that his dog kept me up? My premises could be wrong: John might not have a dog (but he admits to having one); his dog might not have been the one who came in (but John doesn't dispute that). But the notion that "all dogs can bark" is being disputed. Indeed, John's next line could be:

"My dog is a basenji dog, a breed also known as the barkless dog."

That would sink my argument. Knowing that the conclusion was false, he actually shows me why that might have been: one of the premises was a loser – not all dogs can bark. Indeed, his can't.

But unfortunately, my argument was faulty in other ways. It was not quite deductive: I began with premises including: 1) all dogs can bark; 2) John, you have a dog; 3) barks came from your apartment and your dog was home; and concluded 3) your dog barked. But other dogs could have barked, even in his apartment. For example, John's girlfriend might have arrived with a second dog, and hers might have been the dog that barked. In other words, the conclusions don't follow from the premises.

Note now that both things had to work: the conclusions must follow from the premises, and the premises must be true.

But the real power of the deductive argument comes from the case where the premises *do* imply the conclusions and were thought to be true (I believed all dogs can bark) and the conclusion proves false. For then I learn something I didn't know before: I have to revive my premises. In other words, our deduction helps us test our premises.

However, this is a simplification. If premises can't be known to be true (and sometimes turn out quite false), the description above has to be more flexible. Judgement enters in.

One might wonder, if the premises are not true, what is to be gained by generating truth-preserving arguments? From false premises, we can't ensure anything about the truth of our conclusions. And then the conjectures remain just that, and our knowledge really must be understood to be conjectures: claims of knowledge which are well, but not perfectly, justified (see Maxwell, 1972).

Theoretical science, along with its procedures and methods, generates two great benefits. First, the theoretical structure and logic facilitate correctable predictions, and the discovered errors generate questioning that improves our claims of knowledge. These two classes of benefits are quite distinct, but both tie to correctability.

Improving Knowledge Claims

Knowledge claims are all we can ever have from science: knowledge is beyond our grasp. For who really knows when our theoretical scheme will be overturned by a better one that helps account for the anomalies we have had to put aside? But like knowledge, knowledge claims require justification. The criteria of justification might be made a bit more forgiving, but needn't be substantially different if when we say "I *know*," we understand that "I claim to know." A claim to knowledge may not be required to be true, but it must be thought to be true, and still needs justification (Popper, 1959). But then what is to be gained by this shift?

Using derived conjectures that are believed to be true to examine the world, leads to a recipe for weeding out false conjectures and a continual reexamination of our premises. Testing the inferences of our theories and following the clues spurs us to improve the surviving remnants. It helps lead to a growth in both the reliability and the breadth of knowledge claims. In this volume, I develop conjectures of interest about political events justified by the core assumptions of rational choice theory. By having the conclusions "follow" from the premises, the arguments can help us both understand and explain how the conjectured events come about.

To the extent that we have doubts about the status of the premises, the explanations become more conjectural, and corrigibility is again underscored. But this point of view changes our perspective regarding the benefits of logic. Rather than logic being a simple tool for justification, it becomes an instrument in the task of discovery. By developing inferences from core conjectures to new applications, one uncovers possibilities for both new errors, as well as for new extensions of knowledge claims. A theory is no longer a static "argument" but rather a developing and improvable approach to understanding the problems of interest to us.

As pointed out above, the core premises of all theories are quite generalized statements. Imperialistically, research scientists advance arguments by projecting them onto the empirical puzzles they see: "the solar system is a 'Newtonian system;'" "collective action problems are 'prisoner dilemma games;'[9]" and the like. Some of these are better fits than others. But the dialectic that ensues leads to long-term refinements in our understanding of the targets (the solar system and the collective action problems) as well as the theories (our understanding of gravity, and our understanding of rational choice). Hemmed in, at least partially, by our insistence on both greater accuracy in predictions, and by a "more detailed understanding of reality," we work dialectically, back and forth, between improving the theories, and expanding their reach.

In what follows we explore the applications of rational choice theory (see page 14) to political behavior and political questions. In doing so, we might at times bemoan the inaccuracy of the assumptions. This will lead us in the two directions indicated: on the one hand, I detail some of the successes in model development, and on the other, I highlight the research agenda implied by the failings of the predictions that have been found. Hopefully, I will be whetting the appetites of both those who wish to understand politics better, and those who wish to search for better explanations: more accurate knowledge claims.

UNIVERSALS, SYNERGY, AND CONTEXT

What sorts of premises are needed to make for an interesting argument about politics? Premises that are useful in scientific explanations are a collection of generalizations, or universalized claims (e.g., water boils at 100°C; social welfare can't just be the aggregation of separable individual welfare – see Chapter 8) and then some contextual premises that allow one to tie a class of instances to the generalization.

Universality is often misunderstood by social scientists and political theorists. The misunderstanding is helped along by two distinct meanings of universal. First, we think of "universal" as being an "accidental

---

[9] A subject discussed in Chapters 1 and 2.

generalization." For example, a universal social observation could mean "generally done by all Parisians" or even "affecting all in London." Second, universal could mean "applicable to all cases." Logically it is via this bold second meaning (that can subsume the first) that the structure of universal claims is tied to scientific progress. For when one says something is applicable to all cases, then the criteria for the falsification of the claim is clearly set out: the claim is falsified by a non-conforming case. Then falsification of the claim has potentially infinite implications. After all, the original claim had many more implications than the ones that were used in the trial that showed it was wrong. For example, all crows are black is falsified by the existence of a non-black crow, or a set of them that can be observed by those who wish to test the generalization. Simple character-izations of what science is about are often tied to the establishment of "universal laws" (Hempel, 1965). Their ease of correction (in principle) generates a potential continual development of subclasses to take care of the more varied classes of "exceptional" events that one might find. So "all crows are black" might then be changed, after considerable observations, to "non-albino crows are black." Albino exceptions may not prove to be the only ones: that is, this universal statement might also prove false, but the universal continues to develop subclasses until a "better" or more powerful encompassing universalization arises.

The complexity of the world is captured in statements that are universal, but only with clauses that permit the development of more nuanced argu-ments, so that they do not show up to be obviously false. Indeed, we search for correctable, presumably true, law-like statements.

Universal laws in the physical world are usually quite complex, and full of conditionals. Take, for example, the common sense notion that water boils when it reaches a specific temperature. What does it take to change the common sense notion to a "universal law" of some value? Impurities may be found to matter: well water and tap water and salt water are different substances and will behave differently. Adding minerals can impede or facilitate boiling when heating takes place. And altitude matters: at higher altitudes water boils "more quickly." But altitude and impurities aren't sufficiently powerful theoretical concepts[10] to give us a lot of leverage.

---

[10] There is some dispute as to what constitutes a useful theoretical concept. But certainly it has to do with its utility in other accepted generalizations. Altitude is related to boiling in cooking, but not to many other empirical problems.

When altitude is related to the theoretical concept "pressure," we are enabled to combine a number of relations to generate a more general theory of liquids, gases, and state changes. Pressure matters: under lower pressure (and this normally occurs at higher altitudes) water (and liquids more generally) boils at lower temperatures. So under some circumstances we could imagine observing water boiling when cooled: were the cooling accompanied by a sufficient lowering of pressure. And water held under sufficiently increasing pressure may not boil when normally heated. Indeed, boiling has to do with the pressure exerted by the vapor of the liquid becoming greater than the pressure exerted on the liquid's surface. The pressure of the vapor in the liquid is increased by the addition of heat.[11] The utility of the "law like statement" becomes apparent once we have the universal relationship. For example, we can make inferences that were not apparent without it, and construct new realities through technology. With this law-like statement, we were able to manipulate pressure and temperature so as to boil water at a higher temperature in steam engines, espresso machines and pressure cookers.

Conditional clauses, theoretical concepts, and restrictions of precision are needed to transform even the simplest commonsense notions into the laws of the physical sciences. The same will certainly be so in social and moral inquiry. Take for example the strong universal statement at the base of some economic reasoning: "people are self-interested." What does it take to change this to a law-like statement: a universal claim that is presumably true, and empirically testable? Just as in the case of water, we may want to be careful regarding what is the subject or the domain of the claim; "what is water" here gives way to "what are people." Is the claim to include those people who are deranged? Perhaps we would want to be careful to exclude such cases. But also, somewhere, as we needed to clarify boiling, we need to clarify self-interest. And as we need to relate our clarified notion of boiling to theoretical concepts, so must we tie self-interest to broader theoretical concepts. Some might argue all behavior that appears altruistic is actually motivated by self-interest – after all, didn't the person *choose* to behave that way for a reason that they valued?

[11] The relations are captured more precisely in what is known as "the ideal gas law." That law can be checked out at http://hyperphysics.phy-astr.gsu.edu/HBASE/hframe.html and its relation to boiling can be seen at http://hyperphysics.phy-astr.gsu.edu/HBASE/kinetic/vappre.html. In any case, the law expresses more generally the relation between pressure, temperature, and the state change of a liquid to a gas.

So to parse the question further, we need a careful delineation of self-interest. Further, circumstances matter. What do we mean when we claim that someone is self-interested? Is it that all her behavior is self-interested? Or are we restricting our concern to only her decisions? Then, are we saying all her decisions are self-interested or that she is usually self-interested but at other times not?

So we might wish to specify some circumstances but once we do that, there could well be problems of universality. Suppose we note that mothers are less self-interested with regard to their children than with regard to their grocers. Probably true, but to bring grocers into the discussion we give up some generalizable qualities. Our statement is still universal but it is now suspect: grocer is a suggestive category but it appears too restrictive. Not only do we start claiming differences rather than universality but grocers are part of a modern culture: for example, they didn't exist in small agricultural societies. What are we saying about other times and places? And as in boiling and heat and pressure, how would we tie children and grocers into a category that allows us to derive interesting propositions? How does this tie to what we want from these universals?

I said that the premises must contain ties that bind the instances to the generalizations. What does this mean, more precisely? To create a tie, the predicates (or descriptors) that are used in the generalizations must be connected to each other and to the contextual instantiations. So for example, if we are trying to explain why Toby (our pet) frequently sidles up to his mother, using these premises, it is useful to know that Toby is not a young fish, but rather a young puppy. And somewhere, we would want to include that mother mammals suckle their young, and dogs are mammals. The notion that dogs are suckled by their mothers yields a powerful link to the behavior of Toby. Let's call those sorts of hints synergistic. Then there must be synergy among the premises to carry the ideas forward.[12]

Synergy must exist between the premises, but there is more. There needs to be a parent-offshoot relation between the theoretical core and the models that are developed to explain events. We can sketch examples of

---

[12] So, for example the knowledge that Toby is my pet, plus a premise regarding the boiling point of water, doesn't help us go any further in our understanding of Toby's predilection to be near his mother.

what is meant here. Let us assume a very simple theoretical core of behavior: individuals are rational, which we might take in some contexts to mean that they choose behavior to maximize their *expected value* (see the definition). And now let us show how this conjecture could lead to various justified conclusions.

Begin with our core premise. Further, note that an individual's vote is not very likely to determine the outcome of the election. Then a voter motivated by the difference that her vote could make in an election, will have a somewhat greater incentive to vote if the election is close than were it a "landslide" election. So, holding other conditions constant, we expect that voting in close elections will be greater than in landslide elections. Such an argument can be formalized and shown to be deductively valid. What we would have is a simple rational choice model of turnout in elections (see page 82).

Definition – *Expected Value:* the expected value of an item (for example, a door prize ticket) is the sum of each of the values of the contingent possible "outcomes" times the probability of that outcome occurring. If the singular grand prize is a TV or cash worth $400, and only one of 1,000 tickets is a winner, the expected value is $.40. But if there are 10 second prizes of $20 each being given out, then one has a 10/1000 chance of winning a second prize (the expected value is $20/100) plus a 1/1000 chance of the first price giving the ticket a value of $.60. Similarly if you are to receive a dollar for the value of a throw of one die the throw has an expected value of $3.50. The numerical possibilities are 1, 2, ... 6 each with a probability of 1/6. Hence the expected value of the throw is $(\Sigma 1..6)/6$ or 21/6 or $3.50.

The same conjecture regarding expected value rationality could be used to explain why voters are ignorant of the candidates for whom they vote (see page 71). If they choose to spend time absorbing information, they will choose information that will maximize their expected value. Given limited time, they will seek, acquire, and absorb information that is likely to help them. Information about the candidates will only be helpful when their vote makes a difference in the outcome of the election. What we have here is a simple rational choice model of voter information acquisition.

The two conjectures, regarding voter turnout and information, both use some of the same core hypotheses regarding rational choice: individuals behave in accordance with rational choice, self-interest and expected value. It is this deductive extension of the core (parent) conjectures into multiple arenas that make up the consequences of rational choice theory. The extensions are the offshoot models. In each model, there will be different premises. Some will have to do with the environment of choice, and some with the particular problem at hand. But there will also be the core conjectures and the synergistic relation between the premises used to derive the conclusions. So for example, take the turnout model. The synergy comes from using expected value to explain changes in behavior we linked to probability differences regarding the efficacy of the individual's vote in close and landslide elections. Using this notion of rational choice behavior to derive conclusions will require that the other premises concern either values or probabilities. Tests of the many models then all serve as indirect tests of the core, or parent, theory.

This means that one needs to be quite precise about the behavioral premises that we use to construct our models so that we can be sure they properly imply interesting arguments.[13]

For universals to be useful, they need to be interesting – they must get us beyond our starting point and add to our understanding. They do this by their being able to link up to other known facts in our reasoning process, allowing us to arrive at new generalizations and helping us to generate a multitude of models. It is also necessary for them to be correctable, which requires that they are *at least possibly false*. But possibly false is too little: they must be presumably true, *and* possibly false. They must add new bridges between our concerns, weaving together an interesting theoretical fabric.

So universal claims are problematic. They mustn't be too general because they need to be interestingly and presumably true, while possibly false. Further, in order to be interesting they must allow for inferences to be logically inferred that get us beyond our commonsensical understanding of our environment.

RATIONAL CHOICE THEORY: PREMISES
TO UNDERSTAND POLITICS

The arguments and explanations that follow in the coming chapters are based on a core theory that many label the "theory of rational choice." The

---

[13] Luckily, von Neumann (1944) developed, as a foundational aspect of his theory of games, a theory of valuation of options that does precisely this. He develops a mapping of individual preferences into utility numbers in a manner that makes it the rational choice to maximize the expected value (see the definition) of the stakes involved. The exposition in von Neumann and Morgenstern (Chapter 2, 1944) is accessible and lucid, as is the discussion in Luce and Raiffa (Chapter 2, 1957). I will not treat the concept of utility here.

theory presumes decisions to be the result of conscious choice made by individuals to further the realization of their own preferences.[14]

This raises some definitional issues. If one works only to satisfy one's own preferences is one necessarily self-interested? We will say "No." An individual might have preferences for the helping of others: she might prefer to improve others rather than herself. In such a case, she has non-self-interested or other-regarding preferences. But she does *have preferences* and if she chooses using them, she makes her choices in conformity with these preferences. Rational choice theorists usefully append other presumptions to the core notions of rational choice theory so as to be able to infer more precisely what sorts of choices will be made in different contexts. These additional assumptions include self-interest, expected value valuation of alternatives that have probabilistic outcomes, and so on.

Further, theorists about politics are often concerned about behavior in typically political institutions and contexts such as legislatures and elections. Many of these political contexts are quite distinct from those at the center of the other social sciences such as economics or sociology. We will be elaborating models of rational behavior in some distinctly political contexts. But to do so we must clarify the notion of rational choice and a good place to start might be to go back to self-interest.

Self-interest

The notion that anything one chooses to do is somehow in one's self-interest is linguistically plausible, but does not help us separate other-regarding behavior: it doesn't allow us to generate interesting distinctions. Such a definition forces us to say that all rational choice behavior is self-interested. You may (or may not) believe this to be so, but it would appear to be an empirical question: not one to be settled by semantics. We need a definition that allows us to distinguish between self-interested and *other-regarding* behavior. Our definition of *self-interest* is not caring for the welfare of others when their welfare doesn't impact your well-being directly. Then self-interested behavior will be behavior motivated so that an individual would bear no costs to help (or hurt) someone else, unless doing so would lead to some expected benefit for herself. Perhaps such a definition is too restrictive, but it has some positive features: 1) its

---

[14] Our notion of preferences subsumes values and tastes.

falsification *is* operationalizable – it divides all behavior into two non-empty classes; 2) it keeps the tie between preferences and choices over which we have some theoretical leverage. We can imagine, and perhaps observe and study and theorize about behavior that is not self-interested.[15] So doing permits us to study human behavior that goes beyond the commonsensical claim that we are all self-interested. It is likely that the manifestation of such behavior will be dependent upon the institutional environment. Markets may be quite conducive to self-interested behavior; voting booths less so.

Preferences

Preferences are the term we use for values people place on outcomes, and alternatives from which they are to choose. As such, preferences are a relationship that one imposes upon one's alternatives: I prefer coffee to chocolate ice cream means that for me, coffee is superior to chocolate and when faced

> Definition– *Transitive:* A relationship "R" is transitive if when x, y and z relate by R, and both xRy, and yRz, then it follows that xRz. To illustrate: the relationship 'older than' is transitive because if David is older than Jane and Jane is older than Alex, it follows necessarily that David is older than Alex.

with the choice, I will pick coffee ice cream. But preferences don't get us very far unless we make assumptions regarding their properties. For example, if we argue that our preferences vary from moment to moment, that they are unstable, and contradictory we would have a less useful theory of behavior built on the foundation of preferences. A set of assumptions must underlie our concept of preferences. In combination, those assumptions, plus the assumption of preference stability in any choice context or situation, give us some ability to generate interesting inferences about behavior.[16]

---

[15] The conjecture that we do not behave as purely self-interested creatures was put forward by Adam Smith (1759). He said, "How selfish soever man may be supposed, there are evidently some principles in his nature, which interest him in the fortune of others, and render their happiness necessary to him, though he derives nothing from it except the pleasure of seeing it." Indeed, nuanced experimental tests of self-interest have been undertaken. One of the first was Frohlich et al, 1984. More general views of subsequent experiments can be had in Frohlich and Oppenheimer, 2004, and Roth, 1995. Frohlich et al, 2004 expand the findings. I explore this topic further in Part IV of this volume.

[16] Note that this is not the same as assuming that preferences are stable and consistent over all time and contexts. Experiments show that assumption is false (Kahneman and Tversky, 1979, 1982; Grether and Plott, 1979, among others).

First, we assume preferences are *transitive* (see the definition). What does *transitive* mean? Transitive is illustrated by such relationships as heavier than, or older than. "Mother of" is not transitive. If Irving is heavier than John who is heavier than Kyle, Irving is heavier than Kyle (i.e., the relation "heavier than" is transitive). Not so for "mother of:" if Jane is the mother of Isabelle who is the mother of Kathryn, Jane is certainly not the mother of Kathryn (i.e., the relation "mother of" is not a transitive relation). It is also presumed that in any situation, individuals evaluate and compare all the options available to them (i.e., preferences are **_complete_**). This is expressed by insisting that individuals either find one option more valuable than another (i.e., they prefer one of the options to the other) or hold them in equal regard (which is called *"indifference"*). In this sense the preferences can be said to be "well-ordered:"[17] all the options can be ordered from best to worst (with ties) in an unambiguous fashion.

Research Frontiers: Experiments, Doubts, and Ways Forward

But are these assumptions accurate? Are our preferences transitive, stable, and complete? The accuracy of these assumptions has been one of the major issues regarding rational choice theory. The first significant doubt regarding the premises was generated by an in-class experiment run by Kenneth May (1954). He asked 62 male students to make choices. They were to indicate their preferences regarding a hypothetical wife. Three alternative hypothetical partners were given: one was wealthy, one was beautiful, and one was intelligent. The students had to choose between one pair, and then another (e.g., wealthy versus beautiful, and then the winner from that pair versus intelligent). The results were that most students chose intelligence over beauty (39 to 23); beauty over wealth (57 to 5); and wealth over intelligence (33 to 29). These numbers imply that some persons had preferences that did not exhibit transitivity (i.e., were intransitive) – see Sidebar 2.

Would that this was all. Serious doubts were introduced by Kahneman and Tversky (1979) who developed a theory as to precisely how and when choices among risky alternatives would prove to be inconsistent. Entitling their theory "Prospect Theory," it was received with great reservations by economists (Grether and Plott, 1979) but hundreds of experiments later, these hurdles have led to various weaker formulations of the rational

---

[17] It is also usually presumed that preferences are **_reflexive_**: an individual will evaluate any item as equal to itself.

Sidebar 2 – Experimental Evidence of Preference Intransitivity

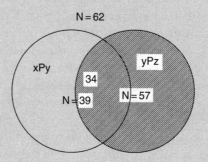

There were 62 people. The results are shown in the Venn diagram. They show a violation of individual transitive preferences. Fifty-seven people (in the striped circle) preferred y to z. Only 5 didn't have this preference. Thirty-nine are in the solid circle (each holding x preferred to y). Since only 5 can be outside the striped circle, at least 34 of the 39 must be in the overlap and hold both x preferred to y and y preferred to z. They must hold (by transitivity) x preferred to z. That would leave at most the others (i.e., 62–34 or 28) who should hold z preferred to x. But 33 express z preferred to x. So at least 5 (33–28) must have intransitive preference orderings.

choice theory being put forward (Regenwetter, et al., 2011; Bendor, 1995; Wendel and Oppenheimer, 2010; as well as the "evolutionary" models of choice as reviewed in chapter 13 of Dixit and Skeath, 2004). These reformulations are useful, and the cutting edge in research and have led to more accurate theories within the same framework: tying choice to preferences.[18]

Choice

Choice by the individual is presumed to follow her preferences, but there are other variables that must be considered. So, for example, you may prefer to win the lottery rather than to pay for a bus ride, but since the cost

---

[18] But see Green and Shapiro, 1994.

of the lottery ticket can also lead you to gain nothing, you may find that the gamble isn't worth it. Your valuation is modified by the probabilities that are involved in a manner reflecting *expected value* as defined above. Similarly, you may wish to purchase both the bus ride and the lottery ticket, but discover that you don't have enough money in your wallet. Thus, your choice is constrained by the resources available to you. (This constraint is referred to as a ***budget constraint.***)

In other words, persons make choices over *actions*, to obtain valued outcomes (a presumption that – except when the actions themselves have positive or negative value – the ends must justify the means). The choices are made in some sort of constrained environment - usually constrained by three things: a defined set of outcomes, a budget or resource constraint, and some set of costs or prices. Social situations involve a set of individuals who presumably each have their own preference.[19]

Can our premises of rational choice help us understand politics? To do this, we must tie politics to conscious choice and preferences. We must see how predicting choice behaviors helps us understand political outcomes. Such macro phenomena of political bargains as policies and outcomes are in part determined by the rational choices of individuals. The premises let us construct arguments and arrive at principles regarding politics.

It is useful to think of politics as arising when individuals can't satisfy their needs without organized collective action – at least organized beyond the nuclear family.[20] Governments aren't the only institutions that organize people for collective action. Political behavior goes beyond behavior about governance. Politics might usefully be defined as behavior oriented to enable a group of persons to work together regarding a shared goal to accomplish what they can't accomplish separately. This perspective leads us to consider the relationship between both individual and collective choice as well as between individual and collective action. It highlights the conflicts between self-gratifying behavior and behavior useful for furthering shared or group objectives. This line of analysis, often referred to as the logic of collective action,[21] is central to much modern analyses of political behavior and has been formalized in numerous places. We explore collective action in Part I of the book. How a society makes a centralized policy decision by aggregating the decisions of a group of individuals is

---

[19] Individuals often influence one another: their preferences need not be assumed to be immutable.

[20] Concerns such as family relations are not our central focus.

[21] The name stems from the eponymous volume by Mancur Olson, *The Logic of Collective Action* (1965).

usually referred to as the field of social choice, and will be explored in Part II of the book.

Because our perspective starts with individual choice, we will need to also consider how specific institutional contexts impact the incentives individuals have. These political institutions differ from the markets which are the central context for economics. In markets, individuals are making decisions to buy or sell usually assumed to primarily affect themselves.[22] In contrast, politics concerns decisions that are being made for groups of people. Most of the time, the group has a select few who are making the decision for the whole group. Such distinctions between those who make the decisions and those who are to be affected by them lead to unique problems for political institutions. For example, what is best for the group? How do we know? What are the unique problems of political institutions in achieving the group's interests? These issues are dealt with in Parts III and IV.

Rational choice theory is of significant help in illuminating the relationship between individual decisions and group outcomes. It allows us to develop models with testable, interesting conclusions. Some of these conclusions seem to be correct, while others will prove to be problematic. The problematic conclusions can lead us to identify frontiers that require further research to figure out how better to formulate the presumptions used in the models. In examining the implied conjectures that appear incorrect, at times I will discuss how experiments have been used to shed light on the question.

FOR FURTHER READING

Logic, Knowledge and Truth

Edelman, Gerald M. (1992), *Bright Air, Brilliant Fire: On the Matter of the Mind.* New York: Basic Books. Edelman gives a great overview of how the brain works in a manner that reflects a correspondence theory of truth. It also touches upon points I develop below requiring a probabilistic relationship between values and choice (see pp. 39, 132).

Jeffrey, Richard (1981), *Formal Logic: Its Scope and Limits.* New York: McGraw Hill. This is just one of many good introductory logic text books.

---

[22] This is, however, a special case. When other parties are also affected, economists refer to those effects as 'externalities.' Both are discussed below. Externalities are usually considered a type of "market failure."

Prior, A. N. (1970), "Correspondence Theory of Truth." *Encyclopedia of Philosophy*. V. 2. New York: Macmillan, 223–232. Excellent introduction to the correspondence theory of truth.

White, Alan R. (1970), TRUTH. Garden City, New York: Doubleday Anchor. A fine essay on truth. The part on the coherence theory is also contained in the *Encyclopedia of Philosophy*.

Philosophy of Science

Giere, Ronald N. (1984), *Understanding Scientific Reasoning*, 2nd ed. Chicago: Holt, Rinehart and Winston. This is a simple introduction to the major questions of what it means to reason scientifically. It focuses on the issue of justifying arguments. Early editions also contain four chapters on logic and statistics.

Giere, Ronald N. (1988), *Explaining Science: A Cognitive Approach*. Chicago: University of Chicago Press. Here Giere presents a very interesting cut at how to explain science. He argues that we should consider both how scientists judge theories, and what sort of "representation" of reality theories give scientists.

Hempel, Carl G. (1966), *The Philosophy of the Natural Sciences*. Englewood Cliffs, New Jersey: Prentice Hall. This is a solid and useful introduction. Not very detailed in argumentation. In some ways Lambert and Brittan is better. But the story of Semmelweis is classically well done.

Lambert, Karel and Gordon G. Brittan, Jr. (1970), *An Introduction to the Philosophy of Science*. Englewood Cliffs, New Jersey: Prentice Hall. They review such controversies as the theory of induction, probabilistic explanation, and the nature of math.

Maxwell, Nicholas (1972), "A Critique of Popper's Views on Scientific Method," *Philosophy of Science*, June, 131–152. Maxwell argues that Popper's motivation of the notion of methods is incomplete: falsification can not be shown to maximize the chances of progress in science. This is an important critique of Popper.

Nola, Robert (2004), "Pendula, Models, Constructivism and Reality." *Science and Education* 13: 349–377. Nola examines the use of models as abstractions. He discusses the role of abstraction in science, and how this creates a problem of "fit" that is not easy to deal with. His argument that much debate in the philosophy of science concerns how to deal with reality given that models are deliberately "inaccurate" is important. Implicitly Nola is arguing against a pure coherence theory of truth, placing a useful threshold need for "realism" in science.

Popper, Karl (1959), *The Logic of Scientific Discovery*. New York: Harper and Row. [First Edition, 1934.] This once-revolutionary approach to the problems of scientific method may not be the last word, but it is a great start.

Weinberg, Steven (2001), "Can Science Explain Everything?" *The New York Review of Books*. V. xlviii, No. 9 (May 31. 2001): 47–50. Weinberg discusses the role of models and theories and the difficulty of claiming knowledge on the basis of explanation. Points out that non-regular (e.g. accidental and unique) happenings can't be subsumed under the formal rubric of modeling.

Rational Choice Theory and The Nature of Politics

Bendor, Jonathan (1995), "A Model of Muddling Through." *American Political Science Review*, V. 89 (No. 4, December): 819–840. This is a remarkable paper on the nature of bounded rationality. Bendor develops three levels of analysis: 1) on the competence of the decision maker (the problem of making a good decision); 2) the search for and evaluation of alternatives to the status quo; and 3) multiple decision makers. He shows the conditions under which the expected value of the alternatives chosen over the status quo improve as a function of the competence and the search and evaluation techniques of the decision maker.

Diermeier, Daniel (1995), "Rational Choice and the Role of Theory in Political Science" in Friedman, Jeffrey, ed., *The Rational Choice Controversy: Economic Models of Politics Reconsidered*. New Haven, Conn.: Yale University Press, 59–70). Diermeier discusses the limitations of the Green and Shapiro citation below. He points out that one can't usually test an assumption directly and that theories contain non-observable, non-directly testable, terms. His opinion is that the biggest problems with rational choice are: 1) how we relate the deterministic predictions of rational choice theory with the empirically apparent probabilistic nature of the behavior and 2) how we integrate notions of learning and evolution in rational choice.

Green, Donald P. and Ian Shapiro (1994), *Pathologies of Rational Choice Theory: A Critique of Applications in Political Science*. New Haven, Conn: Yale University Press. This is a classic criticism of rational choice theory. They argue there has been no serious attempt to see whether rational choice theory can empirically explain things of interest to political science. This is a serious case study as to what it takes to get a theory accepted or rejected. They look at both experiments and field studies. Their arguments are both clear and controversial.

Hausman, Daniel M. (1989), "Economic Methodology in a Nutshell." *The Journal of Economic Perspectives*, V. 3, No. 2 (Spring): 115–127. Hausman looks at the empirical appraisal of rational choice theory and specifically at the variety of approaches of evaluation of the theory. He concludes that we need to heed the tests of the theory and that disconfirmation by itself is not useful as it doesn't reveal how science has progressed.

Kahneman, Daniel (2011). *Thinking Fast and Slow*. New York: Farrar, Straus & Giroux. This gives a very accessible broad view of the anomalies that any theory of choice must eventually deal with. It is written for the general audience.

Kahneman, Daniel and Amos Tversky (1979), "Prospect Theory: an Analysis of Decision Making Under Risk." *Econometrica* 47 (March): 263–291. Theirs is an interesting and by now classic theory of how our expressed choices vary as a function of the context of choice. It is a direct challenge to the presumption of preference consistency.

Nagel, Ernest (1963), "Assumptions in Economic Theory." American Economic Review (May): 211–219. Nagel discusses the pitfalls of pure instrumentalism as a template for the development of rational choice theory.

Shafir, Eldar and Amos Tversky (1995), "Decision Making," in Edward E. Smith and Daniel N. Osherson, eds., *An Invitation to Cognitive Science: Thinking.* V. 3, Second Edition, Cambridge, Mass.: MIT Press, 77–100. They offer a fine review and update of the Kahneman and Tversky "Prospect Theory."

THE LOGIC OF COLLECTIVE ACTION

Politics grabs our attention under two circumstances. Politics is important when we share interests that are worth pursuing as a group but are
too costly for any one individual or family to undertake alone. Politics also
grabs our attention when politicians achieve things that are not in the
people's interests. We begin our examination of politics by analyzing the
positive basis for politics grabbing our attention.[1] Why are political institutions needed when the interests of a group surpass the means of any
single individual?

Politics enables us to achieve together what we can't achieve separately. This view enables us to connect the premises of rational choice
with the political life we all observe. Mancur Olson brilliantly used this
connection to fashion some of the first models of collective action. He put
the point clearly enough to catch political scientists' attention. As Olson
put it in the opening of his 1965 blockbuster, *The Logic of Collective
Action*:

The idea that groups tend to act in support of their group interests is supposed to
follow logically from this widely held premise of rational, self-interested
behavior . . .. But it is *not* in fact true that the idea that groups will act in their
self-interest follows logically from the premise of rational and self-interested
behavior . . .. The notion that groups of individuals will act to achieve their
common or group interests, far from being a logical implication of their individual
interests, is in fact inconsistent with that assumption.

---

[1] Later we will consider how the political institutions can be driven toward other ends.

Since Olson's clarion call, collective action problems have been central to the development of modern political science.[2] Great efforts were spent developing and testing models of collective action in the form of what has come to be called "social dilemmas." These models spelled out the implications of rational, self-interested behavior in collective action situations. Models of individual behavior starkly juxtaposed the potential welfare of the group with the welfare of the individual. They focused attention on the incentives facing individuals in their decisions. Working through the logic of the models one sees how details of institutional structures can lead to more, or less, rewarding outcomes. These models demonstrate the limitations of purely voluntary behavior. In doing so, they also help us sketch a "proper realm" of government.[3] Governments ought to handle those situations where the self-interested behavior of members of the group lead to outcomes for the group that all in the group can agree could be improved and leave everyone better off.[4] Most of these implications and arguments are introduced and discussed in the next chapter.

Before delving into the details of the argument, its premises should be clarified. In its most basic form there are two behavioral premises: rationality and self-interest (see the Introduction). As will become clear, these are important to keep separate. They help us analyze the choices that we as members of a group have, and the historical possibilities that our groups have and have not been able to realize.

The conclusions one can reach with the collective action arguments touch on many aspects of politics including questions of political leadership and the behavior of citizens. There are implications here for observers of politics, activists, analysts, and moral and political philosophers. These extensions will be handled in Chapters 2 and 3. Chapter 1 analyzes why we must, so often, go beyond voluntary contributions to get collective needs met.

---

[2] Olson's 1965 book was certainly not the first analysis of its kind (see, for example, Baumol, 1952).

[3] However, other concerns such as the protection of liberties, property, and support of the needy will be considered and will broaden our normative sketch for the role of governments.

[4] The technical term for such situations is Pareto suboptimal. This notion of optimality was given to us by Vilfredo Pareto, an Italian economist of the late nineteenth and early twentieth centuries.

CHAPTER I

Voluntary Contributions and Collective Action

How did Olson conclude that self-interest conflicts with the obtaining of shared goals? Whether it is some neighbors wanting a stop sign or a clean-up of a trashed empty lot, citizens of a small town hoping the grocery store will stay open, or the population of a city trying to get lead out of their water supply, if one member of the group gets her interest met, so do the others. Each individual can opt-out of the collective efforts, and follow her own private interests. This possibility creates problems for the achievement of shared goals within groups. This is a property of public goods.

PUBLIC GOODS

Consider that cup of coffee you might purchase at your local favorite café. You buy it. You get it. If I want a coffee, I don't get yours: I have to get my own. These sorts of items are the types of goods economists had traditionally thought about when analyzing markets. We refer to them as *private goods*. They have two important characteristics not typical of many of our political objectives: 1) if I want some, I have to get it myself (*excludable*: each consumer can be excluded separately); 2) if I get some and you do too, we don't share the same item (*divisibility*). Olson realized that the shared interests are fundamentally different from private goods.

> Definition – *Public Goods* are goods that, when made available for one person, are available for others. No one can be excluded if someone receives it (*non-excludable*). Each individual consumes the same unit (*indivisible*). A 'public bad,' such as global warming, is a negatively valued public good.

Consider an example of shared interests: a stop sign: Typically, it has two properties: 1) if you get the stop sign, so do I (*non-excludability*) and 2) we both use the same stop sign (*indivisibility*). Goods which share these two characteristics are referred to as public goods (see the definition).

Let's see why the concept of public goods gives us leverage on the logic of collective action. First, note a problem that stems from the combination of self-interest and non-excludability: Recall in the coffee situation, I must buy my own to get one. But to secure a stop sign, I can rely on your efforts, and save my time and resources for other things. If I do this, I will be as much a beneficiary of the stop sign as if I had made the effort myself: I can "*free-ride*" on your efforts.

Second, note a problem that stems from indivisibility: The use of the item by too many persons can lead to a deterioration of the quality of the use of the item, or '*crowding*.' So, with a stop sign, as the intersection gets too busy, and the roads get wider, a traffic signal may be a better solution.

Finally, consider the value of the shared interest. How do we calculate its value to the group? In the typical market case of private goods, it is easy. Your café latte is worth $3 to you. But, to me, *your* coffee is worth nothing. What about public goods?[1] If the stop sign is at a corner that you and I both use, then for the two of us the value of the stop sign would be the *sum* of our valuations. In general, the value of the good to the group of individuals is presumed to be the sum of the values of the good to each of the individuals who gets the good.[2]

Now, there are logically three different possible cases. First, when one adds up the value placed on the public good by the group's members, the value does not exceed the cost of the project. Then the project is not a reasonable goal for the group. One would hope that the group does not undertake it, for it is *not* in the interest of the group to pursue.[3]

---

[1] The distinction here is not to be understood as one in which *items* can be understood to be public or private goods. Most goods have aspects of both. (See Sidebar 4, p. 81, for a fuller discussion.) For example, take a privately owned 2002 Lexus. It may share brake problems with other identically designed Lexus cars. The design is a public good to all the Lexus owners. And fixing a bad design may, therefore, become a political problem about public goods. The original analysis of public goods was developed in Samuelson 1954, 1955.

[2] This is not to say that it will be easy to find the value of the stop sign to each of us. If we are to pay for it collectively, we have an incentive to each downplay our interest in the sign. If the larger community is to pay, we have an incentive to overstate our interests. See Footnote 15.

[3] Note that any shared project will be disliked by some. Since they also get the public good, their 'negative evaluation' of the project would have to be taken into account in calculating the value of the project.

A second possible case is when some individual places such a high value on the good that she provides it to the group as a whole. Olson called groups who are sufficiently lucky to have this happen *privileged* (p. 48). There have been corporations, or wealthy individuals, or large countries that play this role. For example the United States as a member of the NATO alliance[4] turned its private concern for security in the Cold War into a realization of the alliance giving benefits to the larger community. When a group has actors with abnormally outsized interests those actors may be burdened with more than their share of the costs as the others free-ride on the group's behavior – unless the organization is designed to prevent that.

But more usual is the third case where the group would be better off achieving its shared interest and no one places a private value on it more than its cost. Then it doesn't pay for any *one* person to undertake the effort as it would be too costly for a single individual.

In these circumstances the shared objective is 'worth it' (using some 'cost-benefit' notion). Since no one individual's behavior can be counted on to satisfy the group's interests, some form of collective action is required. Now we can see how Olson concluded that group interests will not get satisfied if all the members of the group act in a rational, self-interested fashion unless something is added to the story. This has dark implications for political problems. To properly assess these implications, we will need to do some careful analysis.

To illustrate, imagine a somewhat desolate cul-de-sac. It has a deserted and trashed lot with an empty house on one side, and an occupied house on the other. It is easy to imagine that for the one resident, the time and money needed to clean up the lot would be so great as to make the project not worth the effort. But were the house on the other side to be occupied, the clean-up would become a 'public good.' Perhaps the two neighbors would be able to get together to accomplish the task. And certainly, were other nearby houses occupied, the effort each would have to expend would decrease to accomplish the task. And each would gain something by having a nicer neighborhood. With more neighbors, however, we are faced with the possibility of free-riding.

Russell Hardin (1971) showed that with some simple tools, called game theory, one can develop models of collective action to clarify the alternatives we could utilze to get around the pessimistic conundrums outlined by Olson.

---

[4] Olson and Zeckhauser, 1966, developed the application of this theory to the problem of alliances.

To understand Hardin's contribution, we need a short introduction to game theory.

GAME THEORY

Game theory lets one analyze how people choose when the value of their alternatives depends upon the behavior of others. It presumes rationality or goal-oriented behavior. In some contexts, such as markets, rational behavior can be quite directly tied to choice. Take, for example, that cup of coffee at the café. You are confronted with a number of choices, each of which has a different price attached. Different types and sizes of coffee have different attributes and prices. But once you settle on your preferred item, you pick it out and pay. Such goal-oriented behavior is simple in the modern market. Your behavior doesn't affect the attributes of the options for the next person in line.

The situation gets more complicated when the attributes of the options aren't fixed but depend on the behavior of others. For example, prices might be the result of a bargain – as when buying a car. Knowing this, you may strategically pretend to have a lower budget than you really have and even focus on a different model than you hope to settle on. What is available at what price is determined by the salesperson's thinking about what she can get from you, which depends, in turn, on your behavior.

The great twentieth-century mathematician John von Neumann concerned himself with precisely those situations where the value of an alternative depends upon the behavior of others. He called these situations games.[5] The theory of behavior in such situations is called game theory. Markets in which the prices aren't 'posted' but are rather reached by bargaining have such properties. But so do many other situations including those situations involving collective action and achieving shared goals.

> **Definition – *A Game*** is a model of a social situation where the value of an option is determined by the interaction of the choices that other individuals make. The model must specify the participants (called <u>players</u>), the structure of how their choices (called <u>strategies</u> or <u>moves</u>) lead to <u>outcomes</u>, and finally, via the preferences of the players over the outcomes, lead to the satisfaction of the players (i.e, their <u>payoffs</u>).

A game can be depicted in various ways. Here we show one way, called the normal form of the game. In the normal form, we list all the options of

---

[5] He invented game theory and it was first widely accessible in his 1944 volume coauthored with Oskar Morgenstern.

each player in a matrix (i.e., a box). This is straightforward when there are only two players. Here is a two-player (Jim and Joan) example:

Two people, Jim and Joan, are considering going on a river walk together. Jim is to choose from among his alternatives, each of which we can depict as a different column. Joan chooses from among her alternatives, each of which we depict as a different row. The outcome will be the box selected by their combined choices (see Table 1). We will show the value of the outcome using two numbers in the box. Convention determines that the first number is the row player's evaluation of the outcome, and the second is column's. So in the example, the alternatives for each of the two players are to go (on a river walk) or not. If they both choose to go, they each get their highest payoff (represented by a number higher than that associated with the other outcomes.)

Jim and Joan are two environmentally concerned friends. They like to spend time together. Joan wants to participate in a river walk. She prefers to do it with Jim, and so the evaluation of her choice is determined by whether Jim would be going along. Jim is like-minded. The best outcome for both would be to go together on the river walk. The worst would be for one of them to go, but not the other. Giving the most valued outcomes the highest number, and the worst the lowest (another convention), we depict this simple interaction in Table 1.

The game is symmetric – Jim and Joan, referred to as the ***players*** (participants of a game) face the same options and evaluate them the same way. In the example, both players find that what is best depends upon the choice of the other. For example, 'going' can yield a 4 or a 2, depending upon the choice of the other party. This is a rather simple game to analyze since there is no conflict: True, what is best depends upon the choice of the other, but they can easily coordinate their choices to get the best outcome. Were one not able to go, the other would also prefer not to go.

But games can model less cooperative situations. For example, everyone may find it best to act in one way, but this can lead to problems for all. Such games are more central to politics than the simple coordination game

TABLE 1. *Jim and Joan Consider a River Walk*

	Jim's Options	
Joan's Options	Go	Don't Go
Go	4, 4	2, 1
Don't Go	1, 2	3, 3

TABLE 2. *Jim and Joan Consider Visiting a Relative: Depicted as a Prisoner Dilemma Game*

	Jim's Options	
Joan's Options	Go	Don't Go
Go	3, 3	1, 4
Don't Go	4, 1	2, 2

described in Table 1. One particular family of games is particularly problematic and is usually called Prisoner Dilemma Games. It was this sort of game that Russell Hardin (1971) conjectured could shed light on the logic of collective action.

Specifically, in a prisoner dilemma game each player has a best alternative, but if the players choose it, they find themselves not as well off as they might have been had they cooperated. Take our previous players, who now want a hospitalized relative to receive a visit. But both the trip and the visit are depressing. Each would prefer that the other goes alone, scoring a 4, and each contemplates that the worst would be going alone, scoring a 1 (see Table 2). But they agree, both going is better than neither visiting. Note, that for both, not going is strictly better than going, regardless of the behavior of their friend. For example, if Jim goes, Joan does better not going (it's her best outcome), and if Jim doesn't go, Joan is best off also not going. But, they would rather both go than both stay at home.

Hardin noticed this could be a useful model of a situation where people share a value in getting some public good (the relative getting visited) but share a desire to "let the other guy do it." Recall, this possibility of letting the other do the work stems from the non-exclusionary property of public goods (see the definition, page 27): if one person gets it, so do others. If the group receives the good when the individual does, then there is an incentive for all to "free-ride." After all, one can easily rationalize that one can let someone else do the heavy lifting to get the outcome that you also value. Then something beyond the shared good is needed to overcome this tendency. Of course, in most collective action cases, however, there are usually more than two people. And in large groups it can take politics and governments to attain shared interests and other valued public goods when individuals otherwise might shirk and not contribute to the group effort.

SHARED INTERESTS, COLLECTIVE ACTION
AND INDIVIDUAL BEHAVIOR

To see how self-interest gets in the way of collective action, consider a group of like-minded, self-interested individuals. Everyone values the project the same way. Single out one of them and call her Iris. Let them share a costly goal and assume the "institutional" structure of the group is rudimentary: Individuals voluntarily contribute to the obtaining of the goal.[6] Any equal contribution to the project is equally effective (the returns to the contributions are constant). Now when a shared project is a public good, the benefits of all the contributions go to everyone, while the costs only go to the contributor. A few things are obvious: Were the size of the group to go up, more people would benefit from Iris's contributions. So the benefits to the *whole* group of Iris's contribution would be bigger in a larger group. And of course, benefits to the whole group are bigger than the benefits going to Iris alone. The social effect of the private choice is larger than the private effect. So when Iris makes her decision on the basis of her private costs and benefits, it is not likely to accord with what is best for the group. Consider a numerical case, depicted in Table 3, to understand the logic.

Iris, a typical member of a group, contemplates giving some money, call it x, or nothing (then $x = 0$), toward the achievement of the goal. In keeping with our notion that it doesn't pay for an individual, whatever $1 buys toward the achievement of the good, it must be worth less than $1 to Iris. Say it only generates $.40 worth of value for Iris and for each of the others. (Recall, we assumed all the individuals were like-minded.) We now develop this situation as a game. Assume Iris has only $10 in her purse when thinking about making a cash donation. Iris chooses between giving

TABLE 3. *Value of Donating, Given Behaviors of Others: Illustrating the Problem of Collective Action*

Iris's (Typical Person's) Strategy	Donations by Others in the Group				
	20	10	... 2	1	0
Contribute $x	$18 -.6x	$14 -.6x	... $10.80 -.6x	$10.40 -.6x	$10 -.6x
Give Nothing	$18.00	$14.00	... $10.80	$10.40	$10.00

---

[6] This is usually called a called "voluntary contribution mechanism."

nothing or giving some amount less than $10. In keeping with our premises of rationality, Iris examines her options and chooses the one which she prefers. Assuming that Iris only cares about her own payoff and that the financial calculations properly capture her values, what ought she choose? I depict her options as two rows of a table.

She chooses a row: spending $x or spending nothing: $0. The outcome, however, doesn't depend only on Iris. It depends also on how much everyone else donates to the project. Some of those possibilities are depicted by the columns in the table. Iris can't select the column in which she "ends up." That is determined by the collective choices of others. But we (and therefore, she) can see that regardless of the situation she is facing (i.e., in which column she might end up), the second row yields a better outcome than the first row. This is a consequence of her losing 60 percent of any money she gives. This occurs in each and every column. So for her, the issue is settled: Giving nothing is the better deal.

Assume our self-interested Iris is typical: Each individual has $10 to spend on the project. It is a case where the goal can be partially achieved and as the amount collected increases the value for each member goes up proportionately, as illustrated. Any $1 spent on the attainment of the goal generates $.40 of value that goes to each individual in the group. This gives us roughly the information we need to consider the value of the public good for the group. After all, the benefit derived from a public good is conceptualized as the sum of the value of the good to each of the individuals in the group that is to receive it. In the case at hand, as long as the group has at least three persons, everyone in the group would be better off were they all to give, rather than not give. After all, each person would get $.40 for each dollar spent on the public good. If the group were three persons and each gave $1, each would get $1.20 worth of benefits: an improvement of 20 cents for each of them. A larger group would get more benefits from each contribution. Similarly, a smaller group generates fewer benefits: a dollar spent on the public good in a group of two generates benefits of only 80 cents. Yet in making her decision, Iris compares her *private* costs with her *private* benefits. Being self-interested, she does not compare those private costs *with the benefits going to the group as a whole*. And Iris then notes that for her, it is not worth investing in the group goal. For every $1 she spends out of her endowment, she loses $.60. So Iris, and everyone else for that matter, finds it worthwhile not to contribute to the public good, but rather to shirk, or free-ride.

Recall that while each dollar's partial achievement of the group's goal generates only a return of 40 cents, it does so for each of the members of the group as they all share the partial achievement of the goal of the group. Thus, if there are ten persons in the group, each dollar given buys enough of the public good to generate $.40 worth of benefit for each person, or $4 worth for the group (adding up the difference it makes for each of the ten persons). If each individual gave $1, then each person would have a $4 benefit and the group of ten would have gained $40. It is because the expenditures are not shared (private), while the benefits are shared (public), that we have this difficulty.

Table 3 is an abstract situation. We can give it a context to make it easier to understand. Let the group be 20 residents in an apartment building. Assume there is an alley abutting the building that is choked with garbage. A neighborhood kid has offered to bag the garbage and put it on the curb for collection for $1 per bag. Assume there are many, many (perhaps 200) bags of garbage to collect. Each resident values the removal of the garbage at less than $1 a bag: say 40 cents. Then the table specifies Iris's options: She can contribute some amount, call it $x, toward the goal or not. And without some way of bringing them together to make a collective effort, rather than getting a clean alley they all keep their money, and each save 60 cents on each dollar they might have spent.

> Definition – *Pareto Optimality, Pareto Improvement:* If one can make some better off, without hurting anyone, there is an indisputable improvement for the group. Such an improvement is called a *Pareto improvement.* One has reached *Pareto optimality* when one can no longer make such improvements. So a situation is Pareto optimal when one can no longer make others better off without hurting someone. If no improvement is made the situation is described as *Pareto suboptimal.*

If the residents had a meeting, they could agree unanimously to a system of cost sharing. They would want to set up an institutional context where the residents of the group would not be as likely to follow their 'private' incentives. For when each individual follows his own incentives, it leads to a situation that is not very good; certainly not 'optimal.' The residents could all see that they each would have been better off had they all shared in the cost and supported the clean up. They could all do much better if they could escape the situation where each individual makes no contribution. Such a situation (or outcome) where people could do better without anyone being hurt is *sub-optimal* (see the definition of Pareto optimal). To avoid it, they might even agree unanimously that each of them *must* pay a tax, say $10 per resident) or make a specified contribution to the good. After all, Iris, and each of the others, would be substantially better off were they all forced to contribute: 200 bags could be collected and each person would have a benefit of $80 at a cost of $10.

But without such an arrangement:

1. Iris, and all others, find that it is never beneficial to contribute.
2. Everyone else in the group would prefer that they did all contribute.[7]
3. Without some way of overcoming the impediments to collective action, the group is saddled with a suboptimal outcome.

Some would argue that the situation sketched here underlies many of the dilemmas of politics. To understand the links between individual choice and more general notions of collective action and group patterns of behavior, begin with a simple inference from the above discussion: If individuals are in a group that has no arrangements for the members to share the costs of solving their shared problems, the individuals will usually not find it worthwhile to help achieve shared interests. They will then find it useful to shirk their responsibilities.[8]

We have just sketched why this is likely to happen. Indeed, one of the major contributions of the theory of rational choice is that it gives a relatively simple account of the problem of collective action: Each contribution to a group or collective project yields benefits for all members of the group, but costs accrue only to the individual who makes the effort. Self-interested individuals make their choices based not on the distributed benefits to the group, but on the comparison of the *private* benefits to themselves with the *private* costs their behavior entails. This leads to a general choice of non-cooperation while, for the group and all its members, it is not difficult to see that it would be best if all contributed.

Prisoner Dilemma Games and Collective Action

We have now sketched why the group goal would not be easily achieved until members of the group work out a more complex structure to generate incentives to cooperate. The standard portrayal of this argument has become that of an n-person (that is, more than two people) prisoner's dilemma game (Hardin, 1971).

---

[7] Note the strong relationship between Pareto optimality and unanimity. If a situation is suboptimal, it should be possible to find an alternative that all would prefer (Dougherty and Edward, 2005).

[8] Of course, we might not observe only confirmatory evidence: only shirking. Such is the stuff of science. For a fine, if somewhat dated, overview of the experimental data, warts and all, see Ledyard (1995) who reviews the experimental studies of the subject. But we will have considerably more to say about this in ensuing pages.

The first important property of a prisoner dilemma game is that each participant has an alternative that trumps his other alternatives. Such an alternative is referred to as a *dominant strategy*. When an individual has a dominant strategy the *person* would be in what we might think of as an individual *equilibrium* (i.e., she can't do better by *unilaterally* changing her choice).

> **Definition – *Dominant Strategy:*** A strategy is *dominant* if the outcomes it leads to are 1) always at least as good as those that can be achieved by choosing an alternative, and 2) in some circumstances even better than that which can be achieved by any other choice.

This is what we argued in the example where Iris decides to not contribute, and hence to shirk her responsibilities.

But, what is this sort of equilibrium? No one, *by herself*, can choose an alternative that would be certain to improve her own situation. In other words, in equilibrium, without coordinating her choice with others, a person has no better alternative. If an outcome leaves every player with no way of improving herself by changing her choice, then the situation is said to be in what is called a *Nash equilibrium* (named after John Nash, who first identified it).

It is often a conjecture that the "Nash equilibrium" outcome is a strong claim to stability in choice: hence, a good predictor of behavior. After all, each individual is getting as much as she can be sure of claiming on her

> **Definition – *Nash Equilibrium*:** any outcome when no single individual can ensure herself a better payoff by changing her choice.

own. But there are competing notions that involve individuals coming together and coordinating their choices so as to achieve better outcomes.[9] Why these might be important becomes clear in light of the second property of a prisoner dilemma game.

The ***prisoner dilemma game*** models a situation where, although every individual has a dominant strategy, when they choose it, these choices collectively lead to an outcome that is *not* Pareto optimal.[10] The participants have missed the mutual advantage of cooperation. The group optimum is not achieved because each individual's possibility of cooperative behavior is strictly dominated by the opportunity of defection. There are mutual gains to be had were players to cooperate rather than defect.[11]

---

[9] There are other problems with the concept of the Nash equilibrium. Many games have too many outcomes that would be in equilibrium for this to be a useful concept. But I shall not go into these questions here.

[10] An n-person prisoner dilemma is one which involves more than two individuals.

[11] A final property of the prisoner dilemma game is that the outcome of the dominated strategies must yield a bigger payoff than some 50–50 coordinated mix of the two

The prisoner dilemma game was invented by Flood (1952, 1958) to depict a situation that forced players to consider the trade-off between the Nash equilibrium and the cooperative outcome. He developed the game to see whether individuals would behave in a manner to reach the group optimum or whether individuals would act as autonomous non-cooperating individuals, choosing their dominant strategy (leading to the Nash equilibrium). He then performed laboratory tests. He had two individuals face off in a many-times repeated form of the game, and had them each keep a "diary" regarding what they were doing and how they felt about it. Interestingly, the Nash outcome was not the most frequent outcome reached. Indeed, with 114 decisions tabulated, the cooperative outcome was reached 60 times (see the 1958 reprint, Table 3, p. 14), while the non-cooperative, or Nash equilibrium, was reached only 14 times.[12] But the non-obvious empirical outcome of these two person games stands out: Cooperation does much better than expected.

The theory of the prisoner dilemma game, as a model for the public good problem, took on its own life. And the prisoner dilemma analysis leads us to our first principle of politics regarding collective action:

AN UNORGANIZED GROUP CANNOT OPTIMALLY SATISFY ITS SHARED OR COLLECTIVE INTERESTS.

(Olson, 1965)

In other words, when a public good is worth supplying, and there is no institutionalized means for members to share in its cost, the amount of the public good which will be provided will be suboptimal. Various interpretations of the finding are possible, but the most obvious is that when individuals have shared values and interests an anarchic structure will not be adequate. Volunteers will not be sufficiently forthcoming to

---

strategies. This ensures that the parties do not have an alternative form of coordinated cooperative strategy choice that they both prefer to cooperating.

[12] The frustrations and anger expressed in these diaries (see Flood's 1952 and 1958 papers) constitute insightful illustrations of the tension that such cross pressures put people under. But his experiments are inconclusive: Flood didn't realize that when the game is repeated the players can use their moves to communicate their intentions, thereby giving players a possibility of cooperating over time. This changes the analysis. Indeed, there is a folk theorem that asserts that virtually any outcome could be in equilibrium in a repeated prisoner dilemma. This change is often argued to explain the unusually high cooperation rate. I present other experimental evidence and analysis below.

generate an adequate supply of public goods to meet properly the needs and interests of the individuals involved. Rather, the existence of public goods ensures that people need to organize to overcome the tendencies of free-riding that a purely self-interested view of the situation encourages.

Successfully organizing a group involves giving sufficient incentives for members to contribute enough to group efforts. Such organizing is needed to supply solutions to satisfy the shared interests of the members. The need for groups to supply themselves with such basic public goods as security, water supply, fire protection, public sanitation, health, and more, only point to the need for people to be organized in a manner to satisfy their basic needs. A controversial way of putting this is that the incentives associated with the public good alone are insufficient to secure behavior to get the public good. As Mancur Olson (1965) put it:

A GROUP CAN ONLY GET MEMBERS TO CONTRIBUTE TO SOLVE ITS SHARED PROBLEMS BY PROVIDING INCENTIVES INDEPENDENT OF THE PUBLIC GOOD.

Although this is clearly an overstatement,[13] the implications of the first conjecture go well beyond this preliminary analysis and interpretation of it. They fly directly against the implications of the minimalist government and free market anarchist advocates' positions that often creep into public debates regarding the appropriate nature of governmental scope. We will discuss this more fully below. (page 143) For example, as Olson noted, the workers at a unionized plant might well unanimously vote for a requirement that they join the union and pay union dues, as a solution to the problem that they might neither join nor pay on a voluntary basis. This also shows why "right to work" laws (which prohibit such agreements by unions in the United States) have been so effective in weakening unions.

Corollaries and Further Implications

If nothing else, our analysis to this point gives a solid justification for both taxation and liberal political orders. Of course, there is no "ought" derived without a normative presumption. In this case, the normative presumption, which we argue is inherent in the justification of democracy, is easy to state. A political order is to be judged by its ability to improve the well-being of the

---

[13] It might hold for unorganized groups. But, for example, assume there is a local neighborhood swimming pool association. We could imagine a successful finance committee raising funds for improvements of known costs by promising to return any extra monies to the donors and also to return the funds if they don't raise enough to make the improvements. The incentive of the good itself then could be sufficient to obtain the result.

individuals in the group. (We might understand this as a minimalist form of consequentialism.[14]) Since decent individual well-being requires the satisfaction of shared needs, it follows that people should have such basic freedoms as are required to organize themselves for satisfying these needs. Such requirements include the standard freedoms of press, speech, and assembly. Without such freedoms, even the identity, and certainly, the aggregate value of the shared interests, will likely remain unknown.

Given the logic of collective action, to justify governments by the welfare they afford their citizens implies that people must have basic civil liberties. Otherwise, the demand for many valued public goods will neither be manifest nor factored into public decision making. This proactive justification for liberties goes beyond a more traditional justification, which turns on the need for "negative" protections from governmental intrusion. Often, groups will not even know that there are common interests without the possibility of free communication. Indeed, the importance of free communication in the identification of shared needs has been made apparent by what the internet's low communication costs have wrought. It has led to greater awareness of the shared interests of such groups as gays and lesbians and other oppressed individuals.

For groups to politically and socially demonstrate their needs they must be capable of bringing attention to the harm of current policies. Often harm is imposed upon those who try to bring attention to need for change. Even the threat of such punishment can prevent individuals in a group from effectively mobilizing others to show its plight to the wider public. Since a means of sharing the costs of achieving or even articulating shared goals is organizationally difficult, an important corollary can be developed:

FOR GROUPS OF PEOPLE TO MEET THEIR SHARED NEEDS OVER TIME THEY MUST HAVE THE FREEDOM TO ORGANIZE THEMSELVES POLITICALLY.

But liberty alone won't let us know the aggregate value of a shared interest. A strategic problem known as the 'revealed preference problem' (Samuelson, 1954, 1955) prevents this. The revealed preference problem can be seen by imagining yourself being 'polled' about your concerns regarding a particular public good (e.g. bike lanes). If the pollster is asking

---

[14] In political philosophy, consequentialism is the notion that an arrangement's value or worth is to be judged by its consequences. The most well-known form of consequentialism is utilitarianism.

you how much you care about it, and you want (or dislike) the program, you have every incentive to *overstate* the value you place on (or not having) the program. But, if the issue is going to be tied to your taxes by what you say, then you have every incentive to *understate* your value of the program. In sum,

INDIVIDUALS DON'T HAVE AN INCENTIVE TO GIVE THEIR TRUE VALUATION OF A PUBLIC GOOD.
(Samuelson 1954, 1955)[15]

Further implications can be developed from our simple model of public goods. Remember, the value of the good to the group is (roughly) the sum of the values of the good to the members of the group. Consider how the value of the good to the group increases with size. For simplicity, let us make four initial assumptions to simplify the analysis. First, put aside the problem of 'crowding' that can occur when the scale of the public good is insufficient for the population being served. Second, assume that the cost of increasing the scale of the good provided is constant. Third, assume that 'more' of the public good is valued at a constant rate. Fourth, continue with the assumption that each individual has the same valuation of the good. Then it follows that the larger the group, the bigger will be the social benefit each individual's contribution yields, as it gives benefits to a larger number of people. This is so even as the individual calculation of private benefits and costs remains constant, leading to the same choice of non-cooperative private action.[16] And hence, the larger the group, the bigger the social cost of any individual *shirking*. This gives us another principle regarding collective action:

THE LARGER THE GROUP, THE FURTHER FROM OPTIMAL WILL BE THE AMOUNT OF A PUBLIC GOOD WHICH AN *UNORGANIZED* GROUP WILL SUPPLY ITSELF.
(Frohlich and Oppenheimer, 1970)[17]

But there is another way of thinking of "suboptimality." Recall from the definition (page 35) that suboptimality implies that everyone can be made better off without hurting anyone. The greater this distance is from optimality, the greater is the potential reward for achieving optimality. This

---

[15] Tullock, 1977 contributed to a special issue of *Public Choice* that dealt with some innovative ideas to get people to reveal their preferences (called demand revelation mechanisms). These were subject to considerable scrutiny and finally found to also be no certain solution (Miller and Hammond, 1994).

[16] Indeed, we might think of a prisoner dilemma game as a game where the externalities (or effect on others) of each player's choice is bigger than its "internality" (or effect on self) (Kuhn and Mores, 1995; Frohlich and Oppenheimer, 1996; as well as Kuhn, 1996).

[17] Olson saw that there was a relationship to size, but misspecified it.

gain is shared by the entire group. That being so, we might identify another law-like implication regarding collective action:

THE FURTHER FROM OPTIMAL THE GROUP IS WITHOUT ORGANIZATION, THE GREATER WOULD BE THE POTENTIAL PROFIT IN ORGANIZING THE GROUP TO SATISFY THEIR "COMMON INTERESTS" OR TO SUPPLY THEM WITH PUBLIC GOODS.
(Frohlich and Oppenheimer, 1970; Frohlich, Oppenheimer, and Young 1971; and Wagner, 1966)

This implies that, holding other conditions constant, larger groups with shared interests are more attractive to organize as organizers can reap bigger rewards for their efforts in such groups. After all, the group would find it is gaining more by being effectively organized and would then be more willing to reward those who enabled it to gain these benefits. This leads to corollaries:

POLITICS IS POTENTIALLY MORE PROFITABLE FOR POLITICAL LEADERS IN LARGER GROUPS.

Hence, one has an explanation why larger groups are more likely to have successful political efforts to supply basic collective needs. Leadership can be rewarded better. But it also follows that politics can get nasty in larger groups. For if there is 'more to be had' in larger groups, then:

POLITICAL COMPETITION WILL BE STIFFER IN LARGER GROUPS.

Graphically, the collective action problem can be displayed in a form that will give us an easy way to get beyond the simple prisoner dilemma game story. Take a still simpler case than the one presented in Table 3. As in the table, each person receives $.40 for each $1 spent on the good. And each is presumed to have an endowment of $10. But, to make the relation between donors and contributions simpler, let us assume each person can either give $1 or nothing and that the group has precisely ten members.

This gives us the graph shown in Figure 1.[18] In the graph, the number of other individuals who are cooperating varies along the horizontal axis; the value of a person's choice varies along the vertical axis. Two lines show the payoff or value to a typical member of the group for her two possible choices, given the number of other cooperators:

[18] This sort of diagram is referred to as a 'Schelling' diagram because Thomas Schelling, Economics Nobel laureate in 2005, invented it. See Schelling, 1973.

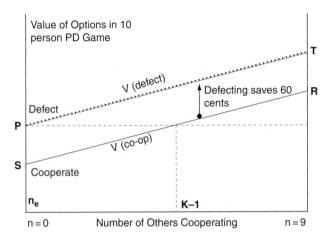

FIGURE 1. Graphing the payoffs of a 10 person prisoner dilemma game

- The value for defecting, labeled **V (defect)**, going from **P** (the value of defecting when everyone else also defects) to **T** (the value of defecting when no one else does).
- And the (lower) value for contributing, labeled **V(co-op)**, going from **S** (the value of cooperating when everyone else defects) to **R** (the value of cooperating when everyone else does).

The lines show the value of the individual's choice given the possible number of others in the group who choose to cooperate. Note that, in keeping with our 'story,' the line for *not* contributing is always above the line for contributing. This is because in our story the strategy of not contributing has a higher payoff than contributing regardless of the number of others who contribute: It is, therefore, a dominant strategy. Defecting is always $.60 more valuable than cooperating. So the lines are parallel: the vertical distance between them represents $.60. The graph depicts the same sort of n-person prisoner dilemma that we discussed earlier. If each person chooses her dominant strategy, and each keeps her original $10, they each get **P**. That is worse than if each of them made the $1 contribution. In the graph, that is shown as **R**. **R** is higher than **P**, showing that **R** is a better outcome. When ten people each give $1, the total benefit from the ten contributions is 10*.40, or $4 per person. And each person still has $9 of their initial endowment. Hence, each would get an outcome worth $13. In Figure 1 this is depicted by having the right-hand end of the bottom line (depicting the value of contributing when everyone else does) above the left-hand end of the top line (depicting the value of not contributing when no one else does). And this comes about because the outcome of everyone doing nothing is worse for the donor than giving when others all do. No one giving is Pareto suboptimal: one of the defining characteristics of a prisoner dilemma game.

Notice that the more other people who give, the better off everyone is, including those who give. So one question might be, how big must be the group of contributors so that none of them are worse off than if they had not contributed? We can see on the diagram the minimum size a group of contributors would have to be to break even: How many others would have to be giving $1 for you to find yourself better off joining them than having no one give? Call that level of giving by others K-1. It is identified by the point at which the height of the cooperation line is equal to P: When enough others cooperate to generate a value for each of the cooperators equal to the value of their non-cooperation choice. This is shown by where the dashed horizontal line (representing the value of P or the Nash equilibrium outcome) crosses the V (co-op) line.

If some subgroup can get together as many as 'K' to give, they will all find it better than everyone doing nothing and hence worth the effort. (Schelling, 1973, defined this a 'K-group.') Were fewer than K to cooperate, cooperation would be a losing proposition. The relative size of the number needed, or "K", to break even, gives one a partial idea of how difficult a minimally successful job of organizing would be. Of course, the game *is* a prisoner dilemma and so it would still pay for the individual to defect were he able to be sure it didn't affect the behavior of others: Defection is, after all, a dominant strategy. This leads to another conclusion about political organizing.

IN MOST COLLECTIVE ACTION PROBLEMS THERE WILL BE A BREAK EVEN POINT, SUCH THAT IF MORE THAN THE BREAK EVEN NUMBER OF PEOPLE CAN BE ORGANIZED TO GIVE, THEY WILL FIND IT REASONABLE TO GIVE, EVEN THOUGH THEY HAD A DOMINANT STRATEGY TO NOT GIVE.
(Schelling, 1973)

This leads to a proposition regarding political organizing in general:

POLITICAL LEADERS CAN USUALLY SUCCEED IN TURNING A COLLECTIVE ACTION DILEMMA INTO SOMETHING OF A COLLECTIVE SUCCESS BY ORGANIZING JUST A SUBGROUP OF INDIVIDUALS.

Since the incentive to free-ride exists even inside a K group, the difficulty of organizing such a subgroup should not be underestimated.

Note that the 'break even' point (expressed in number of donors) will be determined by the average return on the donation. In the example, where one gives a dollar or nothing and the return on the dollar is a "constant" 40 percent, the size of the contributing group of others has to be two for the individual to find it worthwhile to contribute. In the real world what one contributes to any collective effort is variable. If the group is made up of poorer individuals they are likely to make smaller contributions, and it will therefore take a 'larger' group to be successful. Or, we might say the job of political organizing is more difficult in poorer groups than in wealthier ones.

In Figure 1, the lines are parallel, implied by the cost of contributing to, and the valuation of each bit more of, the public good remaining constant. If these assumptions are violated, the lines would no longer be parallel. Let us see how this comes about and examine the real world contexts that would be modeled by such changes in the assumptions.

Changing the productivity of a contribution

In the previous 'story,' as illustrated in Figure 1, both the cost of contributing and the value of a bit more of the public good remained constant. But this is quite restrictive. Relaxing the assumption of constant valuation of the public good is certainly a move toward realism. For many things, the more we have of it, the less we value a little bit more of the same thing. Economists refer to this as decreasing marginal valuation (see the definition of marginal benefits and costs). If this were to be so for the public goods in question, the graphs would look different. The benefit line would not be "straight" but rather would rise ever more slowly as it rises to the right. Assuming the costs per unit were to remain constant, the

> Definition – *Marginal Benefits and Costs:* marginal refers to 'the next' or 'last' unit. So marginal benefits are those associated with getting the next unit and marginal costs are those associated with procuring it.

cost line would stay a straight line. The two no longer would be parallel. Since each unit is less valuable than the previous one, the more units others supply, the less valuable is Iris's act of donating a dollar to the cause. So, the more who give, the larger the incentive to free-ride.

This is depicted graphically in Figure 2. Here, the strategy of contributing is, again, never as valuable as that of not contributing. In other words, not contributing is a dominant strategy. Second, if everyone withholds support (i.e., everyone gets $10) the outcome is worse than if everyone gives (the right hand intercept of the contributing line **R** is above the left

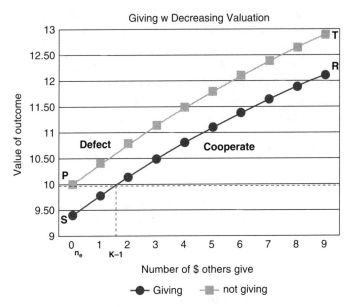

FIGURE 2. The Value of Donating with decreasing marginal valuation.

end of the defect line **P**). This implies the equilibrium outcome is not Pareto optimal. So this situation is still a prisoner dilemma game.

What then are the solutions to a prisoner dilemma game? Traditionally the prisoner dilemma story was solved by an enforcer: If you don't do the right thing you are punished. An enforcer would change the relative payoffs of defecting by taking away benefits from the defectors. But there are other solutions as well.

POSSIBLE SOLUTIONS

The prisoner dilemma game has received more attention from analysts than any other game theoretic subject. If it is a good model for social problems, we must ask how is it that these problems are solved. Or, to put it another way, what might be the solutions to a prisoner dilemma situation? Needless to say, there are a number of solutions that have been proffered to explain why groups have successfully gotten around the problems of self-interest that are endemically sapping contributions to the community. We can classify the main solutions that have been discussed as:

1. Changes to the payoffs or structure of the game to affect the choices of the players. The payoff changes could come from other-regarding preferences that value the group's welfare, altruism, a sense of ethics, a notion of social obligations or mores, and the like.
2. Repetition of the game which generates multiple equilibria (see Footnote 12).
3. Communication among the participants.
4. Organization of the group so that choice isn't purely voluntary. This could involve taxes or other designs of obligations which usually also require some form of leadership. I discuss leadership in the next chapter and institutional problems more generally in Part IV of the volume.

Transforming the Game

Rewards and Punishments

The proposal most commonly put forward to improve the outcome of a prisoner dilemma is that the game itself is transformed. This usually involves altering the payoffs associated with either cooperation or defection.[19] The object in both cases is to change the game so that non-cooperation is no longer dominant. An enforcement agency such as the Mafia is a good example. It must be sufficiently likely to catch up with the non-cooperative person to make it worthwhile to cooperate. Such enforcement changes to the model originally shown in Table 3 are displayed in Table 4. Again, a contribution gives each person a 40 percent return. As long as the punishment is big enough (more than 60 percent of each contribution, or .6x in the table) the new game has a dominant strategy to cooperate.

Thomas Hobbes may be interpreted as an early advocate of such an approach. His hypothetical state of nature analysis was, by many accounts, an n-person prisoner dilemma.[20] His solution was to set up an enforcer: a governor with full power to punish those daring to not cooperate.

An alternative approach to such dilemmas was adopted by Mao Zedong during early phases of the Chinese Revolution. Recruits for the

---

[19] Indeed, this is the move that is made implicitly by Mancur Olson when he concludes that there must be separable or incentives independent of the public good itself to solve the collective action problem.
[20] See, for example, Binmore, 1994 or Hardin, who dissents from this view, 1999.

TABLE 4. *Value of Donating, with Punishment*

Iris's (Typical Person's) Strategy	Donations by Others in the Group				
	9	8	... 2	1	0
Contribute $x	$13.60–.6x	$13.40–.6x	... $10.80–.6x	$10.40 –.6x	$10–.6x
Give Nothing and Be Punished	$13.60 – P	$13.40- P	... $10.80–P	$10.40–P	$10.–P

revolutionary militias were offered arable land. In their absence it would be tilled by the recruit's family who would then get the crops.[21] Such a reward for a contribution creates a change in the relative value of volunteering. It upped the payoffs associated with contributing.

But there are other ways that were often overlooked by economists, by which payoffs can be altered. Social mores and ethical motivations can change values and preferences, and hence alter the collective action problem.

Moral Incentives

Human (and apparently other animals as well, cf., de Waal, 1991, 1996) ability to be motivated by more than self-interest can alter the basic collective action problem. Thinking about one's choices as moral problems, with moral obligations to cooperate, changes one's payoffs. The adoption of a moral point of view creates a reward for cooperating, or guilt for defecting. This can transform the game from the standard prisoner dilemma.

A variety of ethical solutions have been developed to apply to situations that were traditionally considered prisoner dilemma games.[22] Two of these ethical solutions might serve to illustrate the approach, and to show how the adoption of other-regarding outlooks can transform the decision calculus of the players.

[21] "Red soldiers, like their commanders, received no regular salaries. But every enlisted man was entitled to his portion of land, and some income from it. This was tilled in his absence either by his family or by his local soviet." (Snow, p. 258)

[22] A number of pieces have been written about the role of adopting a moral point of view in decision making and its role in ethical theory. See, for example, Baier, 1981; Frankena, 1983; or Frohlich and Oppenheimer 2001.

One of the first solutions put forward for collective action problems was by Colin Strang (1960). He argued that a social norm of 'doing one's fair share' could solve the free-rider problem.[23] In simple situations, such a behavioral norm could lead to improvements and even, at times, to an optimal outcome. And in more complicated situations, the notion of fair share could still be calibrated so as to solve a social dilemma. In larger groups with widespread adoption of the norm, some social dilemmas might take care of themselves without further ado. Hence, for example, basic forms of small social insurance are offered for "free" all the time. For example, people who need help crossing streets often get it from the 'kindness of strangers.'

Another sort of moral point of view shows that a prisoner dilemma can be transformed into a purely cooperative game if the participants use impartial reasoning to calculate one's choice of action (Frohlich, 1992). Impartial reasoning is important since individuals often use it to calculate the right thing to do (for an example, think of the 'golden rule'). How does it work to transform the dilemma? The problem of collective action stems from the would-be contributor bearing costs greater than his individual benefit but not as big as the benefit going to the group. With impartial reasoning one takes into account these (larger) group benefits. Then, as shown in experiments (Frohlich and Oppenheimer, 1996), individuals adopt such reasoning and the dilemma goes away: Cooperation becomes the dominant strategy.

More recently, a number of empirical approaches to game theory have included moral decision making as a factor in the analysis of empirical outcomes of experimental evidence regarding behavior in social dilemma experiments (see Ostrom, 1998; Ahn, Ostrom and Walker, 2003; Epley and Caruso, 2004; Moore and Lowenstein, 2004; Tenbrunsel and Messick, 2004). The results support the conjecture that taking a moral point of view helps overcome the free-riding problem.

For 'moral suasion' to be effective, there may need to be a social norm, or 'persuader,' to lead people to rethink the value of their alternatives. In the absence of very strong acceptance of social norms, this isn't likely to happen by itself, and so, the group might need to be 'united' or 'organized,' at least informally. A group's reliance on social norms to solve social dilemmas will

---

[23] Strang does not fully address what one's fair share would be. He is best when considering a situation where everyone is to contribute in the same way and has an equal stake in the outcome. When inequalities of contributions and stakes are involved, each person's "fair share" may be neither equal nor easily comprehended.

work best when the group is dealing with repeated problems: helping out others in your family or community (village, workplace, etc.) who have been placed in need due to no fault of their own, or helping out at a moment of trouble (fire, accident, etc.). But in the modern world, problems take on new social forms involving multiple groupings of individuals amongst whom there may not exist established relations. Then social norms are less emphatically invoked and the moral points of view they suggest are not likely to be adopted without some advocacy leadership.

Thus the transformational power of social norms, and any moral point of view they induce, is unlikely to have strong applicability to the social dilemmas our societies face without conscious efforts by advocates. Rather, the use of a moral point of view to induce solutions to a prisoner dilemma is likely to be an explicit strategy of some players of the dilemma in order to alter behavior of others. Organization will usually be required, as in the rethinking of the environmental problems we face, and the social pressures to do our share that some environmental groups have brought to bear on all of us when we make decisions regarding the size of our houses, cars, and overall carbon footprint.[24] These efforts can have a substantial effect.[25]

Repetition of the Game

In some ways, the most radical transformation of the prisoner dilemma game, and its analysis, comes from the possibility of repetition. Since most opportunities for social cooperation involve individuals whose interactions continue over time, it is important to investigate how repetition of a prisoner dilemma game effects our analysis.

With repetition, the options expand beyond cooperate or defect. Players can signal their intents and trustworthiness by their choices. Over time one can respond to the choices of the other. For example, with two players, and two rounds of choice, one's choice of how to play in the first instance may

---

[24] As leadership and organization are often involved in 'organizing' groups to solve their social dilemmas we should recall the conclusion that the further from the optimal the group falls, the more profitable it is for a leader or organization to solve the problem (see above, page 42).

[25] Baumol and Oates (1979) discuss the lasting (though also limited) power of such appeals to solving such problems as recycling. The problem limiting the power of the appeals is related to their conflict with other values. See Besedes et al, 2011; Frohlich and Oppenheimer, 1984; Frohlich, Oppenheimer, and Kurki, 2004.

signal something to the other player for the second round. One can choose in the second round either conditioned on the decision of the other player in the first round or not. Non-conditional behavior could be to cooperate (or not) in both rounds, or to first cooperate (or not) and then to switch. Similarly, conditional behavior could be listed as to cooperate (or not) in the first round and then either do as the other did or as the opposite of the other.

It turns out that in repeated games, two situations must be distinguished. In the first, the individuals know that the situation will be terminated after some specific number of rounds. In the second, the repetition has no known endpoint. We consider both of these in turn.

Repetition and knowledge of the termination point
First, consider what happens when the players know the interaction involves a specified number of repetitions. Consider the case with one repeat. Presume the two-person prisoner dilemma game as depicted in Table 5. There it pays to defect: Non-cooperation is the dominant strategy. Regardless of the other's behavior, one loses by cooperating rather than defecting. Now what if both know the game will be repeated once. What is one to do? To analyze this, you might begin by considering the last repeat (i.e. second round). In that situation a player can cooperate or not, but need not consider any future response or 'signal' of intent. So, in the last round, it simply pays both players not to cooperate. It is the Nash equilibrium outcome. That settled; consider choices in the preceding round. Given that the other is sure to defect in the second round, no amount of signaling by cooperating is going to make any difference to her behavior in that last round.[26] So the game unravels: The last round can be analyzed as a simple prisoner dilemma game as we had considered earlier, but then, working backwards, so do the previous rounds.

Things change if one can't be sure when the situation will end. Without that knowledge, perhaps your behavior will be responded to in the next rounds, and lead to better payoffs. This then becomes the more interesting case. Now with no defined termination point one player can punish the other for non-cooperative behavior. One could, for example, begin by cooperating, and if the other doesn't cooperate, one can switch to

---

[26] This method of analyzing what to do by asking how things will "play out" in the last move, and then thinking back to how to get to the best last choice available, involves strategizing from where you want to be at the end of the game to how to get there from the step before, all the way back to the starting point. It is a general method for figuring out "what to do." It is commonly referred to as ***backward induction*** or ***rollback***.

TABLE 5. *Two-Person Prisoner Dilemma Game*

	Other's Choice	
Your Choice	Defect	Cooperate
Defect	10, 10	26, 4
Cooperate	4, 26	20, 20

non-cooperative behavior. By then mimicking the partner's behavior, she would find herself rewarded for cooperating and punished for not cooperating. (Such behavior is often called ***Tit-for-tat***.) How would a rational person respond to tit-for-tat? Clearly, knowing that you are facing a tit-for-tat player would give you an incentive to cooperate. Would the incentive work? That could depend upon how you evaluate future payoffs as compared to present payoffs. For example, were the prisoner dilemma game to be repeated only once a year, you might care quite a lot about the outcome of the first round, and discount the value of the future interactions by quite a lot. Future benefits are not the same as immediate ones. As they say, "A bird in hand is worth two in the bush."

The usual way to handle an evaluation of future payoffs is to think of the present value of those payoffs one is getting in the future. This involves a transformation of the future into the present by using what is called a *discount rate* (see definition). So, for example, suppose you could buy a certificate of deposit that would pay $100 in one year. Presumably you value today's money more than money to be received in one year; hence, you require compensation for waiting for your money. The more you need money today, the bigger is the discount rate (i.e. the less you would pay for the $100 in a year). For details, see Sidebar 3.

> Definition – *Discount Rate:* the percentage decrease you would accept for a future payoff to be received today.

Now reconsider the prisoner dilemma. To use discount rates we need a different scale for our preferences. A simple 'order' from best to worst won't do. As with expected value calculations, one that allows for multiplying by a discount rate is needed. Monetary values could do, and will be employed, but luckily it isn't required for the results to make sense. Preferences can be translated into "utility numbers" which carry a bit more content than their "ordering" from best to worst and allow us to

Sidebar 3 – Discounting Future Rewards

How does one convert future rewards (and costs) into something comparable to present rewards? One does this by calculating the *present value*, or P, of what will happen in the future. The information one needs is how big a difference the wait makes for the individual in question. The evaluation of the difference the wait makes in her welfare is called her discount rate, d. The process of calculating a future value (F) from a present value, or discounting, is actually just the opposite calculation. To illustrate, if we are talking about one future payment at a specified time (say, next year), then today's value

$$P = F/(1 + d) \text{ or } F = P(1 + d)$$

So with a discount of 10 percent a year, a promise of $10 say in one year is worth $10/1.1 or $9.09 today. A lower discount rate (say, 1 percent) would increase the present value $10/1.01 or $9.91. The same method also allows us to understand the value of a payment over a longer amount of time. Take the case of d = 10 percent, but with a wait of two years for the reward. Assuming that the delay over the second year is valued similarly to that of the first year, the discounting occurs once, and then the discounted value is discounted again. In other words, the discounting is compounded.

$$P = F_2/[(1 + d)^2] \text{ or } F_2 = P^*(1 + d)^2$$

A wait of n years would be similar, with n substituting for the 2.

$$P = F_n/[(1 + d)^n] \text{ or } F_n = P(1 + d)^n$$

use discounting (see Footnote 13, Introduction). But it may be most straightforward to think of the numbers in terms of money.

Return to the illustration above with payoffs as in Table 5. Now add a repetition with discounting. Assume each player places a discount of 10 percent on future earnings. Using the discount rate and adding the payoffs from both rounds together to the value of the total payoff to the player at the start of the interaction gives us the payoffs as depicted in Table 6. To see this, start with the possible outcome that both parties never cooperate. Each player gets a payoff of 10 in each round. But the value of 10 in the

TABLE 6. *Some Alternatives in a Twice Repeated Two-Person Prisoner Dilemma*

	Column's choices		
Your choices	Defect Always	Cooperate Always	Tit-for-Tat
defect always	19.09, 19.09	49.64, 7.64	35.09, 13.09
cooperate always	7.64, 49.64	38.18, 38.18	38.18, 38.18
Tit-for-tat	13.09, 35.09	38.18, 38.18	38.18, 38.18

future second round, would be 10/(10+10%) or 9.09 today. Then adding the value of 10 in the second round with, say, 10 in the first round would give 19.09.[27]

The first thing to notice is that there is no longer a dominant strategy. If Column were to choose Tit-for-tat, then if Row were to always defect she would get $35.09 over the two rounds.[28] If she had also chosen Tit-for-tat she would have done better ($38.18).

Tit-for-tat is but one way to choose conditionally on the basis of the choices of others.[29] And given our focus on collective action we are interested in more than the two-person, once repeated prisoner dilemma game. But the point should be clear, and can be stated in a more general form.

WHEN PEOPLE CARE ABOUT THE FUTURE PAYOFFS FROM INTERACTIONS THAT ARE REPEATED, THERE IS SUBSTANTIALLY GREATER POTENTIAL FOR COOPERATION IN PROBLEMS OF COLLECTIVE ACTION.

The correlates are obvious and swirl around the following generalization.

PEOPLE WHO ARE TRANSITORY MEMBERS OF GROUPS (SHORT TIMERS) ARE LESS LIKELY TO BEHAVE COOPERATIVELY TO SOLVE COLLECTIVE ACTION PROBLEMS.

Even without a termination date (as in exit from the military) their limited time horizon causes them to discount the future more, and hence volunteer

[27] Similarly, a 4 in round two, from cooperating while the other defects, has a present value of 3.64; a 20 in round two, from both cooperating, has a present value of 18.18; and defecting while the other cooperates has a present value of 23.64.
[28] $26 in the first round, and $10 in the second. But the second would be discounted, hence $35.09.
[29] Tit-for-tat, however, is a particularly interesting strategy. In two-person interactions it does exceptionally well, and has a number of other very interesting properties (see Axelrod, 1984; Bendor and Swistak, 1997). Our concern with larger group interactions leaves this subject a segue not taken.

less. Further, if there are a number of short timers with explicit termination dates (as in a political administration that has no chance of being reelected) individuals may exhibit a higher discount, enabling them to "unravel" the cooperative possibilities that previously existed.

RESEARCH FRONTIERS: EXPERIMENTS, DOUBTS, AND WAYS FORWARD

Olson's analysis of the pitfalls to a purely voluntary basis for supporting shared interests has proven very fruitful. It has given political scientists a new starting point for their studies. But as studies increased in scope and claims, some doubts surfaced. The claims seemed over-reaching. People sometimes cooperate without any formal organization. Major problems do sometimes get addressed, even in what appeared to be unorganized groups. These observations created puzzles and led to a multi-faceted research frontier spawning field studies, experiments, and theoretical revisions. It is useful to identify some of the puzzles as they motivate much of the content of the next two chapters. The most basic question is accuracy or correspondence of theory and reality.

Behavioral Evidence from Prisoner Dilemma Experiments

Does the theory really tell us what to expect or do people who find themselves in a prisoner dilemma behave as the theory contemplates? Here the results are ambiguous. To see this consider some experimental evidence.

- The notion that no one will contribute is certainly false under virtually all conditions. People cooperate to some extent. Indeed in the first round there usually is a relatively high degree of cooperation (30–50 percent of what would be considered optimal). This falls off somewhat with repetition. But some degree of cooperation remains (10–25 percent of what is optimal) in almost all experiments.

Many hundreds of experiments have explored the behavior of individuals in n-person prisoner dilemma games. The experiments are called "voluntary contribution mechanism" (VCM) experiments. They are designed to test whether behavior fits the theory. They test many conjectures and some very clear lessons have been learned.[30]

---

[30] Ledyard, 1995 gives an excellent summary of experiments through the mid-nineties.

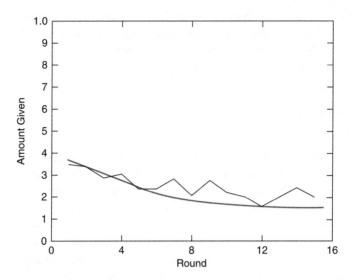

FIGURE 3. Average contributions in 5 person groups in a VCM experiment and a reasonable smoothing over many experiments.

At the level of the group, Figure 3 depicts some of these experimental results. The jagged line represents average individual contributions in a fairly typical experimental situation. The groups in question have five members each and each person has $10 to contribute in each round. The return to each person in the group of a contribution of $1 by anyone is 40 cents. Olson would predict no contributions in this case. The line seems a reasonable "smoothing" of the data, which would be approached by averaging many similar experimental results. What would lie behind such data?

Perhaps people start naive and learn that cooperation isn't in their interest. But then why is there a 10–25 percent floor of cooperation in later rounds? There have been many conjectures. Perhaps some people are suckers and just give, while others fall off. Perhaps some people feel better if they "leave a bit in the pot" – sort of like a tip. Neither of these seems borne out by the evidence on the individual level.

- Individual behavior appears erratic. There are very few "pure" free-riders or purely self-interested individuals. Other-regarding individuals rarely reach a stable decision in their behavior.

The data from these experiments has been problematic. The simple conjectures that the subjects are learning, or "tipping," are simply wrong. The

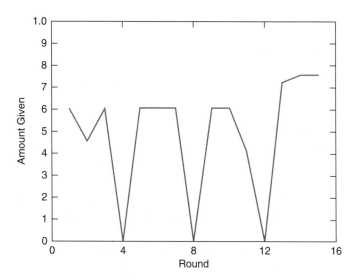

FIGURE 4. Example of a moderately cooperative subject in an n-person prisoner dilemma game experiment.

vast majority of individuals participating in these experiments behave in a manner that appears chaotic (see Figure 4 for an example). Analyzing the data shows[31] that people make their judgments (and hence choices) probabilistically. They want to help each other and to do their fair share. But even more than that: They don't want to be taken advantage of.[32]

Now the first of these findings goes way beyond issues of self-interest and touches upon what we mean by rational choice. Theorists have not readily included probabilistic evaluations as an aspect of their models of rational choice. But to understand how people behave, we must examine how people focus their mind, or pay attention. It has long been known and shown by others (e.g. Standage, et al, 2005) that attention is a winner-take-all phenomenon.

To displace what one is currently paying attention to (i.e. to grab one's attention) an item must appear more important or pass an 'importance

---

[31] A series of three papers reports the results. See Frohlich and Oppenheimer, 2006; Wendel and Oppenheimer 2010; and Oppenheimer, Wendel, and Frohlich, 2011.

[32] Numerous researchers have concluded that people care about the welfare of others and fairness. But in general people care more about not being taken advantage of than either the welfare of others and the overall fairness of the outcome. See Fehr and Schmidt, 1999 and Frohlich, Oppenheimer, and Kurki, 2004. There is considerable research being conducted to understand precisely how best to model these values.

threshold' needed to displace one's current subject. So subjects do not pay attention to their cooperation level unless their perceived short-fall relative to others is 'big enough.'[33] When combined with others, and tied to max-imizing, this leads to the sort of jagged behavior shown in Figure 4. Tests showing this to be likely are given and analyzed in Wendel and Oppenheimer (2007) and Oppenheimer, Wendel, and Frohlich (2011).

- Communication matters a great deal. A little bit of communication among group members goes a long way to solving the social dilemma. Even electronic communication can be a great facilitator. (Frohlich and Oppenheimer, 1998)
- The rate of return of any effort for the public good to the individual (i.e., the cost of cooperation) makes a substantial difference in the level of cooperation achieved.
- The size of the group makes little or no difference in the behavior of the individuals as long as the rate of return to the individual is held constant.

So the experiments show there are empirical anomalies with the traditional theory: People don't behave purely self-interestedly; behavior exhibits a random element in it; and people have a relativized (to others in the group) sense of welfare rather than an absolute one. Some of these will be dis-cussed at later points in the text. Clearly, the theory of the prisoner dilemma game is itself less than a perfect explanation of behavior in collective action situations. Although it has been widely employed, we cannot expect to predict accurately all the collective action phenomena that have been modeled using it. On the other hand, it is a useful starting point. It lets us see regularities that weren't apparent and has created new research questions likely to lead to theory that is better grounded. Finally, note that predictions at the group level are better approximations than those at the level of the individual.

A Further Comment Regarding Communication

Why it works no one knows, but add a little ability to communicate among participants to a prisoner dilemma game, and bingo: One gets lots of

---

[33] The argument is for a sort of "bounded rationality"; evaluations and updating are not happening continually. Alternative forms of bounded rationality have been proposed by Bendor (1995) and Simon (1992). Early proposals are discussed in Zeckhauser and Shaefer (1968).

cooperation. It shouldn't be the case. After all, defecting is a dominant strategy. One might think that communication leads to an ability to identify the others and hence leads to a fear of punishment for non-cooperative behavior. But no, even when great care is developed in experimental settings to ensure that no one can identify the other individuals, communication has cooperative effects. And it matters little what sort of communication: Whether it is face-to-face or electronic communication, the results are similar (see Frohlich and Oppenheimer, 1998). Indeed, so strong is the effect that such marginal forms of communicating as the ability to send an electronic happy face, or an inverted triangle (▼, that some would say looks ever so slightly like the shape of a face) works quite well in inducing cooperation (Wilson, et al., 2001).

What this suggests is that there are difficulties with the original premises: Individuals are more complex. They see themselves both as individuals and as part of a group. Indeed, they act as if there is at least a weak tie between their own well-being and the well-being of the group. But the erratic cooperative behavior is insufficient for most collective purposes: Groups would not get their shared interests satisfied were they to rely on individual voluntary contributions. The prisoner dilemma is a useful model for the thinking about collective action problems in unstructured situations. We now expand the analysis of collective action to a variety of social structures. As a result we will better understand political interactions. In the next chapters we develop other models to get a fuller picture of the possibilities of political action.

CHAPTER 2

Going Beyond the Prisoner Dilemma

Although considerable leverage is gained by modeling a collective action problem as a prisoner dilemma game, many, if not most, social problems are only *similar* to prisoner dilemma situations. Voting is an example of a social institution that leads to situations that are very close, but not actually, prisoner dilemmas. When one votes, quite clearly, the essence of voting is that the vote one casts will be counted and hence counts. Although unlikely, it could make a difference; it could change the outcome.[1]

This possibility, that the vote matters, implies that there is no dominant strategy. For if one's vote can matter, then under precisely those circumstances, presumably, it pays to vote. Thus, voting is fundamentally different from the standard prisoner dilemma game.

It follows that there is more to be understood about collective action than we can model with the prisoner dilemma. And yet, as we shall see, the fundamental similarities between our expanded set of collective action cases helps us use the tools we have already developed to understand the situation. Our analysis of simple modifications of these new situations leads to some surprising results.

COLLECTIVE ACTION BEYOND THE PRISONER DILEMMA

Recall that a prisoner dilemma game requires two things: first, each actor must have a dominant strategy. Second, the collective choosing of the

---

[1] Indeed, this notion that a vote counts and can make a difference is behind numerous definitions of democracy. An elegant starting point in pursuing this literature might be Farquharson (1969).

players' dominant strategies leads to a suboptimal outcome. What might collective action look like when we don't conform to these fundamental attributes of the prisoner dilemma game?

No Dominant Strategy

Begin with an illustration. Imagine a small suburban block with four houses on it. The group of four neighbors includes three younger families and an older fellow with some handicaps. They all would like to have some shade in their backyards and would like to plant a few trees of substantial size between them in the corner where their plots meet to generate that shade. They have already agreed to split the cost of the trees; what remains is the task of planting them. As anyone who has planted a tree of substantial size knows, the effort of digging the hole, placing the tree therein, staking it, repacking the soil, and then watering the tree is a real job. The trees have been delivered and the three healthy neighbors are planning to plant them on Saturday. Any delay would mean at least a week until they have another day off, and the trees would slowly deteriorate. Each of the neighbors can either show up or make up some excuse and not help on Saturday. That means that there are precisely three scenarios that could occur. Consider the depiction of this example in Table 7. There we have pulled out one of the neighbors, Jim, to depict his decision calculus.

He could show up to help with the work of planting the trees (or not), and his two neighbors could also be there, or only one of them could be there, or, finally none of them might be there. From Jim's perspective, if the other two show and he doesn't go, some of the job will get done and he will have the day off; we depict this as a +10. But with both of his neighbors by his side, he can not only have a good time, they can get all the trees planted, thereby preventing any deterioration in the quality of the trees (a +20 for him). Clearly, if the others show, he's better off showing also. But if no one else shows up, Jim can't do a good job. The effort of digging a big enough

TABLE 7. *Neighbors in an Assurance Game*

Jim's Strategic Options	Number of Others Who Show Up		
	2 others show up	1 other shows up	No others show up
Show up	20	5	−10
Don't show up	10	−2	−5

hole in the rocky soil is just too much for the weekend gardener. And so, although part of the job would be done, the planting might not go as well (the trees might be planted neither straight nor deep enough, for example) if there is no one else to help. In other words it would be a losing situation: he'd score it a −10, and it would be better, under those circumstances, not to have showed up at all. (Then he'd have the day off, although the trees would certainly deteriorate.) If one other neighbor were there, then probably it would be better to be out there working than staying home. They could then do some of the work quite well: +5. Sitting at home with one person working would mean that the work wouldn't be done right, and so staying home would be worse than going out to help then also.

Once again, here we have a simple collective action problem, but no longer is there a dominant strategy. This time what any one player will want to do depends upon the behavior of others. It doesn't pay for a neighbor to show up to work if none of the others show up. But were even one of the others to show up, it would be worthwhile showing up to do the job. In this sort of situation, what is one's best choice depends upon what others do. If sufficient others cooperate, it is worth cooperating. Otherwise, not. This sort of situation is called an *assurance game*.

The Assurance Game

More generally, we can expand the analysis to that of a larger group with a variety of collective interests. What is required is only that it is only worthwhile contributing if enough others do. In these cases, there would be no dominant strategy and the graph would look something like Figure 5.

In such cases, passing some threshold level of help from others, marked here with an **A**, it would be the case that even for one individual, cooperation "pays" or is worth more than defection as a choice. At this point, the line depicting the value of cooperation for each level of cooperation by others crosses the line depicting the value of noncooperation. Below **A** other contributors, it pays for the person to defect. In Figure 5, there is clearly no dominant strategy: what is best for any player depends on the pattern of behavior of all the other members of the group. What one would want to do depends on what one has assurance that others will do.

Each member of the group would find it worthwhile to make their choice depending on whether the number who cooperated was above or below **A**. The final outcome could well be full participation. On the other hand, were the number of others who show up *below* **A**, those who showed up would change their minds and quit. If no one else showed up, then the Nash equilibrium would occur were no one to show up. But if more than **A**

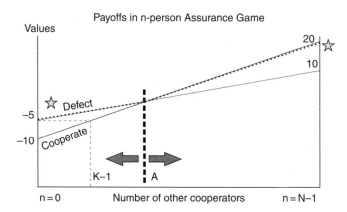

FIGURE 5. An n-person assurance game where equilibria are shown by a ☆, and the best strategy choice is 'dotted.'

show up, then everyone has an incentive to show up another and we see another Nash equilibrium: universal cooperation. As indicated by the two ☆s there is no *single* equilibrium: there are two.

And let us notice "K-1" too. In Figure 5 as in Figure 1, if a subgroup with as many members as **K** can all agree to give, they will all find it better than everyone doing nothing and hence worth the effort. Once the group gets past **K-1** each of the members finds it paid for them to contribute to the group effort: they each got more than they would have had none of them contributed, even though, as in a prisoner dilemma, it would pay each of them to defect on the others in the **K** group. A simple inspection of the graph should suffice to let the reader understand that **K** is always smaller than **A**. Above **A** it pays for everyone to jump on the "cooperation" bandwagon. If the size of Schelling's **K**-group (see Chapter One) depicted one measure of the difficulty of organizing a group, the magnitude of **A** gives another. A group involved in an assurance game is easier to success-fully organize if **A** is a smaller proportion of the group's size. After all, only below **A** does it pay for each of them to free-ride. It is probably important to keep clear the meaning of these two parameters, **A** and **K**, as both are important for organizing a group's solution to many collective action problems.

Some analysts have argued that the trick of political organizing is to transform collective action from a prisoner dilemma to an assurance game and then to get enough people to contribute to get beyond that threshold **A**, where it no longer pays to be a free-rider. But as Schelling pointed out, it might well be that there are plausible supporting tricks: one can begin by organizing a large enough subgroup of **K** to stick together, to "get the ball rolling" on a self-sustaining basis. Note, again, in Figure 5, **K** is the size of the subgroup that needs to cooperate for all to be better off than they would have been if no one cooperated.[2] This leads to an insight regarding political organizing in general:

SOMETIMES POLITICAL LEADERS CAN SUCCEED BY TURNING A COLLECTIVE ACTION DILEMMA INTO AN ASSURANCE GAME, AND THEN BY ORGANIZING A SUFFICIENT SUBGROUP, GENERATING A BANDWAGON EFFECT IN THE GROUP AS A WHOLE.

Unlike the incentive to free-ride that exists even inside a **K** group, passing the threshold of an **A** group generates an equilibrium for people to contribute. Still, the difficulty of organizing such a large subgroup should not be minimized. But, as indicated in the previous chapter, if people can communicate within that group, and if there is some recognition of the identity of others in the group (as with, for example, neighbors or friends, etc.) the job is made easier. In a large scattered group, one might be able to organize a number of local subgroups, each exceeding size **K**, and in so doing, create a total level of cooperation that can move one beyond **A**, the level that makes it worthwhile for all to get on board.[3]

The Chicken Game

Social dilemma situations without a dominant strategy aren't all assurance games. Indeed, just making a small change in our tree-planting example fundamentally alters the situation: what if it only took two to do the job? Then the new situation is that the best outcome for Jim would be that the other two do the job while he stayed home to watch football. Further it could be that one can do the job (not as well) and that Jim would prefer to see it done than to watch the game and have no one plant the trees. Then the payoffs might look more like what is shown in Table 8. Again, there is no dominant strategy. And a reasonable way to look at this situation is that Jim would hope others would show up, while he stays home. But if no one else is going to be there, he'd prefer to do the work than not have it done. This sort of game is known as a "chicken game." Each player is hoping the others will do what they don't want to do. Like the assurance game, there

---

[2] In general, this is found in a Schelling diagram when the height of the "value of cooperation" line gets above the intersection of the value of not cooperating with the left axis.

[3] Dennis Chong (1991) develops and applies a similar argument to analyze the very successful strategic work by the leadership of the civil rights movement in the 1960s.

TABLE 8. *Neighbors in a Chicken Game*

	Number of Others Who Show Up		
Jim's Strategic Options	2 Others Show Up	1 Other Shows Up	No Others Show Up
Show up	10	2.5	−5
Don't show up	20	5	−10

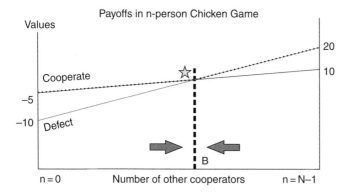

FIGURE 6. A chicken game where the equilibrium is shown by a ☆.

are two different conditions to consider. When no one else cooperates, it pays to cooperate, and when others do, it pays not to help. In such situations, if contributions by others fall short, people will give.[4]

But if contributions from others get beyond a sufficient level, individuals will free-ride. There is, however, a single equilibrium level of giving as can be seen at **B**, marked by a ☆, in Figure 6. Unlike the situation in the assurance game shown in Figure 5, this Nash equilibrium is precisely where the two lines cross. For when there are fewer than **B** cooperators, some defectors find cooperation is now worth more than defecting (i.e., cooperation pays, pushing the number of cooperators up). Similarly, when

---

[4] Perhaps this should be contrasted with the typical depiction of a two-person chicken game. There each player can either "swerve" or not, as in the classic "who is more macho" automobile game of the 1950s. Then the worst outcome would be for both players not to swerve and to meet in a head-on collision. In that case there are two Nash outcomes: in each case one swerves (loses) and the other doesn't (wins). But note that there is only one Nash number of swervers. Here in the *n*-person collective action case, there are incentives to let the others "lose" by contributing, but if no one is contributing, it pays to jump in.

there are more than **B** cooperators, the value of defection is higher than the value of cooperation and some cooperating individuals find they would prefer to defect – pushing the number of cooperators down.

Now let us put these pieces together to get to a more general analysis.

The General Case

Our analysis is now populated with prisoner dilemma games, assurance games, and chicken games: the world appears to be getting more complicated by the page. But a general pattern of collective action underlies a good deal of this analysis. In larger groups, cooperation by the very few first individuals is not very helpful in itself, but each individual can move one toward a more valuable range of collective effort. Virtually all costly collective efforts require some minimum to get off the ground. Consider a bridge over a brook. A minimalist bridge may cost one thing, but many embellishments, such as increasing the capacity or durability, or improving the aesthetics of the bridge, can be added at greater cost. On a smaller scale, a project may appear hopeless until a few people have put their shoulder to the wheel: then it appears achievable. We have now developed models that show how individuals come to understand that their contribution can make a sufficient difference to motivate them to chip in. But then, usually, beyond some point, the value falls off again. It often takes a certain threshold of others to make your contributions worthwhile. And then, also, if too many others give support to the cause, once again, your contribution becomes less valuable.

This is certainly the case in voting. There is a range of behavior of others that leads you to feel that your contribution can be valuable, indeed, maybe even essential, for the project to go forward. We model this more general case to get more leverage on the problems of political action.

The general case being outlined is similar to what we have just discussed regarding decreasing marginal valuation. But more generally, there will first be a level of increasing marginal benefit to one's donation and then a range of decreasing marginal benefit. That would mean that the slope of the payoff lines, for either a contributing or withholding strategy, will become steeper as others give more (indicating the value is increasing faster) and then will become flatter.

To understand the more general case, we first consider the most extreme version of this story: giving is worthless for a while, and then, if enough others also cooperate, and if you help, the problem is solved. If still more contribute, their effort is unneeded. This is similar to one's vote making the difference in the outcome. There is a range in which your action solves the

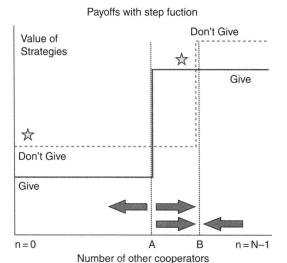

Payoffs with step fuction

FIGURE 7. The value of cooperating with a step function with equilibria marked with a ☆.

problem: it "pays" to act. This is depicted in Figure 7. Because of the shape of the valuation lines, they are called "step functions." Now clearly, when the lines are so steep, they will cross: at some point and for some range (depicted as from **A** to **B**) cooperation pays for the individual. Neither strategy is dominant; so the situation is not a prisoner dilemma game. To the left of **A**, and to the right of **B**, it doesn't pay to contribute. There is a noncooperative equilibrium for everyone on at the left. But between **A** and **B** there is a range of others' behavior where the individual would find her contribution would make enough of a difference to her so as to be worth making. There, contributing is more worthwhile than withholding support. This makes **B** and zero equilibrium levels of cooperation.

Generalizing the situation is straightforward. What sorts of situations have these characteristics? To answer this question, we need to think of how resources that are allocated for projects translate to their success. Typically this is via a project's "production function." Projects often take substantial effort to start and only then are resources "productive." This is a notion that there is a start-up cost that then leads to a period of "increasing marginal returns." After some further investment, the project can't be made much more useful or successful by having more resources thrown at it (decreasing marginal returns). Rather than suddenly making a bigger

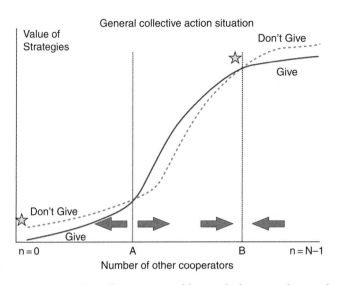

FIGURE 8. Contributing to a public good: the general case where equilibria are shown by a ☆.

difference, as is depicted by the lines turning at right angles in Figure 7, usually the efficacy builds rather smoothly and then the lines bend toward becoming flatter smoothly. This makes the production function S-shaped, as in Figure 8. Again, if there is any hope of making a difference, the lines must cross. In such cases, the cooperative line could not remain below the line depicting the value of noncooperative behavior. It is illustrated in Figure 8. Here we see the lines depicting the value of not contributing and contributing cross each other at two values of others' efforts: **A** and **B**. Neither strategy is dominant, so the situation is not a prisoner dilemma game. Doing nothing is an equilibrium when everyone does the same. When too few cooperate (i.e., to the left of **A**), the dotted line, "don't give," lies above the solid line, "give." It doesn't pay to contribute.[5] And when "too many" cooperate (to the right of **B**) it also doesn't pay to cooperate. Between **A** and **B** is a region where the individual would find her contribution would make enough of a difference to her so as to be worth making. In other words, just a means-ends calculation regarding efficacy will lead her to only contribute when her contribution is sufficiently effective. Different individuals value the public good differently and hence have different thresholds for being cooperative:

---

[5] Note that although here I do not discuss the Schelling K group concept, one could. Doing so would increase our leverage over the collective action problems.

the value of the difference they make must be greater than the cost of making the contribution.

In these situations, **A** is directly analogous to our level **A** in the assurance game in Figure 5. Indeed, from the left and toward point **B**, the game is like an assurance game. Consider the nature of the situation when the behavior of others aggregate to **A**. This is the dynamic of many social dilemma games referred to as assurance games. In such games, there is a threshold: were a group to achieve **A** they would have gotten "over the hump," and members would find it worthwhile to support the group effort. Such a threshold is not in equilibrium, for if it is achieved, it will generate more support and contributing will go up toward **B**. If **A** is not achieved, support is likely to collapse. But **B** *is* in equilibrium. Small deviations above or below **B** lead back to **B**. Below **B**, individuals give more, and above they draw back their support. Indeed, above **A** the situation is analogous to Figure 6 of the chicken game. **B** has the same properties in both diagrams.

But we can be more precise. To do so, recall that rational individuals are making trade-offs between different values in order to maximize their expected value (see the Introduction). People behaving so as to maximize their expected value will be more prone to contributing when the probability of being in the range of **AB** is higher. Individuals discount the difference they will make by the probability of making a difference. Of course, people only approximate such theoretical behavior,[6] but this is all our conclusions require. So, looking at the simple case of the step function, as in Figure 7, to consider the likelihood of making a difference means considering the probability of being in the range **AB**. The expected value of a contribution, then, is this probability times the difference in value between getting the valued public good and not. This needs to be greater than the expected value of holding onto the resources and making no contribution if the individual is to contribute.

The lessons for political leadership are clear:

EFFECTIVE POLITICAL LEADERS "ENGINEER" SITUATIONS TO EXPAND THE RANGE OVER WHICH A CONTRIBUTION WILL MAKE A DIFFERENCE.

---

[6] Indeed, there has been a great deal of research undertaken about how people make choices in risky situations. Nobel prizes have been given for research in this area (as a starter, see the works by Kahneman et al., 1979, 1982, 1986; and Tversky et al., 1973, 1981, 1986, 1992). Those who doubt that humans think carefully about these matters may find Gopnick's *The Philosophical Baby* instructive. She points out that experiments show that even preverbal children make decisions on the basis of probability estimates.

One way of doing this is to tie particular contributions to highly valued differences. Examples are appeals from charities such as "A $20 donation will feed a child for two months" or "For $100, you can give a family farming tools and seeds that will feed them in perpetuity." Another approach is taken by expanding the probability that your donation will be helpful by "matching" or expanding donations. This is done by PBS fund-raisers claiming, "Give now while your contribution is matched 3 for 1. Every dollar you give will give $4 to our station."

A second lesson can be learned.

EFFECTIVE POLITICAL LEADERS ENCOURAGE INDIVIDUALS TO BELIEVE THE PROBABILITY THAT THEIR CONTRIBUTION WILL MAKE A BIG DIFFERENCE IS HIGH.

This can be done by creating goals. PBS again uses such goals as, "This hour's goal is only $5,000, and we are almost there, so there is no better time to give!" Here the goal is not a budget to make a viable station: who knows what that would be? Rather a goal is defined that is made significantly more achievable by even a $100 gift. Similarly, politicians emphasize the closeness of the race: "every vote makes a difference."

One of our earlier conclusions should now sound more likely: more complicated and costly efforts at satisfying shared interests will require some incentives beyond the public good itself. Although there may be some ability to mobilize many people for bursts of giving and help, sustained efforts are going to require the political and governmental organizations and their inevitable taxes that we all expect. These will be needed to sustain efforts to satisfy the needs and maintain the welfare of the members of the group.

CHAPTER 3

Collective Action Applications to and Beyond Democratic Politics

Public goods are received by a group of individuals: if one gets it, so do the others. Many things such as laws, judicial appointments, and foreign policies (in general, the outcomes of political as opposed to personal decisions) can be viewed as public goods. This means that the previously reached conclusions have significant implications for how individuals relate to political and governmental outcomes. Here we use these same models to deal with relations between citizens and government. This is especially important for politics in democratic systems, where one of the objectives of the design of political institutions is to help relate citizen behavior with control and responsiveness of the government. We will show that implications of the above arguments for the behavior of citizens run counter to some traditional expectations of both the democratic public and political science professionals.

RATIONAL IGNORANCE

How do people inform themselves regarding electoral politics? Getting accurate information regarding candidates can be difficult. Information acquisition and processing about other political things (such as the goings on in a legislature, or reasoning behind judicial decisions) is likely to be even more difficult. We might say political information, and its processing, is costly.

Consider Heather, a subscriber to, and reader of, her daily local newspaper. Perhaps Heather, like many of us, reads the paper for about half an hour at breakfast: she has constraints. Heather notices the variety of things to read and chooses within her constraints. Perhaps half of her scarce minutes were spent on page 1; now she skims the headlines noticing several items of interest. On page 4, something that looks negative and important concerning a candidate she was going to vote for in the next election, and there also, on the same page, is an item on water pollution at the beach Heather was planning to go to for vacation. She is torn, wants to read both, but must run. How to decide?

Let's consider why Heather is so likely to read about the beach and not the candidate. Getting information about the candidate can lead her to avoid the error of voting for the wrong candidate: someone she would rather not see win. Getting information about the beach can lead her to avoid the error of going to the wrong beach, someplace she would rather not swim. If it is an important office, probably the election could have a bigger impact (higher taxes, loss of programs that matter to her, even a war, etc.) than a somewhat less nice vacation, *but* ... gathering all the information in the world about the candidate isn't likely to do more than prevent *her* from making a mistake in her voting. It is very unlikely to change the outcome of the election.[1]

Tying this more directly to the discussion in the previous chapter, Heather is faced with two activities. One has a very big prize (voting for the right side were her vote to change the outcome of the election) with a very small probability and the other has a smaller prize (having a better vacation by choosing a better beach) as an almost sure thing. Using the logic of expected value Heather decides not to invest in gathering information either concerning politics, or public goods.

The models of collective action then let us see that the rational voter decides not to invest in the information about the public good: not because of self-interest, but because of lack of sufficient efficacy (Downs, 1957). It is rational for Heather to remain ignorant about the political choice, while actively consuming information about private choices.

Reviewing experimental results is revealing; running one in a class is eye opening. John Pisciotta, an economist at Baylor University, designed a simple in-class experiment[2] about rational ignorance that is also a learning exercise for the participants. Students are given a budget to spend on gathering information. They have a choice as to whether to purchase information about which might be the best private purchase or about

---

[1] Of course, voting in elections is not the only way to use your political knowledge to change political outcomes.

[2] All the materials are available at http://business.baylor.edu/John_Pisciotta//

which alternative might be the most advantageous to vote for in a referendum. The values can be similar for the outcomes in the two classes of choices. Students purchase two bits of information: either about the public good, or about the private good, or one bit regarding each. Round one typically finds students purchasing both types of information. Quickly the typical student shifts to buying only the private decision as she becomes aware that there is less to be gained in gathering information on what to vote for than what to buy. After all, what the individual purchases is received. But what she votes for needn't make a difference. The outcome may be decided with a margin greater than one vote.

Further, to solve the obtaining of shared outcomes groups usually need to provide incentives independent of the public good for members to contribute to solve the problem (e.g., punishments for not paying taxes). This leads people to have information about the incentives but not the programs, since it is the incentives that have been designed to motivate the behavior. The argument in this section leads to another principle of politics: the expectation of rational ignorance.

INDIVIDUALS HAVE A DISCOUNTED INTEREST IN ACQUIRING INFORMATION ABOUT POLITICAL AFFAIRS AND WILL, IN GENERAL, REMAIN RATIONALLY IGNORANT REGARDING POLITICS.

(Downs, 1957)

Not all individuals have the same lack of interest in staying politically informed. Individuals' wealth, profession, and so on will help determine the utility they have for political information: the information might be useful for strictly private decision making. So, for example, a "producer" needs to make investment decisions informed by tax laws, information regarding importation of substitute factors of production, etc. A car buyer may wish to acquire details regarding a tax incentive to buy fuel-efficient cars. A wealthy person may wish to know about foreign policy so as to better assess risks regarding international investments. A poorer person may have little use for such knowledge. The mobility of capital means that those with it will want information about the "exit" strategies they can employ to save tax monies, gain higher returns, etc. Those without capital will be less interested in acquiring such information.[3]

---

[3] Two asides here are useful. First, Hirschman (1970) points out that there are often private strategic responses to "public good" problems. Whites who didn't want to be subject to the public good of integration sent their children to private schools and had their towns sell off their public swimming pools to private clubs that could exclude blacks. He calls such responses "exit." Also, Boix (2003) developed a very useful model based on the notion of

Because wealth gives one private interests to acquire political news, we can identify a few corollaries to the above principle:

THE WEALTHY WILL BE BETTER POLITICALLY INFORMED THAN THE POOR. THEREFORE, WITHOUT MASS ORGANIZATIONS SUCH AS UNIONS OR CLASS-BASED PARTIES, THE POOR, MORE OFTEN THAN THE WEALTHY, WILL MISIDENTIFY THEIR POLITICAL INTERESTS.

We can develop another corollary from this argument regarding the performance of democracies: again, define "better" policies as those that in some way have more positive consequences for the welfare of the individuals involved. Voters and citizens are not likely to seek adequate information about their candidates and governments. They are more liable to collect information by direct observation. They observe the direct effects of acts of governments rather than seek out political information on their own. Domestic consequences of governmental policies are more observable by citizens than are foreign consequences. So citizens are more likely to observe directly the domestic acts of governments than their acts abroad (unless the foreign policy involves the country in a costly war). There is little in even very bad foreign policy to create a cheap stream of information for most voters. To illustrate, in the fall of 2005, all the citizens of New Orleans, and the gulf coast region of the United States, directly observed the effects of Hurricane Katrina. Many of them also directly experienced the failures of the response of the government in giving aid. In Louisiana, people could not avoid knowing that the levees gave way, that rescue efforts were dismal, that poor blacks were virtually left to fend for themselves, and that FEMA failed in delivering adequate help. Voters who felt that they, too, could have been abandoned need not have more information than that to know they want the government to change.[4] We can compare the ease of these painful observations to the difficulty in discovering the real state of affairs in the run-up to the war in Iraq. This leads to the second corollary:

DEMOCRACIES ARE NOT LIKELY TO HAVE MUCH "BETTER" FOREIGN POLICIES THAN NON-DEMOCRACIES; THE BENEFITS FROM DEMOCRACY WILL MAINLY BE IN THEIR IMPROVED DOMESTIC POLICIES.

capital flight as an exit strategy that serves to restrain redistributive policies (see below, p. 159). Second, instrumental calculations aren't all that affect the acquisition of political information. Cultures vary and some place higher values on political discussion, etc. Such things as media coverage also help determine how much political knowledge is shared.

[4] Note the empirical finding of Amartya Sen (1981), that famines have *never* happened in a democracy. His theoretical discussion of this (in chapter 7, "Famines and Other Crises" 1999a) is in the spirit of this essay. But note the great variability of democracies in the quality of their response to natural disasters.

DOING THE RIGHT THING

When it comes to politics, and things political, the incentive to be informed is small. The same argument has implications for another major aspect of citizen behavior: willingness to stand up for the moral or "right" thing. There are at least two reasons for this, one direct, another indirect.

We have already shown that individuals have substantial reasons to be and remain uninformed. What are the ethical implications of rational ignorance? Ignorance weakens the tie between responsibility and action. After all, ethical responsibility requires that a number of conditions be filled. Certainly, ignorance is not a barrier to responsibility, but it is a mitigating circumstance. Those who are ignorant and guilty are not as responsible as those who are knowledgeable and guilty. Ignorance decreases one's moral stake. Individuals are rarely totally ignorant, but rather informed by freely available sources, with a focus on those all important "independent incentives" that they are faced with that are designed to channel their behavior. Consider a costly but relatively ineffective political action, such as volunteering for a revolutionary militia. The choice can be expected to be made, not on the programmatic nature of the revolutionary movement, but on the incentives given to join the militia. There is not likely to be much incentive to acquire costly information about the public good characteristics of the movement. And one would expect that the normal person would be careful to get the information regarding the private incentives right while accepting a propagandized story that fits to justify the behavior.[5]

If one takes efforts that are reasonable and rational ignorance leads one to not include the public good effect of one's behavior, the tendency is to sever, or at least greatly weaken the perceived ethical responsibility for one's support of, or opposition to, public policies and other public goods efforts. Since political behavior is more concerned with public goods than is personal and economic behavior, we can conclude that:

POLITICAL BEHAVIOR BY CITIZENS (ALTHOUGH NOT LEADERS) CAN BE EXPECTED TO BE SUBSTANTIALLY MORE AMORAL AND IRRESPONSIBLE THAN THEIR ECONOMIC AND PERSONAL BEHAVIOR.

(Oppenheimer, 1985)

---

[5] The communists were one group that put out a lot of "free" and entertaining one-sided portrayals of political issues. See Gage(1983), Hinton (1966), Johnson (1962), and Snow (1968) for many descriptions of popular agitprop theater tied to increasing support for political action.

Indeed, when accurate information is more costly to acquire (as in dictatorial states that control the media) the effect will be larger:

THE GREATER THE COSTS OF ACQUIRING INFORMATION FROM COMPETING SOURCES, THE LARGER WILL BE THE MORAL GAP BETWEEN POLITICAL AND PERSONAL BEHAVIOR.

(Oppenheimer, 1985)

This means that ethical factors are likely to be weaker motivators for costly behavior in politics than in other activities. So successful political organizing is often about giving people private reasons to do "publically" oriented things; or, rephrasing this, getting people to do the "right things" for the "wrong reasons."

Of course, we daily witness moral appeals in politics. But the real connection of these moral crusades to the policies pushed by the elites is often weak or selfishly instrumental.

Finally, another barrier prevents individuals from acting morally in politics as frequently as they do in their private affairs. Much of modern ethical theory has been built on notions of consequentialism: that one must morally justify one's behavior by its consequences. This leads to a notion that "if there is no can, there is no ought." (If you couldn't help, you had no moral obligation to do so.) But in politics this is a slippery slope, for we noted (consider Figures 7 and 8) that with collective action often one can only make a difference in a range of situations defined by the behavior of others. Expected value behavior leads one to ask, "How likely is it that I can make a difference?" And if the chance is smaller, the moral obligations are attenuated. So the tendency for rational individuals to have only marginal control of the political outcomes means that regardless of the rhetoric people employ, people can be expected to be less morally involved in politics than in other spheres of their behavior.

Democracies have a system of voting coupled with competitive sources for information and open campaigns for office. They invite individuals to be more ethically concerned with their political environment than would be the case in other systems. Yet in democracies we have found individuals are likely to be quite amoral in their political behavior. In non-democracies, the propaganda lines of the governments are more likely to be accepted, and individuals are likely to engage in behavior that is generally supportive of the system regardless of its moral opprobrium. In other words, the deep structure of politics invites us all to be "good Germans." Only by removing virtually all costs of dissent and making accurate information readily available can one hope to make any dent in this general amorality of the political. Fortunately, technology has greatly helped to increase the availability of information and decreased the ability of governments to control the information citizens receive.

BEHAVIORAL CASCADES AND POPULAR UPRISINGS

In some contexts, modeling collective action as a game among individuals who share no organizational coordination is quite realistic. Under such conditions, how can collective action succeed? The answer that one must always have an organization, or a leader, is to dismiss the chicken and egg quandary: the "what came first" problem. For how is an organized group to get started? "Communication!" might be the simplest possibility, but in oppressive situations, explicit communication can't be the elixir for collective action. Collective action in repressive situations may require action without explicit communication. Yet in recent years we have witnessed some of the greatest revolutions against tyranny in history. How we might make sense of this was shown by Suzanne Lohmann (1994, 2000). She modeled the emergence of protest in the Soviet bloc in the late 20th century. She analyzed how protests were able to topple such a powerful regime when most forms of communication regarding the protests were forbidden. Lohmann modeled how trickles of protests can evolve into powerful rivers of political revolt and cast light on the possibilities of effective unorganized political action.[6]

Lohmann starts with a status quo sufficiently awful so that even a repressive regime would have trouble containing unrest. She assumes no public information is available regarding the regime's unpopularity. It is precisely the squashing of indicators of such public feelings that unpopular regimes attempt. Lohmann notes that both those who do and do not show up at a demonstration communicate regarding the degree of their alienation by their attendance. These signals are received privately by other citizens who use the signals to "update" their understanding of the support for the status quo. Each citizen then decides what action she will take regarding the status quo in the next instance.[7]

Expressing any desire for change by people involves taking costly action to express discontent. It is precisely the costliness of the action that tells bystanders how strongly the protesters feel about the conditions. People

---

[6] Other situations that would invite applications of the model include the recent uprisings that have come to be called the "Arab Spring," as well as riots of the poor in many countries, as discussed in the introduction to Piven and Coward (1977).

[7] This is actually just one sort of model developed from game theory usually referred to as the theory of "signaling games." See Rasmusen (1989) for an introduction.

also take information about the situation from the size of the protest over time. The size of the protest gives a public signal of the discontent that lies otherwise unknown as disaggregated feelings dispersed among the citizens. This information leads the other discontents to decide whether to support the protests or be free-riders. This feedback loop, powered by the signals of the protest's size, reflects both the feelings held by others that the status quo is malign and the expectations of the individual for possible further support from other citizens. If enough people protest, the government collapses.

Since the status quo is overturned by the size of the protests, one's participation merely modifies the probability that the threshold for efficacy will be reached. The signal one sends is by attending, or not. How that is received by still other individuals depends on estimates that each has in their head, regarding who (and hence how many) might be participating. Lohmann assumes there are four categories of others to which people react:

Pro status quo extremists: they won't participate no matter what they thought others were doing.

Apathetic anti status quo citizens: they also don't participate regardless of their private information about others; but they would support regime change.

Anti status quo moderates: they would participate if, based on their private estimations, it was "worth it." And finally,

Anti-status quo extremists: they will participate no matter what their estimations regarding the behavior of others.

No one knows precisely who is participating but each bystander discounts some as extremists and estimates the proportion of the protesters who are anti-status quo moderates. The question remains, how do they make these estimates as to who is participating, and how vulnerable the status quo is to their participation (i.e., what's the chance that they can make a difference). As more go to the protests, others decide that more of the anti-status quo moderates exist than they had reason to believe. This changes their estimate that the status quo can be maintained. As signals mount, a "bandwagon" effect develops and the coercive power of the regime is overrun. Often the situation is triggered by covert leadership that has helped organize the protests from a somewhat independent base of power and resources. Note that the basic argument only requires an expected value form of evaluation along with updating of these estimates based on the size of the protests to generate the bandwagon from individual choice.

COMMON-POOL RESOURCES AND ENVIRONMENTAL DEGRADATION

Fish and timber would not appear to be public-good problems. But the analysis we have sketched is directly related to problems of resource degradation. Indeed, one of the most fruitful applications of rational choice theory over the last few decades has been to the problem of common-pool resources. These are resources that are available without exclusion, but each person is consuming his or her own units privately. Often such resources are renewable and sustainable with careful harvesting. Problems arise when there is a threat to sustainability because harvesting occurs faster than the renewal rate of the resource. Common examples are fish stocks, underground aquifers, open or public pasture, and so on. Because the stock of resources is available without exclusion it takes on many of the properties of a public good. Indeed, the deterioration of the stock of resources stemming from too speedy harvesting can be thought of as a form of "crowding."

The simple analysis is that the exuberance of the harvester is fueled by her gleaning all the profit of her excessive harvest to herself while the cost (i.e., the deterioration of the asset) is shared by all users. Early analyses of these problems were dire in their predictions and severe in their prescriptions (see Garret Hardin, 1968).[8] Faced with despoliation of the stock the typical prescription was to privatize the resource (e.g., sell the common property and let the new owner arrange to sell access if they so wish). Certainly such changes help get rid of the problems of excessive harvesting, as the private owner will be eager not to have her asset devalued by excessive harvesting. But privatization of commons, especially when the commons resource is vital to community welfare, as in the case of pasture, fish, or water, has its own problems. These were well analyzed by Amartya Sen in his breathtaking work on famines (Sen, 1981, 1999a, 1999b). In these works, he showed that famines come about not from a lack of food, but rather from a lack of purchasing power. So, any privatization of truly vital commons resources must be coupled with the development of programs to ensure economic security in times of shortages, when prices are liable to rise, and thereby lock out access of the less fortunate (also see Frohlich and Oppenheimer, 1994, 1996b).

---

[8] The classic paper on this problem is Garrett Hardin's (1968) "The Tragedy of the Commons."

If common-pool resources that are vital to life are to be privatized, then programs are required to ensure the less fortunate economic security or access to these resources in times of shortages when prices are liable to rise.

(Sen, 1981)

On the other hand, privatization is not the only answer. As the pioneering work of Elinor Ostrom[9] has shown, humans have engineered a variety of responses to common property problems. Typically these come about because the affected group of individuals are aware of the deterioration that comes from overuse. Ostrom has shown that a commons can be governed quite successfully under a variety of conditions. Her observations are useful in our understanding of how to solve problems of collective action more generally. Restricting access to individuals known in the community certainly is a start. After all, it facilitates communication of expectations, mores, and the consequences of cheating (Ostrom and Walker, 1991). But successful arrangements go beyond that: for example, observability of prohibited behavior is vital. For example, farmers sharing water resources can rotate the fields to be irrigated and if a farmer's field is "wet" out of turn, it presents evidence of a violation. More generally, Ostrom finds communal arrangements to prevent depletion are successful when detection of violations and identity of violators is relatively easy. And beyond this, the benefits of these arrangements must be sufficient to outweigh the costs of setting up the monitoring, otherwise the communal effort will end up a victim of neglect.

These observations regarding what is needed to prevent the deterioration of common-pool resources are quite relevant to our understanding of how to deal with environmental degradation more generally. After all, environmental degradation is a form of spoiling the commons. Often this takes the form of dumping more degradable waste than the environment can absorb (such as fertilizer runoffs in watersheds, or greenhouse gasses in the atmosphere). Note the similarity of the logical structure of all these situations to the standard n-person prisoner dilemma and the problems of public goods (see Sidebar 4). In each of these situations, the individual has a dominant strategy to exploit the commons, and the outcome is socially degrading. As reported above experiments have been run to see what leads to greater, and to less, cooperation in such games. But other experiments have been more directly related to policy structures to prevent the

---

[9] Elinor Ostrom, Economics Nobel laureate in 2009, is the scholar who has done the most to advance the analysis of common-pool resources. See Ostrom (1990, 1994, 2003, 1998), Ostrom and Walker (1991), and Ostrom et al. (1992 and 1994).

Sidebar 4 – Types of Goods

The two properties that we have used to define the distinction between public and private goods actually can help us define a topology of four categories of "goods." One must be careful before thinking of these goods as particular "objects." A meal, for example, is certainly individually consumed. But even if the food appears to be a meal for one, we can imagine a poor mother sharing it with her child. Then it is more of a "club good." And a car may be thought of as a private good, but its design is given to all its owners who jointly "consume" it. Hence the recalls affect the owners. And some design defects (a bad braking system, for example) may affect more than owners and may have pure public good aspects. Still, it is useful to think of the four-fold distinction, and the problems implied by their properties.

TABLE S4. *Types of Goods*

	Excludable	Non-Excludable
Individually Consumed	Private Goods bottle of soda, food	Common-Pool Resources fish stocks, wilderness
Jointly Consumed	Club Goods toll roads, movie shows	Public Goods clean air, election outcomes

continued deterioration of the environmental commons. Plott's (1983) pioneering study of market regulation forms shows the superior power of privatized incentives such as those that are in markets for pollution rights (e.g., "cap and trade" schemes) or in pollution licenses, rather than the less effective regulation by general rules and standards.

BROAD VERSUS NARROW, INTENSE INTERESTS

We can usefully distinguish a particular class of public problem: a large group of individuals each either incurs a small cost or stands to gain a small amount while a few stand to gain or lose a great deal. This becomes a public policy problem when the collective value to the large group each with small interests outweighs the value to the small group of high stake holders.

For any member of the large group, any substantial costs of action, or often even information acquisition, are just not going to be worth it. On the other side, the small party of intensely interested individuals find it very worthwhile to take costly action. And so, even in cases where the summed interests of the large group may be many multiples more significant for the overall population, it is most often the small group that wins the day. Or

A SMALL GROUP OF INTENSELY MOTIVATED INDIVIDUALS IS FAR MORE LIKELY TO TAKE ACTION TO ACHIEVE A SHARED GOAL THAN IS A LARGE GROUP OF INDIVIDUALS WHO ARE EACH NOT VERY SERIOUSLY AFFECTED BY THE OUTCOME.

As an example, consider tariffs such as the sugar tariff. Sugar is not a major budget item for most American families. Indeed, many are not aware there is a sugar tariff. On the other hand, there are a handful of sugar producers in the United States. Indeed, their actions have been so effective in keeping up the price of sugar that manufacturers using sugar move to Canada, so as to be able to buy sugar more cheaply. So big has been the effect that high fructose corn syrup is substituted for sugar in many commercial products in the United States.

Another class of general problems that fit this rubric are NIMBY (not in my back yard) issues. The overall community may need a half-way house, or a homeless shelter, to solve a problem. But in a NIMBY situation the intense feelings lie with those who don't want the facility near them. Take the example of the important NIMBY case of Yucca Mountain. Clearly, spent nuclear fuel needs to be stored. But the potential cost to the inhabitants of Utah was sufficient to stop its deployment.

When the issues involve private companies and consumers, as in cases of design flaws, it is often only via the possibility of class-action lawsuits that a large group of less affected individuals can take remedial action. Their lawyers sue for damages for each of the multitude of small claimants, thereby solving the collective action problem with a profit motive.

VOTING AND THE PARADOX OF VOTING

Even with other-regarding behavior as the rule, were voting undertaken for only instrumental reasons, most people would not vote (unless the group provided incentives for individuals to vote[10]). This is because the chance of any one vote making a difference is so small. Hence, the expected value of voting is too small to motivate most voters most of the time. But

---

[10] As, for example, is done in Australia where citizens who don't vote have to pay a modest tax.

many citizens do vote. This theoretical difficulty has been labeled the *paradox of voting.*[11]

Can one square a rational analysis of voting with observed behavior? Or is the very fact that people vote *en mass* an irrefutable barrier for rational choice theory's acceptability?

The Instrumental Incentive to Vote

First, let us consider voting as instrumentally rational behavior: voting that makes instrumental sense. This occurs when a single vote makes a difference. As we mentioned earlier, (page 66), this possibility implies that with voting there cannot be a dominant strategy. Graphically, the lines must cross. As in Figure 9, voting mirrors the situation shown in Figures 7 or 8.

For a voter (call her Iris) to vote because of the instrumental effect of voting, the benefits of the vote must outweigh the costs. Voting must yield a bigger value than not voting. Let's agree that in a well-functioning democracy, the stakes of the election are virtually always greater than the cost of voting.[12] But this hardly ensures a positive incentive to vote. For only rarely would Iris's voting change the outcome. To see this, consider the incentive she has if she votes only to change the outcome. (Here we need some definition of the rules: presume Iris is faced with the sort of 'first past the post' electoral systems prevalent in the United States and Canada: the candidate with the most votes wins.) In such cases the chance of making a difference is that of snatching victory for her candidate by her vote: "making or breaking" a tie among the two leading candidates.[13]

Figure 9 shows the relative values of voting and not voting as we have described it. The dashed line is the value of not voting. The lines depicting the value of each of the strategies of voting and not voting

---

[11] This anomaly was, I believe, first noticed and addressed by Downs (1957) and has remained a continual topic of research in rational choice literature. Critics of rational choice have continued to use it to point to the weakness of the theories (for example, see Green and Shapiro, 1994).

[12] In modern democracies, costs of voting are usually set to be very low. At times, such as during the 2000 presidential election in the United States, this is violated. In 2000, Florida deleted many persons from the lists of registered voters saying they fit the profiles of criminals. By so doing, the Florida officials were able to increase the costs of voting for those taken off the rolls. That they happened to be overwhelmingly black and Democrats yields a plausible explanatory incentive for the policy for the Republican state officials.

[13] We might presume that a "tie" leads to an outcome that is a 50–50 gamble between the two leading candidates.

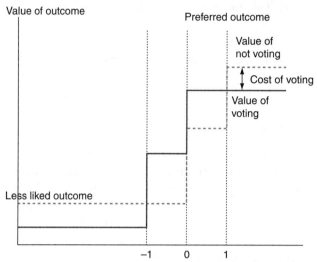

FIGURE 9. Display of the value of voting and not voting

cross each other at two values. That means neither strategy is always more valuable or dominant: the situation is *not* a prisoner dilemma game. At both ends of the line, when there are either too few or a surfeit of supporters for Iris's preferred candidate, it pays not to vote. Under the other circumstances, only when Iris's vote *does* change the outcome, does it pay her to vote. When her preferred outcome loses by more than one vote, or wins without her, it doesn't pay to vote. Between these values there is a region where Iris would find her vote would make enough of a difference to her so as to be worth casting. Under other circumstances, Iris saves the cost of voting by abstaining. But she doesn't know the pattern of others' votes when she casts her own vote.

To evaluate her options, Iris decides on the basis of her expectations regarding the pattern of voting by others. These expectations are likely to be probabilistic estimates. Iris uses these, in conjunction with her values of the outcomes, to compare the value of going to the polls with not voting. She sums the values of the possible outcomes that would be associated with each choice weighed (i.e. multiplied) by the probabilities of those outcomes occurring. Finally, Iris decides by comparing the values of the two possible choices (see the definition and discussion of expected value on page 13).

TABLE 9. *The Calculus of Purely Instrumental Voting*

| | Others Vote So That Your Preferred Candidate | | | |
	Loses by More than 1 Vote	Loses by 1 Vote	Ties	Wins
Chance of This	P1	P2	P3	P4
Don't Vote	0	0	.5 W	W
Vote	0-C	.5 W-C	W-C	W-C

In Table 9 we identify the elements needed to develop an expected value of instrumental voting. Noting the value of having your preferred candidate win as W and the cost of voting as C, we identify the value of each strategy. Each strategy has a different value in the four possible "zones" defined by the aggregate voting behavior of others: the first and last (winning or losing by more of a margin than your vote); and the second and third, where your vote makes a difference. Given your expectation of the chance of each of these four possibilities being realized, you can calculate the expected value of either voting or not. Presume a tie leads to a 50–50 chance for your candidate winning. The incentive to vote is precisely the difference in the values of voting or not (see Sidebar 5).

In other words, the incentive to vote boils down to the product of the (small) probability of making a difference and the value of the difference one makes. From this it follows that:

TURNOUT WILL BE HIGHER IN ELECTIONS THAT APPEAR TO BE CLOSER AND WHERE THE STAKES ARE LARGER.

It also follows that:

TURNOUT WILL GO DOWN WHEN VOTING BECOMES MORE INCONVENIENT OR MORE COSTLY (I.E., BY PLACING POLLING BOOTHS FURTHER FROM THE VOTERS, HAVING INCONVENIENT HOURS, REQUIRING REGISTRATION OF VOTERS, ETC.).

It is not likely that this is the precise form of weighing outcomes individuals undertake, but as long as it is a pretty good approximation, the above conclusions would hold.

But if this eases the problem of explaining the voting behavior of a few (after all, it is not *very* costly to vote and the difference between outcomes can be large), it doesn't seem to be sufficient to explain why most people vote. And here in lies a quandary.

To deal with this, Downs (1957), and then some others in the tradition of public choice, have added a notion that people vote also to support the

Sidebar 5 – The Incentive to Vote

Let us analyze this using the notation in Table 9.

Call the value of voting U(V). $U(V) = P_1*(o-C) + P_2*(.5W-C) + P_3*(W-C) + P_4*(W-C)$. This can be simplified by noting that the voter loses C, and that o times anything is o. Then we have:

$$U(V) = [P_2*.5*W + (P_3 + P_4)*(W)]-C.$$

And the value of not voting, U(NV), can be written as:

$$U(NV) = P_3*.5*W + P_4*W.$$

But we are interested in precisely the difference between these two, as that is the incentive to vote (or not vote). So consider U(V) - U(NV):

$$U(V)-U(NV) =$$
$$[P_2*.5*W + (P_3 + P_4) * (W)]-C-P_3*.5*W + P_4*W$$

Or, simplifying:

$$U(V)-U(NV) = [P_2 + (P_3)]*.5*W-C.$$

In other words, the incentive to vote is precisely the probability of making a difference (the sum of P_2 and P_3) times the value of the difference one makes voting and transforming a tie to a victory or a defeat to a tie: ½ W.

system. In the first instance, this would be based on the notion, "what if everyone did that?" But not everyone will stop voting merely because one person stops. So we have to ask, "What difference will a motive such as 'saving the system' add to the expected value of one person's vote?" And this will be very small indeed.

Indeed, the prevalence of voting would appear to be a falsification of the set of premises that were used to "explain" collective action. And this falsification of a simple inference raises serious questions regarding the status of those premises (see Sidebar 1). How can one make sense of mass voting behavior from within a theory of rational choice?

Research Frontiers: Experiments and Ways Forward – Voting as Expressive or Symbolic Behavior

Most voters say they vote "because they ought to." As citizens they have an obligation to vote. Theorists have used that observation to "fix" the predictions (starting with Riker and Ordeshook, 1968). But adding notions of obligation to the set of premises complicates theoretical arguments considerably and these complications have been resisted by some public choice theorists (Barry, 1970, was among the first to argue against this idea). They argue having preferences, or values, for particular sorts of acts takes away from the power of rational choice theory.[14] But if we are to use the theory to deal with the behavior of actual people, it would seem that we must take people as they are: not purely self-interested, other-regarding individuals with values that lead them to act in manners that go beyond the purely instrumentally rational. This is more likely to occur when the costs are low (as in voting in modern democracies) or the incentives are high (as in the rebellion cascades discussed above on page 77).

Obligations can be understood within rational choice theory as mandates, or rules, that unless there is a dire reason, one just follows. That wouldn't mean that other considerations aren't relevant, but it does raise difficulties: when do these obligations outweigh the instrumental motivations of the individual? If obligations are also evaluated at times, and won't always be met, when does this occur? If we introduce social obligation, is it a function of governmental legitimacy? More generally, how does one make decisions about obligations and ethical matters? Do we make these in a rational fashion? These would be the sorts of elemental questions that would grow out of taking seriously the extension of rational choice to moral questions, some of which were raised earlier.

Naturally, the sort of difficulty that we are referring to has led to some serious reformulation of the foundational assumptions behind the theory. For example, Stephen Knack (1992) has studied voting behavior and found that incentives to vote are primarily in the form of social norms. Furthermore, the need to report one's behavior to others (as happens when one has a spouse) is a major factor in conformity to social norms. One can think of such reporting as increasing the costs of non-conforming behavior. In an experimental study we confronted individuals with moral choices with variable costs attached to them (Frohlich, Oppenheimer, Bond and Boschman, 1984). Costs proved a major determinant of the choices. Indeed, people seemed to set a specific "price: they were willing to pay to deviate from self-interest. Further research probed for the depth and meaning of other-regarding preferences in the face of costs in "dictator experiments" (see page 245). Costs being often important, people who feel

---

[14] Goldfarb and Sigelman (2010) discuss the issue wisely.

obliged to vote can be expected to vote as long as the cost of voting is below their personal threshold.

Two (strongly intertwined) branches of theory have developed in response to such falsifying data as in the case of the paradox of voting. The first, developed primarily in psychology, is referred to as cognitive choice theory and may be thought of as trying to understand how "framing" elicits preferences.[15] The thrust is to relativize preferences to the context of choice, noting that the informational and social contexts will determine the preferences that are utilized by the individual in her choice making. The conjecture is that there are "cues" in the framing of a choice which evoke one sort of preference structure or another. Some cues, such as those in market institutions, elicit self-interested preferences. Other institutions, such as elections, may elicit a less self-interested point of view (Mackie, 2003).[16] This line challenges the presumption that preferences are well-ordered, unique, and stable.

A second branch of research that has developed in response to this and other problematic findings is based on experimentation, and is usually referred to as "behavioral game theory."[17] The idea here is to take a more relaxed attitude toward goal-oriented behavior so as to better capture what we observe in actual decision making.[18] Like the work in cognitive theory, much of this work is developed in response to results of laboratory experiments. Here the experiments have tried to understand what is going on when people adopt other-regarding and other ethical preferences.[19] More discussion of this research follows in subsequent chapters.

---

[15] The literature here is vast. One might begin with Kahneman and Tversky, 1982, 1979; Kahneman, Knetsch, and Thaler, 1986; Knetsch, Thaler, and Kahneman, 1987; Tversky, and Kahneman, 1981, 1986, 1992; Tversky and Kahneman, 1973.

[16] Mackie also argues that the politicians have a lot to do with the orientation of the voters. He reports how the self-interested appeals of the Reagan campaign in 1984 ("You should ask yourself if you are better off today than you were four years ago") increased the correlation of self-interest and vote choice.

[17] Here a useful place to start is with Camerer (2003). The field uses experimental games, and who uses psychological principles to develop theories of fairness, reciprocity, limited strategizing, and learning, to help predict how people behave in strategic situations. Elinor Ostrom (1998) has also written a classic piece here.

[18] Amartya Sen argued for this for many years (1970, 1977). His chapter 2(1970) formalizing the properties (he called them α and β) of "maximizing behaviour" pointed out that more relaxed notions of goal orientation could be formalized and might lead to fewer problems, although he was primarily applying this to group choice, rather than individual psychology. In 1977 he discussed ways to think around the obvious falsity of strict self-interest in rational choice theory. Bendor (1995) presented a full-blown understanding of how to model goal-oriented behavior in a less fragile fashion.

[19] Some of this is reviewed in some detail in Frohlich and Oppenheimer (2006).

In any case, it should be clear that only rarely can one form theories out of whole cloth. Tests find even the most solid candidates wanting, and then requiring further work: careful reformulation that can occur, at best, only over time.[20]

CONCLUSIONS

Two lessons seem central to our explorations. First, we have only begun to scratch the surface of how models developed from rational choice theory can help us make sense of the politics of collective action. Second, as one explores these subjects, the difficulties of theoretical anomalies define new research frontiers and cast doubts as to the structure of the enterprise. These are the very dynamics of scientific inquiry, and help the development of more powerful approaches to our understanding. It would seem that we must deal with an expanded notion of rationality: one which encompasses non-instrumental as well as non-self-interested behavior. As I hope to make clear, these expansions have implications for our pursuit of normative questions regarding politics. We will return to the subject in other chapters when we have added other tools of analysis so as to be able to sketch more complex situations. But hopefully you have found some of the tools of analysis sufficiently beguiling to think of how they might be used to develop applications to political problems in your own environment.

FOR FURTHER READING

Prisoner Dilemma Games

Flood, Merrill M. (1952), "Some Experimental Games," Rand Corporation Research Monograph, RM 789-1, June 20. Although considerable literature has developed regarding two-person prisoner dilemma games, the original paper by Flood is still full of surprises and is of great historical interest.
Axelrod, Robert (1984), The Evolution of Cooperation. New York. Basic Books. Axelrod gives us an eye-opening examination of the power of repetition to change the analysis. He was one of the first to take an evolutionary approach to game theory. The follow-up literature is enormous. It is, however, of limited direct interest to us as it focuses on two-person games. On the other hand, the expansion

[20] An example of the sort of testing that allows us to determine what contextual cues generate changes in behavior can be seen in Frohlich, Oppenheimer, and Kurki (2004). Careful and insightful discussion of the evolution of rational choice theory in light of experimental and other challenges can be found in Hausman, 1989, 1995, 2008.

to n-person analysis by Bendor and Swistak, 1997 allows evolutionary game theory to gain substantial leverage over issues of collective action.

Logic of Collective Action

Theory

Olson, Mancur (1965), *The Logic of Collective Action.* Cambridge, Mass: Harvard University Press. Although there are some errors (especially regarding group size) in this classic, it is a brilliant exposition of the theory with numerous suggestive applications.

Frohlich, Norman, Joe A. Oppenheimer, and Oran R. Young (1971), Political Leadership and the Supply of Collective Goods. Princeton, New Jersey: Princeton University Press:. We develop an entrepreneurial solution to the problem of collective action.

Schelling, Thomas C. (1973), "Hockey Helmets, Concealed Weapons, and Daylight Savings: A Study of Binary Choices with Externalities." Journal of Conflict Resolution, v. 17, No. 3 (September), pp. 381–428. Schelling develops a graphical analysis of cooperation in multi-person situations where the value of cooperation is a function of the choices of others. Reprinted in Schelling's (1978) *Micromotives and* Macrobehavior. New York: W.W. Norton.

Applications

Boyer, Mark (1993), *International Cooperation and Public Goods: Opportunities for the Western Alliance.* Baltimore: Johns Hopkins Press and **Todd Sandler,** "The Economic Theory of Alliances: A Club Approach," *KYKLOS.* 30 (3, 1977): 443–460. These both build strongly on Olson's relating the theory of collective action to problems of alliances and cooperation among nations.

Chong, Dennis (1991), *Collective Action and the Civil Rights Movement.* Chicago: Chicago University Press. Chong develops a nuanced interactive model of leadership strategies to explain how the massive civil rights campaign was sustained. It is an excellent example of empirical research leading to theoretical insights.

Downs, Anthony (1957), *An Economic Theory Of Democracy.* New York: Harper and Row. This book was the first to examine voter turnout as a paradox. Downs also develops the first examination of rational ignorance.

Ostrom, Elinor (1990), *"Governing the Commons. The Evolution of Institutions for Collective Action."* Cambridge: Cambridge University Press. This is to the common property resource problem what Olson is to the collective action problem. It is full of theory and insight and applications.

Ostrom, Elinor (2003), "How Types of Goods and Property Rights Jointly Affect Collective Action," *Journal of Theoretical Politics,* V. 15, No. 3, 239–270 (2003). Ostrom discusses the interaction of our social and legal arrangements with the potentialities of effective collective action.

PART II

COLLECTIVE CHOICE

In Part I we examined how groups can overcome inherent difficulties involved in providing themselves with public goods. Another aspect of the problem was not discussed. Solving dilemmas to achieve shared goals usually requires collective choice: a centralized decision. Just because unanimous support for *some* collective solution should always be possible, as all observers of politics have witnessed, rarely is collective choice of any sort – much less by unanimity – easy to come by. Frequently more is needed than making sure the group is organized to collect and apply resources needed to carry out collective projects. Collective, binding decisions are required regarding what is to be done. This process is anything but simple. Some of the roadblocks that make for these difficulties are analyzed in this (and the next) part of this volume.

We humans have a long and difficult history of trying to engineer "good" political systems to reach collective choices. We have ruled ourselves with various sorts of regimes, which we might divide into two overly broad classes: authoritarian and democratic. And here, in spite of the contemporary Western bias to democracy, looking at the landscape of political history, one notices that people have prospered under a variety of regimes. Civilization did not require democracy. But it did require an element of decent government. Since a degree of general prosperity is needed for the leaders, even the rare Stalins and Caligulas of the world have to consider constraints to their behavior in order to bolster the welfare of their citizens.[1] Although, in most situations, the fate of

[1] If as Napoleon observed "An army marches on its stomach," (c.f. http://www.brainyquote. com) then welfare must be attended to, at least enough so that the soldiers can fight (see

governments is at least loosely tied to the interests of the citizenry, the requirements of prosperity seem quite constraining.[2] In modern times the attempt to tether governments to the interests of the citizens has been intimately related to the establishment and design of democratic governments. Much of this effort has proven successful. Modern democracies have had quite a track record at improving the conditions of their citizens.[3] In this section of the book, I explore some properties of democratic governments that help us understand their potential, and their difficulties.

The justification of governments has certainly shifted over the millennia. From the satisfying of lofty demands of gods, we have come down to the satisfaction of the terrestrial needs of citizens. With such a general loss of celestial grandeur, and such strong findings, it is not surprising that there has developed a considerable degree of consensus regarding the preferred form of government: democracy. Both classes of political system, authoritarian and democratic, have many variations, but modern times and empirical methods have tended to confirm that democracy yields substantial benefits (see, for example, Halperin, et al. 2004). These benefits include:

- fewer militarized interstate disputes causing less battle deaths with one another;
- fewer civil wars;
- virtually no refugee crises;
- much less murder by government;
- higher average citizen happiness.

Democracy is associated with better health indicators (life expectancy and infant and maternal mortality, for example). These indicators have a stronger and more significant correlation with democracy than they do with per capita income, size of the public sector, or income inequality. Even if we only consider poor countries, liberal democracies are associated with

---

Frohlich and Oppenheimer 1974) and the polity has sufficient bounty for the leader to plunder (Olson, 1993). More on this can be found below (p. 151).

[2] The observations of de Waal (1982) regarding power and governance among chimpanzees are instructive. Certainly, chimps have no form of democracy, but when the basic functions of their governance (such as protecting the young) are not properly performed, protesting behavior leads to coalitional shifts that overthrow the alpha male and his "gang."

[3] See, for example, the overview by Mackie, 2003; Sen, 1999a; and Halperin et al., 2004. Also, note the seminal work of Sen on this subject (c.f. fn. 4, chapter 3)

better education, longer life expectancy, lower infant mortality, better access to drinking water, and better health care than dictatorships.[4]

Perhaps arguments still exist supporting other governmental structures for some economically developing states, but for the stable of developed states, the debate is over. So in considering the problems of collective choice, in this and the next part of this volume we focus mainly on democratic regimes. But we will show that even in democracies, we still find road blocks to reaching collective decisions that could benefit everyone.

Imagine a group that proposes to make its decisions by majority rule. One might believe that translating a majority's preference into a social choice is simple. Indeed, the uninitiated reader is unlikely to imagine the complexity of the difficulties one faces in translating individual preferences to social choice. But there are clues that our problem might be big. For example, note that there are different majorities in any group. Indeed, a group of three has four different majorities (three different two-person majorities, and one all-encompassing majority of everyone). A group of five has sixteen different majorities. Needless to say, these many different majorities may not have consistent desires. It might seem commonsensical to presume a direct connection between democracy and the will of the majority. But when there are multiple majorities, this notion may be far more difficult to interpret. Hence, relating a group's choice to the preferences or the welfare of the individuals could be difficult. Even if there may be unanimous agreement that, say, the status quo is not good, and that some particular alternative is better, each of the majorities may have a preferred way of beating the status quo that can lead to obstacles to change. And what if the rules don't call for majorities?

Assuming that individuals reach their decisions through an individually rational process, what can we say about the relationship between rules and outcomes in decision processes? Certainly the details of the rules must make a difference to the quality of the outcomes. I approach at least two aspects of this puzzle: first, how the rules and structures of the political institutions interact with the individual decision makers to determine the outcomes, and then, mainly in Part IV of this volume, the relation between the institutions and the achievement of some metrics of the welfare of the group.

---

[4] See http://en.wikipedia.org/wiki/Authoritarianism#Authoritarianism_and_democracy for an accessible summary and citations to some of the major studies supporting these findings.

These relations have been central to the perennial struggles of politics. The next chapters explore some of these relationships and questions by looking at a special case: when preferences are constrained so that we can analyze them geometrically. More specifically, preferences will reflect how far the proposed outcomes are from one's ideal point: as if the alternatives could be arrayed along a line, or in a space. This permits democratic decisions to be analyzed by what is called a "spatial model" of political decision making. In Part IV of this volume I consider social choice without this constraint. There, we will discuss some of the seminal results of Kenneth Arrow, Amartya Sen, and others regarding social choice, social welfare, and social justice, and we consider how better to tie outcomes to the welfare of citizens.

Rational choice theory gives us a set of useful tools to look at how the design of institutions and other trappings of the political system affect the quality of deliverables from the political system: policy outcomes. If we do not demand too much, generally acceptable decisions can be shown to be a reasonable expectation of a functioning democracy. And careful institutional design can further improve on our expectations a bit.

As in Part I, we begin with a simple story, and then milk it for all it's worth. We then pursue some more difficult problems. Chapter 4 will examine political and electoral outcomes in a radically simplified, one dimensional, spatial world. After establishing some fundamentals, in Chapter 5 we move on to the more complex and at times more disappointing implications of relaxing the presumption of one dimension. We end Chapter 5 with some findings that touch upon general democratic outcomes.

CHAPTER 4

Individual to Collective Choice in One-Dimensional Politics

Consider a block meeting called after a number of fires have occurred: some with tragic consequences. The last fire consumed three houses because the local hydrant was broken. The neighbors on U Street North East, a relatively long dead-end street bordering a park (see the map in Figure 10), are upset. The street has no hydrant. They are meeting to decide what to do about it. Lobbying the town government regarding the placing of a fire hydrant on the street seems to be winning the day when Tim (who lives about halfway down the long block, at number 10) wonders where they will ask the government to place the hydrant. He also proposes that in front of his house would be as good a place as any. An argument breaks out, as each resident sees an advantage in having the hydrant as near as possible to their house. Where will it be placed?

Understanding how to analyze such a problem will help us figure out the effect of voting rules on the outcomes of group choice.

The above example has some properties that we can sum up. We will relate the geometry of the situation to individual preferences. This will often give us leverage on predicting outcomes. We might say that the set of possible policy alternatives are the points on the street where the outcome could end up. (See Sidebar 6.) If, as in the U Street story, the individuals' evalua-tions of any outcome are determined by its position in the possible space, we will be able to relate the distribution of indi-vidual preferences over the possible out-comes. This will give us leverage over the

> Definition – *Ideal Point*: is used in spatial models and represents an individual's best possible outcome. It is the point on a line, or in space that she most prefers.

choices that the group is likely to make. We assume each person has an ideal point (see definition). In the example, each person's ideal point is for the

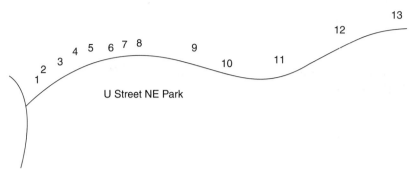

FIGURE 10. Map of U Street.

hydrant to be in front of her house. She prefers those outcomes in each direction which are closer to her ideal point to those that are further. That is, they have what are called *single-peaked preferences* (see the definition) along the street.

To predict what will happen in our U Street block meeting, we need two kinds of information: what people want, and what are the rules by which the decisions are to be made. Regarding what people want, at U Street everyone wants the hydrant as close as possible to their own house: the further the collective choice is from the voter's ideal point, the worse off the voter is. (This is a presumption of symmetry of evaluation: ten yards to the left or to the right is equally good.)

And how will our citizens make their decision? The status quo is no hydrant. Like many citizens in democracies, our U Street citizens use majority rule at their meetings. A simple procedure that is often used works as follows: Anyone can make a proposal; the proposal has to run against the current status quo. If it wins, it is the new status quo. Any other proposal then has to beat the new winner. The contests are all "pairwise." Beaten proposals may not be reintroduced. This goes on until there are no more proposals or they agree to adjourn.

> **Definition – *Single-peaked Preferences*:** As you move from your ideal point in any direction you never prefer an outcome that is further from the ideal to one that is closer in the same direction. Any outcome that is further is less preferred to an outcome that is closer in the same direction. So, for example, imagine a mountain top. If when we climb down the mountain along any straight line to the bottom (i.e., in any single direction from the top), we never go uphill, then there would be a "single peak" to the mountain. If there were some rises along some of the straight line paths, there would be multiple peaks.

Sidebar 6 – One-Dimensional Policies

For a policy choice to be considered "one dimensional" the individuals involved should have preferences as if they all perceive the available alternatives as being ordered in a fashion along a line (as in the example of the geography of U street in Figure 10). This means the people must agree on the relative positions of the items along such a line. Think of the problem as follows: is there a line that can capture the group's diverse preferences so that all voters can have single-peaked preferences on that line? For all preferences to be single-peaked everyone would have to agree, at least, that one, or the other, end is a "worst" outcome for them. For an example that doesn't conform, if the voters i, j, and k have preferences over outcomes A, B, and C as follows:

i	j	k
A	B	C
B	C	A
C	A	B

there cannot be a line on which the ideal points of all of the three voters can be drawn and from which the further the voter is, the worse off the voter is. How do we know this? This is illustrated in Figure 11. Think of a line; it has two ends. Say the ends are A and C. B is in the middle. But in this example three outcomes, A, B, and C, are each listed as worst for one of the voters. Thus if we put the points on a line, (for example a line that goes from A to C) for one of them (in this case i) the worst outcome, B, would end up in the middle. Given that the three voters have three different worst points, they can't all be at one of the two ends of the line. So the voters do not have single-peaked preferences over these outcomes. Single-peaked preferences can come about by various happenstances: a simplified geographical, or ideological situation, or a two-party system. In this last case all individuals might judge the distance of the party's platforms from their ideal points.

SIMPLE SINGLE-DIMENSIONAL ISSUES, SINGLE-PEAKEDNESS, AND MAJORITY RULE

The major result of the analysis is that with simple pairwise majority rule, the social choice will turn out to be in agreement with the voter who is in the *median* position in the set of voters.[1] Let us see why.

---

[1] Or between the median voters' ideal points if there is a tie or because the number of voters is even, etc.

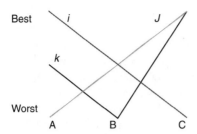

FIGURE 11. Violating single-peaked preferences.

On U Street, there are a set of thirteen numbered houses. Each household wants the hydrant as close as possible. Tim led off the discussion and proposed his house (No. 10) as its location. There would be rapid agreement that this was better than the current situation (no hydrant). But next, Diedra, who owns the last house on the dead end (No. 13), proposed her end of the street as the hydrant's location. In accordance with our assumptions, those whose houses are closer to No. 13 than to No. 10 will vote for Diedra's extremist proposal. But looking at Figure 10, this is only the occupant of No. 12. No. 11, Tim, and all those west of him are further from Diedra's place than they are from Tim's. For example, Tim's neighbor, Nina, at No. 9, would vote to defeat the dead-ender's proposal. Indeed, looking at the situation, since a majority lie to the left (west) of Tim, no proposal to the right of Tim can beat Tim's place. But at No. 9, Nina could improve her situation by proposing her house as the location of the hydrant. After all, everyone to the west of Tim would find No. 9 closer to them than No. 10: and that would leave Nina with nine votes to Tim's four. And going westerly down the block one house at a time, this would continue to be true: until we go "too far." Assuming an open agenda where anything can be introduced, what is too far? Certainly not No. 8, which beats Nina. What ultimately wins? The final winner is always something closer to the house that is in the "middle of the distribution," or the median. In this case, that would be No. 7. It has six houses on each side. So a proposal to move the hydrant east of No. 7 toward the center of the street (which was Tim's place) will be blocked by the majority 1 ... 7. And any proposed move westward toward the start of the street will be blocked by the majority 7 ... 13. Assuming the preferences have the structure we have posited, the median wins: and nothing beats it. It is the equilibrium outcome. Eventually the individuals will move on to other matters of business or adjourn. In other words:

WITH SINGLE-PEAKED PREFERENCES IN ONE DIMENSION, THE EQUILIBRIUM OUT-
COME OF A MAJORITY-RULE, PAIRWISE VOTE WILL BE THE MOST PREFERRED (OR
IDEAL) POINT OF THE MEDIAN VOTER.

(Black, 1958, see Sidebar 7)

We can tie this result to a concept of stability. The concept is called the **core**, and is defined as the set of outcomes that no winning (here, majority-sized) coalition would want to defeat because the members of the coalition couldn't agree on an outcome that would make them all better off. Any outcome that is not Pareto optimal would not be in the core since a (winning) coalition of everyone could form to defeat it. The concept is one of "hyperstability:" If an outcome is in the core, *no* coalition that has the power to change the outcome would want to.

In the voting situation we are considering, any winning coalition must be a majority. If the members of the majority coalition are all direct neighbors (there are no gaps, as occurs with single-peaked preferences in one dimension), each majority coalition would have to include the median voter. One can easily see why the median voter's ideal point is in the core. Any suggested move from the ideal point of the median voter will lead her to be against the suggestion. So will all those who have an ideal point on the side of the median voter which is opposite of the proposed move. Hence, the members that could do better don't form a majority: they are not a winning coalition. So there would be no winning coalition that could agree to change the outcome from that of the median voter's ideal point. Any other proposal could be defeated. Only the median voter's ideal point is in the core. So we can see that:

Sidebar 7 – The Median Voter's Ideal Point is the Equilibrium Outcome

With an odd number of N voters, each with an ideal point, there will be a median ideal point. Call the median voter's ideal point x_{med}. Consider x_{med}, and j's (some other voter's) ideal point, x_j to the left of x_{med}. Now all ideal points (z) at or to the right of x_{med} are closer to x_{med} than they are to x_j. By definition of x_{med} there are therefore more voters who would prefer x_{med} than would prefer x_j, hence, if voter's "vote their preferences," they would defeat any $x_j \neq x_{med}$. (Similarly, were x_j to the right of x_{med}.) No majority could form which could guarantee itself outcomes better than that of the ideal point of the median voter.

WITH SINGLE-PEAKED PREFERENCES IN ONE DIMENSION, AND PAIRWISE MAJORITY RULE, THE MEDIAN VOTER'S MOST PREFERRED (OR IDEAL) POINT WILL BE THE CORE.

After all, no position to the left or right of the median can be closer to a majority of the voters. Hence, the median voter position not only wins, but is hyperstable. It beats all comers.[2] However, not only is the median voter's ideal point the core, but if we assume that a status quo is *not* at the median, then the trajectory of winning proposals can be shown to steadily move toward the median voter position. With pairwise contests, we have the following corollary:

THE ALTERNATIVE CLOSER TO THE MEDIAN WILL ALWAYS WIN IN PAIRWISE MAJORITY RULE.

(Enelow and Hinich, 1984 p. 13)

In other words, the pairwise, majoritarian process drives relentlessly toward the median.

Performance

How well does such a system of majority rule perform, given single-peaked preferences in one dimension?

Note that the result of the process in our U Street example is not totally capricious. It does not lead to a choice that is in some "outlying" area of the city, but in the neighborhood of the people. Even better, it is rather close to some notion of the center of U Street. True, it is *not* the "geographical center" of the street, but it *is* the center of the voters' ideal points on the street. Thus, in some very rough sense, the system hits the target: in front of the median house, a somewhat central location. This is not the same as conforming with some other desirable characteristic – such as minimizing the average distance from the hydrant to the homes; nevertheless, by choosing a median outcome, it does move in the direction of moderation. It does decrease the average individual distance from the

[2] Condorcet was the first person to see that the ability of a socially chosenproposal to beat all of its alternatives is an important property for democratic decisions: something we will come back to. He was a French philosopher and mathematician who was concerned with the theoretical properties of democracy and tried to influence the design of the political institutions of France at the time of the French Revolution. As the revolution became more violent and dictatorial, he was hunted down and imprisoned by the revolutionary government. He died in jail. He was the first to note the potential of majoritarian choice cycles (see part II of Black, 1958). Other voting systems get around the problem of cycles by introducing other elements of arbitrariness. Mackie (2003) has a good discussion of these alternatives.

policy as compared to a more extreme outcome. This could decrease the number of people who would be really upset by a more extreme outcome (Epstein, 1999).

> **Definition – *The Pareto Set*:** The set of all the alternatives that are Pareto optimal.

The U Street voting also satisfies Pareto optimality (see page 35). When a situation is *not* optimal, or is suboptimal, at least some of the individuals could be made better off without hurting anyone. That means, if a situation is optimal, to make someone still better off would require that some others in the group are hurt. Look at Figure 12. It depicts five voters, each with an ideal point on a line. The group is to choose a point on the line for some project. Each of the voter's valuations of the possible points goes down as the points are further from her ideal point in either direction. What outcomes are Pareto optimal or in the Pareto set in this case? It consists of the segment of the line that includes all the voters' ideal points. Consider a point such as X or Y, beyond the interval on the line that includes all the ideal points of the voters. They are not part of the Pareto set: everyone can agree to move from them to the closest ideal point of one of the voters.

On U Street, Y would be the equivalent to a point to the left of the first house on the block. Imagine that someone suggests another point for the hydrant, call it *p*, between Y and 1: Everyone in the group would find *p* closer to their house, and hence better, than Y. They would therefore prefer *p* to Y, and thus, Y is not in the Pareto set. Everyone could be made better off by choosing some point in the interval that includes all the ideal points. The Pareto set is not outside that interval.

To see that the points in Figure 12, between 1 and 5, are in the Pareto set, consider a point, *q* between 1 and 5. Does there exist some other point, call it *s*, which everyone would prefer? What if *s* is to the left of *q*? Then

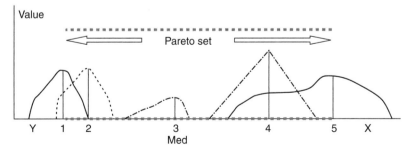

FIGURE 12. Pareto set given N = 5, single-peaked preferences, 1 dimension.

those voters with their ideal point at q or to the right of q prefer q to s. And what if s is to the right of q? Then those at or to the left of q prefer q. So once the outcome is in the range defined by the set of ideal points, there is no point that the group could adopt that would make everyone better off. More generally:

MAJORITY RULE, WHEN ALL VOTERS HAVE SINGLE-PEAKED PREFERENCES, DELIVERS PARETIAN, OR OPTIMAL, RESULTS.

Applications

Although the results regarding the median voter are "easy" to understand, their power is enormous. There are numerous complex models constructed much like tinker toy structures by putting together the elements of the above simple one-dimensional policy idea plus some institutional structure. A few examples will easily demonstrate this to be so. The examples illustrate how a median voter model can help us understand the effect of institutional details in elections and legislatures. The models can help us determine the outcomes we can expect from alternative institutional rules.

I begin by developing a model that applies the above principles regarding the median voter to democratic elections. We then turn to analyzing a system of legislative committees. The committees report bills out for consideration by the whole legislature. Then I develop models examining bicameralism, the power of the chairman of a legislative committee, and finally to see how the senate's filibuster rule restricts the possibility of changes to the status quo.

Two Party Competition in a One-dimensional Political Space

In our real world, democracies are not just collections of voters who come together to vote on outcomes. We have governmental institutions, such as legislatures, committees, and executives. But we also have parties. There have been a number of seminal contributions to our understanding of how democratic politics is modified by the existence of political parties. Some of these have been developed to consider party competition in spatial terms. The original work in this genre was by Anthony Downs (1957). He dealt with party competition in a one-dimensional space.

Downs presumes parties were federations of politicians, working together to win elections. Parties want to maximize their vote. We can use the tools we already have developed to see what happens when two parties compete for votes if voters have single-peaked preferences and choose for whom to vote considering only the relative distance between themselves and the two competitors.[3] Assume the contest is along a single dimension. Downs arrives at a conclusion somewhat similar to that which we have made about the median voter's ideal point being the stable equilibrium in one-dimensional majority rule contests. But he is able to go beyond that quite quickly.

Consider a distribution of voters along a line on which the parties position themselves. Let one of the parties, D, be able to select a position on the line. How is it going to decide where to place its "platform"? The position determines how attractive it is to each voter (how far it is from each voter's ideal point). Judging from the previous arguments, it should be apparent that the position of the ideal point of the median voter is a particularly prized position. After all, if each voter only cares about the distance between her ideal point and the parties' positions, then moving to the midpoint in the distribution will ensure the party half of the votes regardless of where the second party chooses to place itself. If the other party, R, moves to a position that is not identical to D's, then D would be in line to wind up with more than half of the votes. Simple arguments lead to a strong tendency for both parties to opt for the middle of the distribution.

IN SIMPLE TWO-PARTY ELECTIONS, CANDIDATES WILL HAVE A STRONG TENDENCY TO ADOPT A POSITION NEAR THAT OF THE MEDIAN VOTER.

(Downs, 1957)

Note that without further considerations, we do not need to know how the voters are distributed around the median voter. So, for example, in Figure 13, it would make no difference whether the distribution of voters were symmetric and unimodal (as with the distribution), or bimodal and asymmetric, as with the black distribution in the graph. But there are also modifications of the assumptions that show conditions can lead to weakened central tendencies.

For example, the analysis changes if the elections are two-staged affairs: in the first stage the candidate must gain a majority of the party's members (a primary system). Then:

IN PRIMARIES THERE WILL BE A TENDENCY FOR THE COMPETITORS TO ADOPT POSITIONS NEAR THE MIDDLE OF THE DISTRIBUTION OF THEIR OWN PARTY'S VOTERS. GIVEN CONSISTENCY AND CREDIBILITY REQUIREMENTS, THERE WILL BE LIMITED ROOM TO MOVE AWAY FROM THAT POSITION TOWARD THAT OF THE MEDIAN VOTER.

---

[3] In the ensuing arguments, it is assumed that voters have to believe the party is going to deliver its promises for them to base their vote on the announced positions of the party. Forces such as credibility and reputation prevent parties from taking positions and making promises and then abandoning them in subsequent phases of the contest (Downs, 1957).

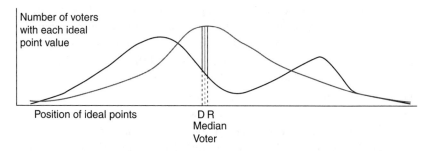

FIGURE 13. Tendency toward matching platforms around the median voter's ideal point regardless of voter distribution around the median voter.

The more similar are the electorates in the party primaries, the less likely it is that voters will be given a diverse a choice in the main election. It follows that holding all else constant, "open primaries"[4] lead to more of a convergence of the party positions than do closed primaries.

But voters may not only vote on the basis of closeness to the candidates. After all, voters have two choices to make: first, whether to vote, and then, who to vote for. Certainly many voters make up their mind to vote on the basis of how enthusiastic they are about one of the candidates winning rather than the other. Those voters may be interested in two different distances: one from her ideal point and the other the distance between the two candidates. If the distance between the two candidates is too small, the voter is likely to feel *indifference* and stay home.

But the voter can also stay home because of *alienation*: she might find that even the closest of the candidates is just too far from her ideal point and thus the outcome is not of the sort she wants, regardless of who wins.

Either of these feelings, *indifference* or *alienation*, could jeopardize the voters' motivations to turn out for the election. These effects modify the arguments regarding the central tendencies in the party platforms. With widespread tendencies of alienation and indifference among the voters, we can get the same diverse platforms that stem from (closed) primary elections. Compare the graphs showing plausible party positions in elections with and without this set of features in Figure 13 and 14. If the voters' ideal points are distributed in a more or less symmetric and unimodal fashion (as by the line in Figure 13), alienation would be most likely for those voters at the tails of the distribution. In this case, with some symmetry the

---

[4] An open primary is one where voters can choose in which party's primary they will participate.

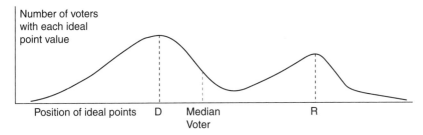

FIGURE 14. Tendency toward diverging platforms with closed primaries, indifference, or alienation.

alienated voters at both ends of the distribution are likely to offset one another. The centralizing tendency of the median voter could drive many more to stay home because of indifference, however. On the other hand, when the median voter position is less similar (as with closed primaries and a bimodal distribution, as in Figure 14), both indifference and alienation would appear to be less systematic.

Two-Party Competition in a Multidimensional World

Above, we assumed that parties are organizations that compete in elections and have the sole goal of maximizing the votes for their party (or its candidate). This limits some of the arguments, but perhaps not as much as we might suppose. To argue that party competition takes place in one dimension needn't mean that politics is restricted to one dimension. This is in part because when two parties compete in a multidimensional space, it can lead to a one-dimensional political competition.

If there are only two parties, and both take an unambiguous stand about the issues of the day, the parties may each be thought of as represented by a single point in some larger (multidimensional) space. And voters, each with single-peaked preferences in this issue space, may reasonably support the party with the position closest to them. To see this, note that the difference between the two parties (we might call them D and R) can be represented as a distance along the line stretching between the parties' platform positions. When the political space is two dimensional the situation can be represented as in Figure 15. There the voters' ideal points, we can call these *i*, *j*, and *k*, can be depicted as points on the surface. Some of these ideal points may be on the line, such as *i*, or on the projection of the line, past the party positions, such as *j*. Finally some of the points (*k*) may be off the line altogether. In each case, if the individual is closer to, say, party D than to

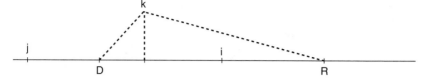

FIGURE 15. 2 Party competition reduces the space to one dimension.

the other, then the projection of that position of the voter's ideal point on the line DR will be closer to D than to R.[5] So, in general:

IF THERE ARE ONLY TWO PARTIES IN AN ELECTION, AND BOTH TAKE AN UNAMBIG-
UOUS STAND ABOUT THE ISSUES OF THE DAY, THE PARTIES MAY EACH BE REPRE-
SENTED BY A SINGLE POINT IN SOME LARGER (MULTIDIMENSIONAL) SPACE. VOTERS
CAN BE EXPECTED TO SUPPORT THE PARTY WITH THE POSITION CLOSEST TO THEM.

Our analysis of this multidimensional situation seems to be reduced to the two-dimensional world of the previous chapter.

But not quite. After all, we have not determined what leads to the political positioning of the parties in the multidimensional space to begin with. There is no reason to presume that this decision is "stable" in itself. So the line "connecting" the platforms of the two parties in a more complex political space may shift around. Voters will continue to support the party they are "closest" to. The forces of credibility and reputation that were referred to above (see Footnote 3) may prevent large shifts: after all, voters would have to believe the party is going to deliver its promises for them to base their vote on the announced positions of the party that is closest.

Legislative Committees and the Protection of the Status Quo

Shift your attention from parties to legislatures. Imagine a legislature that uses simple majority rule with procedures such as Roberts' Rules of Order. Assume it is considering a change of a law. The relevant parameters are the placement of the status quo, the distribution of the preferences of the legislators, and some structural details.

First, consider the difference specialized legislative committees might make if they have the initial task of writing and proposing the final bill that is to be voted upon. We need to presume both the rules and the preferences

---

[5] One's projection on the line is found by drawing a perpendicular line to the line DR (or, if needed, its extension, DR+). Now the point at which the perpendicular line crosses the DR+ is the individual's projection on the line.

of the actors. So assume that both the legislature and any such committee have to reach their decisions by majority rule. The committee's proposal is to be voted up or down by the legislature; it cannot be amended. Again, legislators are presumed to value distance from their ideal points equally on either side of the ideal point: the further an alternative is from an ideal point, the worse it is. Now let's predict outcomes.

Consider next the preferences in the committee, where the proposed change to the status quo must be hammered out.

Assume the range and median of the committee members' ideal points are as shown by the short dotted line in Figure 16. The longer line shows the range of the ideal points of all the members of the legislature (and hence the legislature's Pareto set). On the black line we show the status quo and the median ideal point in the legislature. In this illustration, the committee's members are distributed to the right of both the legislature's median ideal point (marked as L_{med}) and the status quo. You might think that the committee's median voter (C_{med}) would win the day, and that the committee would report out a bill at C_{med}. But in Figure 16, C_{med} is further from the median in the legislature than is the status quo. The status quo would defeat C_{med}. But the committee members would want to seize the opportunity to move the status quo toward their preferred outcomes; they must put forward a bill that appeals to the majority more than the status quo.

By proposing L_{med} to the legislature, the committee members can move the status quo to the right. But they can do better. To do this, they can select a proposal (C) that is not quite as far to the right from L_{med} as the status quo is to the left of it. Then all those at the median and to the right of the median will find themselves closer to the committee proposal than they are to the status quo. They constitute a majority and would prefer the committee's bill to the status quo. That would be the best that the committee can achieve.

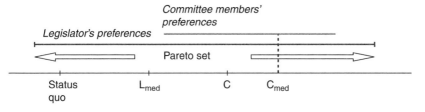

FIGURE 16. The Power of a Legislative Committee.

Consider the performance of such a system. Recall that when we first considered the median voter result, we were enthusiastic: the outcomes would be "moderate," and "in the middle of the distribution." They were shown to be in Pareto set and in the core. With the more complicated rules, the status quo can end up being altered, but not in a manner so simple, and intuitively "benign," as we found above. With a little institutional structure, the result is not necessarily a significantly better outcome than the status quo. With a committee packed in one policy direction, we can get a move that appears to be a manipulation of the system for the special interests represented on the committee. Still, the results will be Pareto optimal, and any changes will be to move the status quo *closer* to the median voter's optimum.

With different preferences on the committee, changes to the status quo may be totally blocked. If C_{med} is on the other side of the status quo from L_{med} of the legislature, as in Figure 17, the committee chairwoman will have no interest in putting forward a bill to change the status quo. Introducing a bill to change the status quo toward the left couldn't get a majority in the legislature. The committee could put forward a bill anyhow, in order to mollify some constituents, etc., but it would not be put forward with any hope to change the situation. More likely, it would just block changes from the status quo.

Using this analysis, we can also see how changes in the procedures (or rules of the game) can change the outcome. For example, imagine that the bill being put forward by the committee can be amended, rather than just voted up or down. If the procedures in the legislature are of the sort that we presumed at the U Street meeting, then any discussion to change the status quo is likely to lead to a move of the status quo to the L_{med}. This being the case, if the median voter outcome on the committee is closer to the status quo than to L_{med}, the committee and/or its chair would not report out a bill to change the status quo.

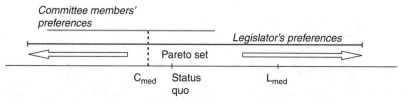

FIGURE 17. The Power of a Legislative Committee to block movement.

Similar models are used to explain why governmental bureaus may be overfunded, how school boards negotiate for bond issues, and the like (see Niskanen, 1971; Eavey and Miller, 1984; as well as Romer and Rosenthal, 1978). Many other models of similar multistage negotiations and votes (often discussed as "structure-induced equilibria," a phrase developed by Shepsle and Weingast, 1981) have been developed to explain other phenomena explained by similar reasoning. Multiple institutions can generate equilibria, much as the legislature and its committee structure can. Numerous models have been developed to analyze the nature of American national legislative/presidential structures (see Miller and Hammond, 1990 for a particularly good example), as well as that of other institutions such as the Federal Reserve Bank (see Morris, 2000).

Bicameralism

In the real world many legislatures have not only committees, but also have two chambers. So let us develop a model to see how a two-chamber legislature changes the situation. To keep things simple, imagine that each of our two legislative houses has three members and that both houses must approve any law for it to take effect. As before, we assume majority rule is used in both houses. Further, assume that the house that reaches a decision first hands the option to the other house that must then choose between either the status quo or the first chamber's proposal.

A legislature with two houses is depicted in Figure 18. There are two different sets of voters: one for each legislative chamber. Each has its own distinct median voter. In the figure we have called the two legislative chambers H and S. H has members (and ideal points) $h_1 = 1$, $h_2 = 2$, and $h_3 = 3$. S has members (and ideal points) $s_1 = 5$, $s_2 = 6$, and $s_3 = 7$. The median voters in each chamber are h_2 and s_2, respectively. Assume each chamber uses simple majority rule as we have described it above. The status quo is at 0.

What happens when H chooses first? The proposal that would win in accordance with our earlier analysis is that H's median voter's ideal point would be 2. But, using the logic developed previously, the legislators in H need to consider whether their proposal to change the status quo will be worth more to a majority in S than the status quo (which, recall, is 0). Only then would it it pass in S. That is, s_{med} has to prefer the proposal from H to the status quo. Were H to select 2, it would be preferred by s_{med}.

And what if S moves first? The median voter's ideal point in S would be 6. But could 6 win in H? A quick examination of Figure 18 makes it clear that a majority of H would prefer 0 to 6. Indeed, S would have to propose

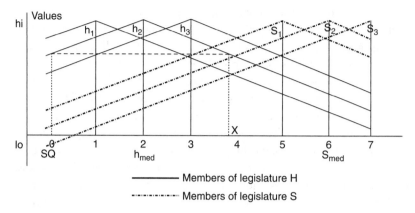

FIGURE 18. Bicameralism.

something that a majority of H prefers to the status quo for S to affect a change. To do so, S would have to make a proposal that H_{med} prefers to the status quo. The range of such proposals is indicated by the dashed line that indicates S would have to propose something between "3" and "4" for the members of chamber H to support the change. Since, in that range, everyone in S wants a higher outcome over a lower outcome, we mark the proposal that S supports as "X" and place it at the right extreme of the dashed line.

Again, the predicted outcome *depends upon the rules and the preferences*, and which chamber decides first. If H decides first the outcome would be 2. If S decides first the outcome will be X. Were the status quo at a different spot, the outcome predictions would also change. This is easy to see. Were the status quo between the two chambers' median voters, the result would be quite different: since either chamber would be passing options that would propose moving the status quo in the direction opposite from that of the other chamber, no proposal passed by one chamber could garner a majority of the other against the status quo.

WHEN THERE IS A BICAMERAL LEGISLATURE, AND THE DISTRIBUTION OF VOTERS VARIES BETWEEN THE CHAMBERS OF THE LEGISLATURE, THEN WHICH CHAMBER DECIDES FIRST MAY DETERMINE WHETHER THE STATUS QUO WILL PREVAIL, AS WELL AS WHAT CAN REPLACE IT.

We could have bicameralism with different rules. It could be that regardless of which "house" made the first decision, the second house could reach any conclusion they wished. If the two houses had differing outcomes, there could be a conference to reach a compromise. Such a rule could lead to the outcome being 2, regardless of which chamber began the action. After all, both chambers prefer 2 to the status quo. But any outcome in the entire range of 2 to 4 would be able to pass the two chambers, and be in equilibrium. Any model to predict outcomes requires as givens the details of the rules, the specification of the options (including the identity and handling of the status quo), and the preferences of the individuals making the choices. If there are multiple committees, and legislative bodies, we have to consider how the procedures constrain the proposals that are effective.

Committees and the Power of the Chair
We have found that the outcome of a committee vote would often be the median voter's ideal point. But committees usually have chairpersons, and a powerful chair can modify this outcome. Let's explore how the rules of a committee can change the equilibrium outcome. To do this, I model a legislative committee similar to the ones we have discussed above. Imagine that only the chair gets to propose agenda items, and the committee discusses them, and then votes them up or down. The chair only votes to break a tie.[6]

Consider a committee where three voting members (V_1, V_2, and V_3) have values for outcomes along a line. Say that each one has a preference that peaks at a value such as those in Figure 19 (20, 50, and 100). The status quo is as marked. If the chair wants to change the status quo (her preference is not represented, as she is a non-voting member unless there is a tie), she needs two votes against the status quo. All the committee members would prefer to move the status quo to the right. Assume she has a most preferred outcome that is also on the right: say at the extreme, along with voter 3. Then the chair can't propose a move too far from the status quo: the median voter must not find the proposal less preferred than the status quo. The dashed line shows the range of points that V_{med} finds preferable to the status quo. Note that a bit to the left of "X" is the proposal that would have the support of the median voter as well being the best obtainable for the chair. The chair then would be expected to propose an item a bit to the left of X. If the chair's most preferred outcome is anywhere to the left of X and to the right of the status quo, she will propose her most preferred outcome; then V_{med} will also find it preferable to the status quo, and it could win. If the chair's ideal outcome is at, or to the left of, the status quo, she has no power to change it. On the other hand, her power over the agenda prevents the majority from moving the status quo to the right.

Let us explore one more example.

---

[6] The following example is taken from Eavey and Miller (1984).

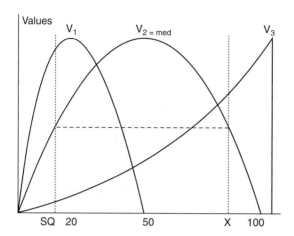

FIGURE 19. Preferences of committee members.

Filibusters, Structure-Induced Equilibria, and Pivotal Voting

Many other institutional details can be shown to change the "equilibrium outcome."[7] After all, institutions don't grow by themselves. They are generated by the value they have to the actors who can establish the rules. But they often have a life that may vastly extend beyond their original purpose, so it is useful to think of how the institutions empower the politicians who use them and how they privilege (by stabilizing or destabilizing in certain directions) some outcomes.[8]

Let's examine how a particular institution, a rule to end debate in a legislature, creates veto points and pivotal voters. Consider the filibuster rule in the U.S. Senate. That rule stipulates that 60 percent of the members have to agree to end debate, to bring a motion to a vote. Hence, a disgruntled 40 percent can prevent any item from being voted upon and prevent the status quo from being changed.

---

[7] A broader view of the findings on how the structure of preferences equilibrate an outcome can be had from Eavey and Miller (1984); Miller and Oppenheimer (1982); Miller and Hammond (1990); Morris (2000); Romer and Rosenthal (1978); Shepsle and Weingast (1981); and Shepsle(1979).

[8] I believe that what we discuss here, although neither novel nor surprising, could be shown empirically to account for many of the great differences in social welfare delivered by the different democratic systems in the economically developed world. See, for example, Immergut (1992, 1998); Maioni (1998); and Birchfield and Crepaz (1998). This is further developed in later sections of this volume.

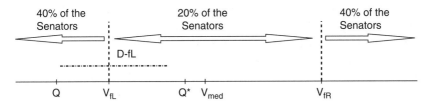

FIGURE 20. The U.S. Senate's filibuster rule empowering 40% to prevent the end of debate on a bill.

How does such an institution work? Again, consider a median voter with an ideal point at V_{med}, and a status quo, Q^*. Without consideration of other rules or institutional constraints, just using majority rule with an agenda process, we would get an equilibrium outcome at V_{med}. But with a filibuster, that outcome may be harder to achieve.

In the example (see Figure 20), the status quo, Q^*, is to the right of the ideal point of the senator who is at the 40th percentile from the left (labeled V_{fL}). That senator is of particular importance because when she, and all those further to the left, don't want to bring the motion to a vote, they can filibuster. A move of Q^* to V_{med} would move the status quo even further from her ideal point. Similarly on the right, when the member at the 60th percentile (V_{fR}), and all those further to her right, don't want to bring the motion to a vote, she and her right-leaning colleagues can filibuster. (Of course, those on the right would not oppose a move from Q^* to V_{med}.) Those members with the extreme positions will be able to prevent a vote from taking place, thereby vetoing legislation that moves the status quo toward V_{med}. There are two cases to consider, defined by the position of the status quo relative to the position of V_{fL} and V_{fR}. The senators with ideal points V_{fL} and V_{fR} are crucial to this story: call them pivotal voters (Krehbiel, 1998), veto players (Tsebelis, 2002), or "play makers."

The first case has the status quo (Q^* in Figure 20) between ideal points V_{fL} and $V_{fR:}$ the two senators with ideal points at the filibuster triggering percentiles. Proposing to move the status quo toward V_{med} from such a position can trigger a filibuster. Therefore, these members can veto changes (hence, they become what could be called "***veto players***"). For if someone proposed changes that moved from Q^* to the right, the left 40 percent of the members would constitute a filibuster bloc and could be counted on blocking the move. The same would happen if Q^* were to the right of V_{med}.

On the other hand, the status quo could be at Q, beyond the space defined by the distance between the ideal points of these two pivotal players. Then a proposal to move Q toward V_{med} could be crafted such that the left pivotal voter, with V_{fL}, would support it, and no filibuster would occur. To garner the support of the 40th percentile voter, V_{fL}, the proposal would have to be closer to V_{fL} than Q is. In Figure 20 we show this distance, from Q to V_{fL}, with a dashed line. The distance is reflected on the other side of V_{fL} as well. In other words, for a proposal to not be stopped by a filibuster, it would have to be no further from V_{fL} than Q is (or within that interval marked by the dashed line). People with legislative interests have to pay special attention to such veto players, noting their ideal points in their calculations as to how to craft legislation.

Concluding Remarks

The above arguments show how a simple theory can be used to develop models to analyze a great many institutions. The models show us precisely how veto players, checks and balances, and other arrangements, restrict the attainment of the median voter's ideal point.

INTRODUCING CHECKS AND BALANCES RESTRICTS THE RESPONSIVENESS OF THE SYSTEM TO THE NEEDS, WELFARE, AND PREFERENCES OF THE MEDIAN VOTER.

We have seen that institutional details such as the specific powers of a committee chairperson, or the specific rules in a legislature, can determine the changes that can be made to the status quo. The average citizen is not likely to have any sense of what these details are: recall the conclusion that the citizen is not going to be well informed. Yet, democratic outcomes are a direct result of the interaction of these "rules" and the choices of the voters.

Indeed, an institutional structure that creates many veto players ensures that legislation to move the status quo toward the median voter's ideal point will often be relatively costly to enact. The institutions will not be particularly responsive to the median voter's interests and positions. If there is a relationship between the institution's median voter's welfare, and that of the citizenry (which is intuitively the case), many veto players will make more difficult a government that responds to the needs of the citizenry. It is only if we believe governments *ought* to be responsive to the needs of the citizens that we would be concerned about too many veto points. We will return to these points in Parts III and IV of this book.

Even though we may be able to think of policy problems that fit nicely into a one-dimensional framework, the reader must have lingering doubts as to the generality of the arguments that were put forward in this chapter. If the analysis in this chapter appears too simple to be general, the next chapter will make some moves to relax the assumptions of the above models. Sure enough, things will get more complex when we do so. Although it will first appear that we are moving from simplicity to chaos, we will discover that there is somewhat less difference between the two situations than first meets the eye. So let us now turn to the more difficult case of multidimensional political issues.

CHAPTER 5

Individual to Collective Choice More Generally

What we passed off as one-dimensional politics needs further elaboration. After all, when there are numerous issues, or even one issue that is very complex, there may not be such a simple metric as a single dimension upon which all, or even most, people can express their preferences in a single-peaked fashion. So the more general case is certainly politics in more than one dimension.[1] In this chapter we shall examine what happens to group choice when there is more than one dimension along which proposals are located. Begin by examining a simple extension of the analysis of majority rule beyond a single dimension. The extension creates problems we have not encountered yet. Very difficult normative questions are raised and the research regarding these issues is extraordinarily rich. It will be further discussed in Part IV. To begin, I use a simple example to demonstrate many of the problems, much as I did with the hydrant story on U Street. I will then move on to discuss non spatial ways of analyzing the outcomes of democratic political struggles in political situations to see what generalizations can be found. This will lead us, in Chapter 8, to discuss the limitations of translating individual preferences to social choice: the Arrow theorem.

Here's the simple example. Decisions are made again with a simple majority rule institution with a binary choice rule: Anyone can make a proposal; it has to go against the status quo. If it wins, it becomes the status quo. Beaten proposals are not reintroduced. This time, the group is to

---

[1] But political parties simplify the political space in which voters find themselves choosing. Hence, the space within which political competition takes place may have many of the interesting properties that we explored in the previous chapter.

decide where to place emergency fire equipment. The possibilities are not points on a road. Placement is anywhere on a two dimensional surface. Add preferences and what can we say about the outcome now?

EXTENDING SINGLE-PEAKED PREFERENCES TO TWO DIMENSIONS

What is the extension of single-peaked preferences to more than one dimension?[2] In two dimensions (think of places depicted on a map) the idea is that one's ideal point is a particular spot (on the map). The further from that spot, in any direction, the worse off one is. So, in the example, imagine that you are one of a small group of farmers on a flat plain. You have decided to place jointly purchased fire-fighting equipment in a place on the plain. You might feel that the closer they are placed to your farm, the better. If distance is the only thing that matters, and you are indifferent between distance in different directions, then we can think of levels of satisfaction in terms of how far you are from your preferred spot. Consider a spot precisely one-half mile from your farm. Then, any place that is also one-half mile away is equally good. The set of all points that are equally good (i.e., to which you would be indifferent) could be depicted as being on a line which is called an *indifference curve*. In this case that would be a circle on a map with the center at your farm house, and with a radius representing one-half mile. Anything inside the circle is better than anything outside the circle. You would be "indifferent" between all points on this "circular indifference curve."[3]

Indifference Curves: The points on the curve are those that an individual finds of equal value. In a two-dimensional situation, where all that counts is distance, the curves would be circles. Since at each distance from the ideal point one could draw a circle, there would be an infinite set of them.

This example has a natural ordering of outcomes determined by the distance from one's ideal point. The distance is measurable in a common fashion by everyone. If each farmer

---

[2] To discuss this, we restrict ourselves to two dimensions for purposes of diagrams and so on. All the major findings hold for dimensions higher than two.

[3] There could be a difference between north-south (along the coast) and east-west distances (inland versus shore). Distances toward the shore might be "more valued" than distance toward the interior, for example. This would mean that connecting points of equal "value" would not generate a circle. But let us leave these complications aside for now. Further development of such complications can be found in Enelow and Hinich, 1984.

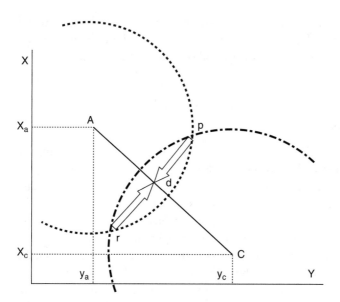

FIGURE 21. A contract curve in two dimensions.

wants the equipment as close as possible to her farm house, each person has a single-peaked preference.[4] They have circular indifference curves centered on the location of their farm. With just two persons, what could they agree to?

In Figure 21 the two farmers, A and C, each indicated by their eponymous ideal points indicated in the X,Y space. The thing to notice is that the two of them could always agree to move from a point off the straight line **AC** that connects their ideal points to some point on the line. That is, they could agree to move from a point such as **p** off the **AC** line, to some points such as **d** on the line. We can see why that is. Each has a desire to have the equipment as close as possible to her farm. So we can represent all the points that A finds equally good to **p** as all the points on the circle with a center at A and that go through **p**. All points closer, for example, to A than **p** will be inside the circle. So draw the two circles centered on both of their ideal point that goes through **p**. The circles of the two individuals that go through **p** will cross, since we have selected a point off the **AC** line and where they cross, they create a "lens." Both A and C will prefer to move to

---

[4] Of course, distance in politics is not as straightforward as distance from a farm house. And we are not usually interested in one individual's preference pattern, but rather those of all the members of a group. It is the group of voters whom we are positing to have single-peaked preferences over the same "two-dimensional metric" or "map."

a point in that lens rather than staying at **p**. Only for a point on **AC** would there be no lens.[5] So the individuals would prefer, that is, could agree, to be on the line: it is the set of Pareto optimal points for the pair of individuals. Such a line is usually called the ***contract curve*** between the individuals.

So now let us introduce a third individual, and majority rule, to see what changes to the analysis this brings out.

MULTIDIMENSIONAL PREFERENCES WITH MORE THAN TWO PERSONS AND SOCIAL DECISIONS

What then are the differences between the world of one-dimensional politics and those of multidimensional politics. Does majority rule still deliver desirable results? And what happens if we relax some of the assumptions about the preferences of the voters – when they have preferences that, though single-peaked, are no longer circular?

The Pareto Set

To begin with, does majority rule deliver Paretian, or optimal, results when voters have single-peaked preferences along more than one dimension? This was so in one dimension. To keep things simple, consider only three individuals: **A**, **B**, and **C**. Each wants the equipment placed as close as possible to their own farm. This ensures, as in Figure 21, that each has circular indifference curves. With three individuals, there will be three straight line two-person contract curves. Those lines represents what for the members of a two-person majority is the set of Pareto optimal points for the pair of individuals. The three contract curves form a triangular space on the map between their homes (**ABC** in Figure 22).

The Pareto set for the three farmers is precisely that triangle. To see this, consider any two points inside the triangle, and then a point outside the triangle. Recall that if an item is in the Pareto set one can't move from that point to another without someone being worse off. Consider any outcome in the interior of the triangle (such as **Y**, in Figure 22) as a useful bench-mark: a good compromise. Recall, each wishes the equipment to be as close as possible to their own house (i.e., ideal point). That would mean that each individual would prefer points closer to their corner of the triangle than **Y**. Starting with a point inside the triangle, such as **Y**, one can't find

---

[5] Given that the radius meets the circle at a right angle, the loci of the tangents of all circles with centers at two points is the straight line connecting those points (see Figure 21).

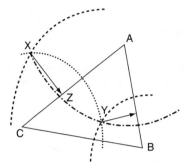

FIGURE 22. The hull of ideal points as the Pareto set.

any points that will be closer to all the corners of the triangle: moving toward any one corner or side will increase the distance to at least one corner. This is depicted by the arrow going from **Y** toward the side **AB**. Notice how a move into the "lens" of **AB** means that one is moving away from **C**.

Now recall the second property of the Pareto set: if one is outside the Pareto set one *can* find an outcome that all prefer. To show that this would be true of all points outside the triangle **ABC**, consider a point such as **X**. Now drop a line perpendicular to the closest side of the triangle to that point (in this case the side is **AC**). Any point along that line will be closer to all three of the ideal points. This is generally the case. And hence we can conclude that the triangle formed by the contract lines between the ideal points of the three individuals forms their Pareto set.[6] Now we can use our finding as to what constitutes the Pareto set with our analysis of majority rule's operation in a political space with more than one dimension.

Majority Rule

Now let us add consideration of majority rule and ask if it will deliver us into the Pareto set, and if it does, will such a point be stable? We continue with the story: placement of fire equipment and three individuals – **A, B,**

[6] More generally, when there are more than three individuals, as in Figure 27, if we consider all the two-person contract lines, there will be some that will form a convex hull that contains all the other contract lines. Convexity is the property that a space has when the straight line between any two points in the space is fully contained in the space. Another way of thinking about it is that there is no "indentation" of the border. One can draw a "convex" hull around any collection of points. This hull that contains all the n ideal points will then be the n-person Pareto set.

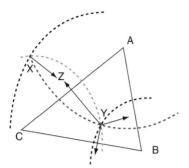

FIGURE 23. Three persons, 2 dimensions when preferences are single-peaked in 2 dimensions.

and C. Any two constitute a majority. Each wants it as close as possible to her own house. As in Figures 21 and 22, we have circular indifference curves, and the three contract lines that form a triangular Pareto set on the map between their homes. Again, consider Y, in Figure 23, an outcome in the interior of the triangle. Since each wishes the equipment to be as close as possible to her own house, each individual would vote for a point closer to their corner of the triangle rather than Y. Each would vote for any point inside that circular indifference curve which is centered at her house, and which has Y as a point on its edge (these are shown with the dotted lines).

What can we predict to be the outcome of a simple majority rule decision? We can see in Figure 23 that for a point inside the circle such as Y, there are three "lenses" (made from where the circles intersect to where they intersect a second time). Each of these lenses stretches from Y to a point outside of each of the three sides of the triangle (X is an example of such a point). Take, as an example, Z, a point inside the lens XY, but no longer even in the Pareto set. Faced with the simple choice of Y or Z, Both A and C would vote for Z over Y, as it is closer to both of their houses. In other words, movement from Y to a point into any one of those lenses permits a majority of the voters to be better off. And any point inside the triangle will have these multiple lenses of indifference curves that extend from it, to beyond the edge of the triangle. It follows that:

WHEN ISSUES ARE MULTIDIMENSIONAL, MAJORITY RULE CAN LEAD TO RESULTS THAT ARE NOT PARETO OPTIMAL.

This is a disappointment. But it isn't the only one. Each lens shows an area that contains the outcomes that would be better than Y for a majority of the voters: and such lenses exists for all points. Clearly, no point inside the triangle, such as **Y**, is a stable outcome. For at **Y** any of three 2-person majority coalitions can form to improve the position of their coalition members. From there, we might presume that each pair could agree to move it toward their Pareto set, or contract line (unlike **Z**, which is not on their contract line). Since there is no point that is on all three contract lines, a majority can always form to move it toward another majority's Pareto set or contract line. There is no point that a majority cannot improve for themselves. Indeed, as shown, majorities that are not careful can even swing the choice outside the triangle (as **A** and **C** can move from **Y** to the point **Z**).[7]

The second disappointing general conclusion is stark:

IN GENERAL, WITH SINGLE-PEAKED PREFERENCES IN MORE THAN ONE DIMENSION THERE IS NO POINT THAT WILL BE IN EQUILIBRIUM WITH THE USE OF MAJORITY RULE.

(Plott, 1967)[8]

This highly pessimistic conclusion has led to a great deal of research, some of which we will explore later. In one dimension, majority rule led inexorably to a result in the Pareto set and the equilibrium outcome was shown to be the most preferred or ideal point of the median voter. But as we examine majority rule in more than one dimension we find there is, in general, no equilibrium.

Take, for another example, a group of five persons, **ABCD** and **E**, to again note the disequilibrium induced by majority rule (see Figure 24). To see this, consider, among the sixteen winning coalitions, those ten with precisely three persons. **ABC**, for example, could get together to prevail. If it did, it could be expected to select an outcome in their own Pareto set, which you can see would be the triangle **ABC**. Note the ten 3-person possible winning coalitions are: **ABC, ABD, ABE, ACD, ACE, ADE, BCD, BCE, BDE,** and **CDE**. Each of these three-person majority coalitions, were they but to form, would be likely to demand results in their own Pareto set. Indeed, were a proposed result not in one of their

---

[7] Recall any point in the lens will beat the mid-point **Y**. And the lens has a portion outside the triangle.

[8] Plott actually showed that one cannot get an equilibrium unless there is point that is a median in *all* directions. The point must be common to all the median lines. A ***median line*** is a line that goes through one or more ideal points and which does not have a majority on either side of the line. That point, that is common to all median lines implies it is a median in *all* directions. that one can draw going through it). That is, for there to be an equilibrium there must be "radial symmetry" of individuals' ideal points: a highly unlikely happenstance.

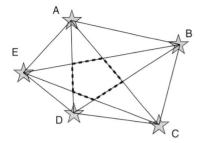

FIGURE 24. Instability with special majority rules.

Pareto sets that coalition would have an incentive to form and change the outcome. But there are no points in the figure that are in more than a few of those triangles: *no points are common to all the triangles*. So there will always be a potentially winning coalition that can do better, were it just to form and push to move the outcome to its own Pareto set. Recall, the core (see page 99) is the set of outcomes such that no coalition has an incentive to form to destabilize the outcome because no coalition can guarantee themselves a better outcome. So another way of stating Plott's result of general instability is that in general, when there is more than one dimension, and one employs majority rule, the core will be empty. Indeed, the outcomes could cycle over time, with no change in the preferences of the voters. So we could go from one coalition's Pareto set to that of another and then a third, only to arrive back where we started.

IN MULTIDIMENSIONAL SITUATIONS AND USING MAJORITY RULE, PREFERENCES ARE LIKELY TO SUPPORT VOTING CYCLES.

With majority rule there is a general instability of the situation. Or,

IN GENERAL, WITH SINGLE-PEAKED PREFERENCES IN MORE THAN ONE DIMENSION AND THE USE OF MAJORITY RULE, THERE IS NO POINT THAT WILL BE IN THE CORE: THE CORE WILL BE EMPTY.

Indeed, we can now examine the conditions under which equilibrium *could* exist (see Footnote 8). Note how things change if the distribution of ideal points were just right: were there a point in common to all the Pareto sets of the winning coalitions. Let us reconsider, for example, the case described by Figure 24. But this time let us place one of the five voters in the "interior" of the Pareto set of the other four. And let us consider two different scenarios. First place E's ideal point right at the crosshairs of the

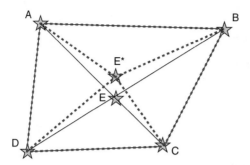

Equilibrium when there is radial symmetry.

diagonals as in Figure 25. In the second case, replace E with E* – off the crosshairs. With E on the crosshair, it (and it alone) sits in all the Pareto sets of each of the winning coalitions. So if E were chosen, one couldn't get a majority to move away from it toward any other point. For example, if B and A wanted to move from E, DCE could form a (winning) coalition to block the move. And here we see precisely the "knife edge" sort of condition that would be required to generate an equilibrium. There must be an ideal point that is common to all of the Pareto sets of all the winning coalitions. If we move the fifth ideal point so it sits even slightly off the crosshairs, say at E*, BDC or ACD could form to upset an outcome at E. Indeed, then no ideal point is in all the Pareto sets of all the possible winning coalitions. And if one of those coalitions formed to overthrow E*, we could expect E* to be part of a coalition with two other voters, ABE*, for example, to upset the winning or proposed outcome, via the new coalition. There would be no equilibrium. But this is not the end of the bad news.

Even more distressing is this: as we saw with the possibility of choosing a point such as Z in Figure 26, there is no guarantee that one stays in the Pareto set, or even in the vicinity of the Pareto set. Unfortunately, some of the points that can beat Z are even further from the Pareto set than Z lies from the Pareto set. This is depicted by Z' in Figure 26.

This property is commonly referred to as the "wildness" theorem. It shows that:

WITH A SET OF ALTERNATIVES THAT ARE IN MORE THAN ONE DIMENSION, MAJORITY RULE CAN LEAD A GROUP TO CHOOSE OUTCOMES THAT ARE ANYWHERE IN THE ALTERNATIVE SPACE.

McKelvey (1976) and Schofield (1978)

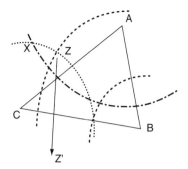

FIGURE 26. With majority rule one can move further and further from the Pareto set (wildness).

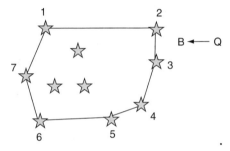

FIGURE 27. The 'pull' of the Pareto Set.

If these three conclusions were the last word on the status of social choice, it would be quite pessimistic indeed. But there are other considerations that will allow us to make a more balanced statement regarding the prospects of competitive politics using majority rule. Other findings bring us back to somewhat more optimistic conclusions. More generally, since individuals with single-peaked preferences on a two-dimensional surface[9] can agree unanimously to move to the convex hull surrounding the optima of the individuals (see Footnote 6), Nicholas Miller (1980) was able to deduce a more positive finding. He showed that although one can go anywhere in the space with majority rule, once one is out of the Pareto set the next move will be toward the set.

To get a feel for why this might be so consider Figure 27. There the ideal points of ten individuals (seven are numbered) are shown on a

[9] This can be extended to more than two dimensions.

two-dimensional surface. We can draw a hull around the entire set of ideal points with a set of straight lines (two-person contract curves) between some of the individual ideal points (**1234567**). If the status quo were outside the hull at a point such as **Q**, then all the individuals could agree to move the status quo to a point closer to the hull, such as **B**. A sufficiently large subset of the voters all clustered on the side of the hull opposite the current status quo could also propose an alternative that is closer to their ideal points but further from the side of the hull. Such opposing majorities could, conceivably, lead to a trajectory of outcomes that get ever more distant from the Pareto set. But that wildness result seems somewhat unlikely given that there could always be unanimous agreement to bring the status quo closer to the hull of the ideal points. Yet wildness remains a logical possibility. One can jump to the far side of the set (as in Figure 26) but the Pareto set is an "attractor" that pulls the results toward it. Think about the analysis of the 3 farmers (see Figure 22) where we saw that points outside the Pareto set (such as **X**) can be defeated. Such points can be defeated only by points that are either closer to the hull or on another side of the hull. Hence, although it is possible for the group to "go astray" and do things that are suboptimal, there is a tendency with majority rule to correct the situation.

WITH MAJORITY RULE ANY SUBOPTIMAL OUTCOME IS LIKELY TO BE REPLACED BY ONE THAT IS CLOSER TO THE PARETO SET AND, HENCE, PREFERRED BY ALL.

(Miller, 1983)

Getting Beyond Simple Majority Rule

The above stories are quite pessimistic with regard to majority rule. But other democratic rules of decision making have "happier" implications. The Pareto set for a group of individuals is the convex hull that encompasses their ideal points. In footnote 7 to Chapter 1 we identified a strong relationship between using unanimity rules and avoiding suboptimal results. With a unanimity rule, a group can be expected to select an outcome that is in the Pareto set.[10] Once they are within the Pareto set they will stay there, as they can't get unanimous support for a move. But there are numerous special majority rules that lie between simple majority rule and unanimity. We can see that they can also lead to some stability.

[10] Dougherty and Edward (2004) show the analysis needs to be more nuanced. Issues of how abstentions are counted matter, for example.

Take for example, the group of five persons, **ABCD** and **E**, that we used to note the disequilibrium induced by majority rule (see Figure 24, p. 123). With majority rule any three-person coalition that can agree on an alternative can win. Any outcome could thus win, but no outcome would be stable. But if we move from simple majority rule to a more demanding four-fifths rule there would be only five winning four-person coalitions: **ABCD, ACDE, ABDE,** and **BCDE.** Each of these coalitions would push the outcome into their own Pareto set. But now, there is a large area in the center of Figure 24, outlined with a dashed line, that is common to all the Pareto sets of these winning coalitions. The result is quite general[11] and we can conclude:

SPECIAL MAJORITY RULES CAN HELP STABILIZE GAINS THAT GROUPS CAN ACHIEVE IN THE MAKING OF BINDING DECISIONS WITH DEMOCRATIC RULES.

(Greenberg, and Caplin and Nalebuff)

In sum, there is a great deal of potential instability in political decisions that are over issues that have more than one dimension. But there are some institutional features that can stabilize the outcomes. These include special majority rules; procedural rules, such as eliminating defeated alternatives from further consideration; giving chairpersons extra power to set the agendas; having multiple decision bodies (as in a bicameral legislature); and the class of things we lump together as "checks and balances." We will address some of the costs and benefits of these rules in Parts III and IV of this volume.

RESEARCH FRONTIERS: WAYS FORWARD

The reasonable reader could be somewhat concerned by the number of assumptions that were required to reach the conclusions in these last two chapters. So let us examine two of these concerns. First I examine the notion of distance and how it relates to those circular indifference curves that lie behind much of the geometry that I have put in place. Second, I consider public bads that may lead to different-shaped preferences. These

---

[11] Greenberg (1979) showed that with single-peaked preferences in n-dimensions demanding a special majority of size $m^* > n/(n + 1)$ ensured an equilibrium outcome. So in one dimension m^* must be larger than one-half, or simple majority rule. With a two-dimensional issue, it would be a two-thirds special majority rule. It goes up as a function of the number of dimensions, with m^* having a limit of unanimity. Caplin and Nalebuff (1988) showed that if the distribution of preferences is itself single-peaked then $m^* > 1 - (n/[n+1])^n$ or 5/9 in two dimensions. It goes up as a function of n, with m^* having a limit of less than two-thirds. If there is a multi-peaked distribution, then this doesn't hold.

alternative assumptions display both the critical role, and power, of the original assumptions, and the potential richness and reward in their relaxation which would enable us to develop models for other sorts of political problems.

Reexamining and Reformulating Distance

"Distance" has been used quite loosely to this point. After all, in the world of politics, there is not "distance": there are issues, and alternatives, and platforms, proposals, and promises. In what I have developed, I have imagined a multidimensional issue space. I further assumed individuals have single-peaked preferences and circular indifference curves. Substantively, this implies that the individuals are indifferent to the direction of the distance that is being specified: or that they value movement from their ideal points similarly whether that movement comes from a disappointment in either one policy or another. But individuals tend to have real lives that dictate their concerns. Jake's children, who are soon to be of school age, trigger his heightened concern for education. A small deviation from what he considers to be a good school policy may leave him more upset than a large deviation from what he considers his ideal military security policy. His neighbor, Jill, worked near the Twin Towers in 2001. This has left her more concerned about security than education. How do these modifications alter the presumptions we have made so far?

Take Jill. A small deviation from what she considers to be a good security policy may leave her more upset than a similar deviation in education policy. Graphically, this would be reflected in the shape of her indifference curves (see Figure 28). A larger displacement (**AC**) in education policy would be less disappointing to Jill than the same size displacement from her ideal point in security policy. In other words, say she had her ideal education policy, but not her best security policy: she finds herself at **B**. Then, she would be prefer an outcome much further from **A** in education (almost as far as **C**) but with her ideal security policy. The greater distance **AC** is of equal value to her than the smaller distance **AB**. This would lead to her having elliptical indifference curves.

But there is another feature of this story that needs discussion. As we have drawn it, what Jill wants in her security policy doesn't change as the status quo in education policy is altered. Jane doesn't define her notions of what should be done in education by what should be done in security. The two issues are independent of one another. In other words, if the actual education policy were as depicted by the dotted line in Figure 28, what she

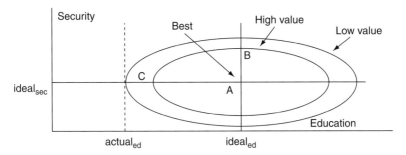

FIGURE 28. Greater concern for one issue (security) leads to elliptical indifference curves.

would want in security wouldn't be altered by education. For any fixed level of education policy (i.e., any vertical line) Jill would want security policy to be set so she could be on the highest valued indifference curve achievable. In the graph the dashed vertical line represents the fixed education policy. It is then clear that Jill to get to the would want security policy to be set at a point of tangency (C) of the vertical line and an indifference curve, in this case B, closest to her ideal point (A). When the axes of the ellipse are horizontal and vertical as in the figure, the achievements on one policy objective don't alter the height of those points of tangency or the ideal level regarding the other policy. If all voters feel the issues are independent, the issues can be dealt with one at a time, without worrying about the implications of one on the other.

Notice that to depict a voter feeling that the issues are *interdependent*, the elliptical indifference curves would be slanted (as in Figure 29). Were this so, for Jill, she would prefer different levels of education, as the level of security changes. The point of tangency to her indifference curves changes its height as we move horizontally. In other words, what she wants in security depends upon what she gets in education. When this is true for voters, any sensible decision on the two issues requires that the issues be thought about and decided as a package.

The ability to "handle" these added nuances let us see that that the models that have been developed are stylized: they can be modified to cover different (at times, more realistic) details to cover different situations. Modifying the models to cover new situations, will, of course, lead to different conclusions. Shifting, for example, from circles to ellipses makes it more difficult to predict the shape of the "contract curves" and hence the shape of the "hull of the ideal points" that were discussed above.

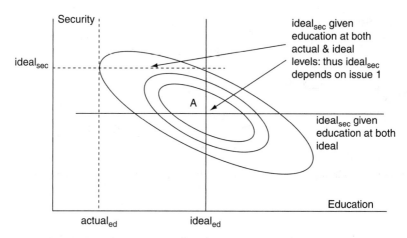

FIGURE 29. Non-independent issues.

So presuming the simpler world is more than pedagogically useful: it allows us to calculate generalizations more easily. But other techniques exist (such as computer simulations) to handle the predicted outcomes of more complex presumptions.[12]

Goods and Bads

All of our discussion to this point has depended upon the notion that one wanted the outcome closer to one's ideal. So the placement of a park or a hydrant might be desired near the home. But when the outcome is a bad, such as a jail or an incinerator, people may want the placement as far from their home as possible (often referred to as a NIMBY – not in my back yard – issue).[13] Then single-peakedness gives way to single-troughed preferences, and we may, once again, get substantial leverage by first presuming that the outcomes are all spaced on a line. As long as the outcomes are along a single dimension, and voters prefer points further from their worst point (e.g., home) the power of the median voter would remain central. The outcome would be at the extreme that was furthest from the median voter.

---

[12] For an example of the use of simulation to discover the inferences one can develop from more complicated (and realistic) preference assumptions see Wendel and Oppenheimer (2010).

[13] Much of the discussion in this section owes its form to the work of Laing and Slotznick (1990).

Most real-world geographical placement problems are not one dimensional. This wrinkle proves quite complicating, as now what happens depends upon the configuration of the geography. If people are concerned with having a facility far away, two things certainly will help determine the outcome: the distribution of the voters in the space, and the shape of the space, relative to their "worst points" (i.e., the shape of the boundary). Geographical and substantive details will further complicate the analysis. So for example, an incinerator's effects will depend upon prevailing winds. But in general, similar sorts of spatial models can be developed, and the probability of an equilibrium is small. But the general centripetal force of voting on bads would hold and we can conclude:

IN GENERAL WHEN THE PLACEMENT OF "BADS" ARE THE SUBJECT OF COLLECTIVE DECISIONS, PLACEMENT WILL BE FAR FROM THE PHYSICAL LOCATION OF THE PREDOMINANT CLUSTER OF VOTERS. IF THERE IS NO SUCH CLUSTER, IT WILL STILL BE PLACED AT OR NEAR THE EDGE OF THE POSSIBLE SPACE.

(Laing and Slotznick, 1990)

Aggregate Actors and the Presumption of Rational Choice

Finally, there is a presumption in all that we have developed, that the actors, or the voters, are each single individuals: but in politics often the actors are collectives, thrown together as some singleton and given institutional identity, such as a nation-state, political party, or province. And then we must wonder, can we even talk of preferences of the collective?

Take for example, the case of the senate, with the filibuster rule. If the collectives act in manners such as that, then they won't necessarily move toward the median voter, then what are we to say of the collective actor's decision? And if there is no equilibrium in the decision processes internal to the aggregate actor, how are we to relate the actor's choices to the preferences of those that make it up? Any evaluation of a real live political system will require that these sorts of problems be tackled. And it should be clear that any progress on this front will require further tools and further analysis. I take this up in detail in Part IV.

THE UNCOVERED SET: STABILITY AND
PREDICTABILITY WITH CYCLES

Go back to circular indifference curves. To this point, things have looked quite bleak. But even though we are stuck with multidimensional politics and its ensuing cycles there is some stability and a strong centralizing

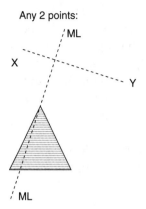

Any 2 points:

FIGURE 30. Closeness to the median line and winning in majority rule.

tendency in the politics of democratic systems. Gordon Tullock (1981) made this observation and conjectured that the relative stability of outcomes would be found to be related to the intersection of the median lines in the political space.

To see why this might be, recall the definition of a median line (see Footnote 8). Recall with circular indifference curves voters are concerned with how far the proposals are from their ideal points. This means that one alternative beats another by majority rule when it is closer to more than half of the ideal points.[14] Now consider two points such as the status quo, X, and a proposal, Y, and three voters with ideal points in a triangle (see Figure 30). Draw a straight line connecting X and Y. Many median lines may be drawn that will intersect this line but only one will be perpendicular to it.[15] Whichever of the points is closer to this median line will beat the other by majority rule – it is closer to more ideal points than the alternative. If all the median lines intersected one point we would have an equilibrium in multiple-dimensions (see Plott's theorem, page 122). Now it should be intuitive that winning alternatives will cluster in the neighborhood containing all the intersections of the median lines.

One other breakthrough was needed to explain the stability and the pull of the center in democracies. That was the work of Nicholas Miller (1980).

---

[14] This is so with circular indifference curves and majority rule. With other majority rules similar inferences can be made.

[15] With an even number of distinct ideal points there could be two such perpendiculars and the claims would be slightly modified.

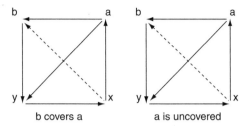

b covers a   a is uncovered

FIGURE 31. Illustrating the covering relation. (An arrow pointing from A to B means that B can beat A.)

In spite of the problem of cycles, it allows us to predict outcomes quite accurately in multidimensional spatial contexts as long as individuals have single-peaked preferences.[16] It uses a relationship called "uncovered."

To understand Miller's contribution, we must understand what "covered" and "uncovered" mean and how they relate to politics. This requires some abstract reasoning about sets of policy alternatives. Call the set of alternatives S and two specific alternatives in them a and b. For a to be *covered* by b (see the left side of Figure 31) means that b can beat a and if any alternative, y, beats b, it also beats a. Note that if there is a cycle that includes a, b, and y it would have to be longer than those three alternatives; it would have to include at least one other alternative, x to get back to a. Thus it would take more than two steps to get back to a. Alternatively, for a to be *uncovered*, either a beats all other alternatives or, if there is something that beats a, such as b (in the right side of Figure 31), then there must be an x that beats b that, in turn, a can beat. Thus it would only two steps to get back to a.

Now the link to politics is quite direct and intuitive. The alternatives in S that are uncovered are called *the uncovered set*. The covered set (the residual) is dominated: it can't beat those things which beat it. Hence the uncovered set is the undominated set. That might constitute a political motivation for the expectation that the political competition is most likely to be found within the uncovered set. If one proposes an item in the uncovered set one need never be in a cycle of more than three: one need never be more than two steps away from having one's proposal regaining a majority (Shepsle and Weingast, 1984). Proposals outside the uncovered set do not have that property. When there are cycles, and the stakes are

---

[16] Both direct experimental tests and field tests of the uncovered have shown it to be a good predictor (Bianco et al. 2004a, 2004b, 2006).

high, serious proposals are likely to be restricted to those in the uncovered set. Politicians who are serious about having their platforms adopted would have a reason to choose items within the uncovered set and to avoid those that are not.

Now, unlike the core, the uncovered set is never empty. Also, when the core is not empty, the uncovered set coincides with the core (as such, it is also part of the Pareto set) (McKelvey, 1986; Miller, 1980). And finally, the uncovered set is always a subset of the Pareto set. Given these properties, Bianco et al (2004b) described the uncovered set as follows:

> The uncovered set captures the fundamental forces driving outcomes in the legislative process: legislators' underlying policy preferences, their ability to foresee the consequences of their actions, and their ability to select agendas. As such, the uncovered set can be thought of as the set of enactable outcomes in a policy space.

Saying that an outcome is likely to reside in the uncovered set isn't very helpful unless we can locate that set more specifically. Luckily its location has been tied to those median lines. The concept required here is the **yolk** (McKelvey, 1986). The yolk is the smallest circle that intersects *all* the median lines. Call the center of this circle c and its radius r. It is the yolk. McKelvey showed that the uncovered set is always contained within a circle which has c as its center, and a radius of $4r$. How big an area this is depends upon how scattered the intersections of the median lines are, but in general, it is a relatively small subset of the space containing S, the set of proposals. An illustration can be found in Figure 32. There we have eight very scattered ideal points (the area in the center is empty). So the intersection of the median lines is quite large.

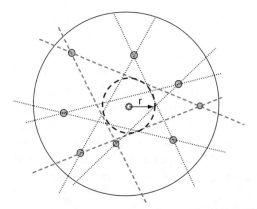

FIGURE 32. 8 voters, r = yoke, 4r contains the uncovered set.

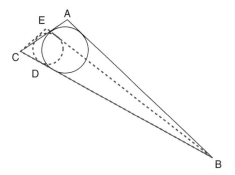

FIGURE 33. Yolks for n = 3 & n = 5.

If the yolk is small, then we'd see a compact space for the competition. Take the case where there is a triangle (three people). If one is far away, the triangle is elongated and the yolk is down on the narrow side. So the far guy's ideal point is out of the uncovered set. (See Figure 33.) Imagine we add two people (**D** and **E**) with ideal points near the line **AC** in the figure. Then the limiting median lines will stem from point **B** to **D** and **C**, and the yolk will be smaller (the circle). Further the analysis can be extended to different sorts of rules, and even to collective actors (see Tsebelis, 2002). We can understand that with the uncovered set, there will be a predictability of outcomes, even if there is no stability. In other words,

DEMOCRATIC PROCESSES AMONG PROFESSIONAL POLITICIANS LEAD TO OUTCOMES IN PREDICTABLE RANGES EVEN IF THEY CANNOT BE SPECIFIED MORE EXACTLY. WITH WIDE LATITUDE OF ARRANGEMENTS THESE RANGES TEND TO THE CENTER OF THE DISTRIBUTION OF THE VOTER'S IDEAL POINTS AND CAN BE EXPECTED TO BE WITHIN THE UNCOVERED SET.

CONCLUSIONS

Hopefully you have come to see both the power and the limitations of spatial analysis. Simplifying assumptions, let us see the wide contours of the possible. And certainly some structures, such as two-party electoral competition can lead to single dimensions in which distance is a salient metric. In such cases, we can see the power of the simpler models in real-world results. On the other hand, the models show that in many cases there is some unpredictability of results: no equilibrium from the preferences of the citizenry. Yet in other environments, such as legislatures and some electoral competitions where agendas are quite carefully manipulated, the aggregation systems of voting are likely confined to the uncovered set. The uncovered set lets us generalize the centralizing tendencies of democracy, even when we can acknowledge the prevalence of preference cycles and wider instabilities.

Certainly, there will be times that we can't utilize spatial analogues for problems of political preference aggregation. In Part IV of this volume I present further models and tools regarding these problems that will let us specify the implications of the findings of non-equilibrium. The analysis will let us compare some of the strengths and weaknesses of alternative voting systems, and it has implications for a slew of ancient political questions regarding liberties, justice, and welfare.

FOR FURTHER READING

Spatial Models in One Dimension

Black, Duncan (1958), *The Theory Of Committees And Elections*, Cambridge: Cambridge University Press. This classic has a historical section (Part II) which is great. Other parts are better treated now in such texts as Enelow and Hinich (see below).

Collier, Kenneth E., Richard D. McKelvey, Peter C. Ordeshook and Kenneth C. Williams (1987), "Retrospective Voting: an Experimental Study," *Public Choice*. v. 53: 101–130. In this experiment of one-dimensional elections, a group of voters vote to keep or throw out leaders. No one knows the underlying payoff functions of the voters, but they are single-peaked. Leaders only know the history of the votes. One quickly gets convergence to the median voter: an astounding result given the lack of information.

Downs, Anthony (1957), *An Economic Theory Of Democracy,* New York: Harper and Row. This is the classic application of spatial models to democratic elections.

Eavey, C. and G. Miller (1984), "Bureaucratic Agenda Control: Imposition or Bargaining?" *American Political Science Review,* 78, September: 719–733. Using an experiment with an agenda setter and a committee that decides a one-dimensional spatial problem, they argue that the institutional equilibria models are too simple. The result is not in the core but rather is modified by bargaining. The agenda setter does not get everything she could.

Hotelling, Harold (1929), "Stability in Competition," *Economic Journal:* v. 39 (1): 41–57. Hotelling was the first to develop the connection of spatial analysis to politics. He also saw how to understand equilibria in spatial competition. This piece is a classic and is the basis for Downs' idea of "matching" strategies by parties.

Morris, Irwin (2000), *Congress, the President, and the Federal Reserve: The Politics of American Monetary Policymaking*, Ann Arbor: Univ. of Michigan Press. Morris uses spatial models to discuss how the Federal Reserve Bank is held in check by Congress.

Niskanen, Wm. A. Jr. (1971), *Bureaucracy and Representative Government*, Chicago: Aldine. Niskanaen uses spatial models to discuss how the head of an agency's incentives to maximize his budget can lead to oversupply of a collective good.

Spatial Models in More than One Dimension

Black, Duncan and R. Newing (1951), *Committee Decisions with Complementary Valuations*, London: William Hodge. This is an early classic which shows that the median voter result is a special case.

Coughlin, Peter and Melvin J. Hinich (1984), "Necessary and Sufficient Conditions for Single-Peakedness in Public Economic Models, *J of Public Economics*, 25: 323–41. Coughlin develops one of the early models of probabilistic models of voting.

Enelow, J. and M. Hinich (1984), *The Spatial Theory of Voting*, Cambridge Univ. Press: Cambridge, UK. Though dated, this text develops the general tools and implications of the spatial models and applies them.

Fiorina, M. P. and C. R. Plott (1978), "Committee Decisions under Majority Rule: An Experimental Study," *American Political Science Review*, 72 (June, 2): 575–598. Using committee experiments they show that you can get core-like results even when there is no core. This would be in keeping with the uncovered set analysis. The results are challenged by other experiments that show "fairness" can upset their results. See Gary J. Miller and Joe A. Oppenheimer (1982), "Universalism in Experimental Committees," *American Political Science Review*, 76 (2, June): 561–574.

Hansen, P. D. Peeters, and J.-F. Thisse, "On the location of an Obnoxious Facility," *Sistemi Urbani*, 3, 1981, pp. 299–317. The problem of siting bads in two-dimensional space is developed. Proposals for social choice methods are discussed, and siting nuclear plants in France are used for data.

Hammond, Thomas H. and Gary J. Miller (1987), "The Core of the Constitution," *American Political Science Review*. Vol 81: 1156–1174. They develop a spatial model of the constitutional structure and show that there is a core to the legislative game. They demonstrate that the core is expanded (i.e., more and more possible outcomes are made difficult to change) by the addition of checks and balances.

Miller, Nicholas R. (2007), "In Search of the Uncovered Set," Political Analysis, 15 (1): 21–45. This is a pedagogic piece that helps one understand the logic of the uncovered set.

Tsebelis, George (2002), *Veto Players: How Political Institutions Work*, Princeton University Press: Princeton, N. J. His development of the uncovered set to complex institutions is important and quite accessible for the mathematically willing.

The Democratic Advantage

Halperin, Morton H., Joseph T. Siegle, and Michael M. Weinstein (2004), *The Democracy Advantage: How Democracies Promote Prosperity and Peace,* New

York: Routledge. Analyzing a lot of statistics, they establish that democracy generates more welfare and peace than autocracy. The book is a careful, direct, statistical portrayal of the rewards of democracy.

Przeworski, Adam (1999), "Minimalist Conception of Democracy: A Defense" in Ian Shapiro and Casiano Hacker-Cordon, eds., *Democracy's Value*, Cambridge: Cambridge University Press:, 23–55. Przeworski argues that nonviolent succession is the real benefit of democracy. This piece is theoretically informed. His review of the literature regarding the benefits of democracy is dated and should be compared with that of Halperin et al. But Przeworski was one of the first to use modern statistics to test if democracy would generate better results. He found the results to be ambiguous and found that the stability of democracy is tied to per capita income.

Sen, Amartya K. (1981), *Poverty and Famines: An Essay on Entitlement and Deprivation*, Oxford: Clarendon Press. This classic shows that the loss of entitlement or market trading power is the real cause of famines, *not* that there isn't enough food to go around. Case studies include Bangladesh ('73–'74), Ethiopia, Bengal (1943), and Sahel (Niger, Chad, etc.). Sen shows how income loss to economically marginal people can wipe out their ability to buy food and lead to starvation. Sen shows that free food can help, and that notions of poverty need to be rethought to take into account survivability in terms of brittleness of the economic situation of the people.

PART III

POLITICAL INSTITUTIONS AND QUALITY OUTCOMES

How can the design of democratic political institutions help, or obstruct, the achievement of such goals as Pareto optimality, responsiveness, and so on? To explore this, begin by considering the general necessity of political institutions and then the general difficulties in holding such institutions responsible to the citizenry.

We have already seen how some aspects of institutional design can affect outcomes. For example, in Part II we examined how filibuster rules and other institutional details can change expected outcomes. We also noticed that attributes of voters' preferences such as alienation can affect electoral outcomes. In Part I we saw how disorganization can affect the preservation of common-pool resources and how, with collective outcomes, there is a tendency for free-riding and rational ignorance. These conclusions stemmed from assumptions about individual behavior. Here, however, we consider particular problems of institutional design per se.

To frame the discussion, I address two big questions in Chapter 6: first, "Are political systems really necessary?" And then, "Why is it so hard to tether political leaders to act in the interests of their subjects?"

Are political institutions necessary? From Ayn Rand, Robert Nozick, and Friedrich Hayek (Economics Nobel laureate, 1974) to Ron Paul and numerous think tanks such as the Heritage Foundation and the Cato Institute and some large segment of the current American Tea Party, there has been an advocacy of something like a minimalist state: a minimalist political structure of free market capitalistic anarchy. Such a vision is deeply flawed.

Until about fifty years ago, one of the major justifications for the state was to correct certain "failures" that naturally occur in markets. One of the most prominent such market failure is called an *externality*. An externality occurs when a market transaction does not reflect all the costs (or benefits) that accrue to those who are not parties to the transaction. For example, consider

> Definition – *Externality:* An externality is an effect (benefit or cost) of a transaction (or exchange) that is not factored into the underlying terms of exchange. For example, were I to consider buying an azalea bush for my front yard, I probably wouldn't take into account the joy that the blossoms bring my neighbors across the street.

the price of an item set in a market by the interaction of the buyer and seller. Presumably, their preferences and interests are taken into account. But if the production of the item causes pollution, there will be costs to others, not party to the transaction, and not compensated by the transaction. They suffer a cost: an externality of the transaction. It was long held that to correct the situation governmental action was required: regulation was needed to ensure compensation and so on. But Ronald Coase (Economics Nobel laureate, 1991) argued this was not necessary. And his argument has served as a foundation for the drive for a minimalist state. The argument is known as the Coase Theorem (1960).[1]

Coase's theorem is easy to restate and discussion of it is available in any number of textbooks: "As long as underlying property rights are defined and enforced, in the absence of bargaining and transactions costs, parties consuming and producing externalities will be able to reach a Pareto optimal agreement among themselves." In other words, governmental action is not needed beyond the facilitation of a bargaining arena. The theorem addressed the many governmental policies that cited cases of market failure and asserted that settlement and amelioration of these problems need not be linked to governmental regulation. Although this argument was shown to have a sizeable hole by Aivazian and Callen (1981), it stayed a bedrock principle underlying many policy arguments for deregulation. So we begin Chapter 6 with a reexamination of both the Coase Theorem and the necessity for governmental institutions.

After illuminating the error in Coase's argument, we move to problems inherent in all political institutions. Many of these problems center on getting professional politicians to take account of the interests of the people or citizens. Using this concern as a template, we think about the

---

[1] The word "theorem" is used advisedly as Coase did not actually derive it. Rather, he told some stories that made it seem plausible.

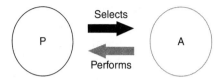

FIGURE 34. Principal-Agent Problem.

difficulties of getting politics to be structured so as to deliver programs that the people need. This will be discussed in terms of a modified "principal-agent" problem.

The ***principal-agent problem*** is one of keeping the hired hand (the agent) responsiveness to the needs of the employer, (the principal): see Figure 34. The main question is, "How can the principal be assured that the agent's behavior will conform to her interests?" This problem is much studied in law, economics, and business administration. Agents – who are making decisions and taking concrete actions for principals – have more complete and better information about the choices they are making than do the principals who hired them. So with such asymmetric information their behavior can deviate from the guidance and interests of the persons who hired them.[2] Further, knowing that the agent has better information, the principal has to interpret the information that is given her by the agent. The principal absorbs the information and it may alter her expectations. This notion that receiving information changes expectations is referred to as ***updating***. Solving the problem of controlling the agent requires finding rules or structures so that the self-interested rational choices of the agent coincide with what the principal desires.[3] This is hard enough. But there are further complications that beset the classical principal-agent problem when it is nested in a political or administrative context.

Once we understand the complexity of the principal-agent problem in political contexts, we will refocus on gaining agent responsiveness. In Chapter 6 we examine one part of this question: the problem of commitment.[4] Some democratic governments have serious difficulties making required long-term policy commitments. An example would be the

---

[2] Madoff's recent financial Ponzi scheme is but one example of distortions that stem from such a conflict.

[3] A rather insightful application of principal-agent models to politics development may be found in Besley (2006).

[4] Notice that long-term commitments often come at the price of responsiveness in the present (Rogowski, 1999).

underfunding of infrastructure maintenance as in building a light rail system and letting the tracks deteriorate. The problem of commitment is also manifest in such "pay as you go" programs as Social Security. This public policy problem is manifest in, but certainly is not restricted to, the United States. Is it a characteristic of aspects of a political system's design?

Since some non-democratic systems have, in some ways, done quite well by their citizens, we might wonder, "Are there improvements that democratic change can bring that are difficult to get from non-democratic systems?" Given these improvements, what can we say about regime change? So I end Chapter 6 with some analysis of the limitations and processes of transition to democracy and regime change.

In Chapter 7, we focus on maintaining and improving responsiveness of democracies and related design and behavioral problems. More specifically, I look into such suggestions as that of Montesquieu to have a separation of powers, the notion of checks and balances, and federalism. Undoubtedly, there are benefits to such arrangements. But all too often the analysis stops without an exploration of the difficulties that ensue. So I examine some of the effects of such properties as checks and balances, separation of powers, and multilayered governments. At their heart, these features imply a division of labor (e.g., she who legislates doesn't administer) and such a specialization can lead to difficulties much like those we have examined previously. These arrangements generate veto points that make the changing of a status quo more difficult. This analysis will shunt us back both to shadows of the prisoner dilemma game and foreshadow the kind of impossibilities reflected in Arrow's impossibility theorem that is discussed in Part IV.

CHAPTER 6

Political Necessity and the Tethering of Leaders

Are governmental institutions necessary? If so, our pursuit of better designs ought to consider the biggest concern for any acceptable political process: the taming of the great violence associated with political competition. To get a handle on how important, or central, this relation is to politics we consider the structure of political competition and how it differs from competition in the market. But wild and violent political competition is not the only sort of political failure we will want to examine.

When competition is constrained, there usually remains a deep problem of getting the behemoth of government to take into account the needs of its citizens: a problem often considered to be a special sort of principal-agent problem. One aspect of this problem will be pulled out for more extensive treatment: the problem of credible commitment. Indeed the nature of political competition can be shown to frame the principal-agent problem in a manner that makes it more acute in politics than in economics. The principal-agent problem manifests itself in politics as a problem best labeled as a constituent-beneficiary-agent problem.

Seeing the problems of tethering political institutions to the citizens' interests leads one to muse on the benefits of democracy. So in a final section of this chapter we examine the leverage rational choice theory has given us regarding the struggle for establishing democracy.

THE NECESSITY OF GOVERNMENTAL INSTITUTIONS

Coase's argument concerns externalities (see page 140). These are usually the effects of market or other transactions on those who are not party to

TABLE 10. *A Two-Party Externality Showing Profits of Both Enterprises*

| | Payoffs (Jam maker, smelter) – When Smelter is | |
Smelter Situations	Producing	Out of Production
Less Profitable	25, 4	32, 0
More Profitable	25, 10	32, 0

the transaction. Some of these are minor, as in the example of planting flowers, but there are also important externalities: the pollution of the Chesapeake Bay from farm fertilizer runoffs, the warming of the globe from the use of fossil fuels, and so on. Such effects that are not "monetized" in the originating market transactions are a form of market failure. The market prices in the transactions do not reflect the valuations of the effects of the transactions. At least since the time of Arthur Cecil Pigou's *Wealth and Welfare* (1912) market failures were considered the fundamental justification for governmental interference in the market.

Coase (1960) argued that externalities did not justify government regulation because the affected parties, if left to their own devices, could and would reach a bargained Pareto optimal solution on their own. He illustrated his point with various stories. For example, consider a jam maker, whose business is conducted next to a smelter. Assume that the smelter's operations cause air pollution that requires air filtration in the jam maker's factory and that the smelter has the right to pollute: others have no "right" to clean air. Pigou had argued this was a perfect place for the government to step in to regulate emissions.

What is of interest to us here is Coase's discovery that the allocation of property rights, though it can change the outcome, doesn't affect the achievement of a Pareto optimality. To help us through Coase's argument, I put some numbers on two different illustrative situations and display them on two rows in Table 10. The table illustrates the two situations in which the two neighboring manufacturers could find themselves.

Consider line 1 of the table. In the first column both companies produce and the jam maker makes $25,000; the smelter makes $4,000. The right-hand column shows the situation if the smelter were to go out of business: the jam maker would stand to make $32,000, or $7,000 more. That $7,000 is the size of the externality: the total lost profit, or cost, imposed upon the jam maker, by the smelter. Also note that the total profit with them both in production is $25,000 + $4,000, or $29,000. But in the right-hand column, were the smelter to stop production, it would be $3,000 more. In other words, stopping the externality is worth more to the jam maker than staying in production is to the smelter. This creates the possibility of a deal: the jam maker buys out the smelter for more than $4,000 (the smelter's profit) and less than $7,000 (the jam maker's increased profit from shutting down the polluting smelter). Such a buyout makes both parties better off.

Now change the situation slightly. Assume the smelter makes more ($10,000 when they are both producing – depicted in line 2 of the table). In this situation, the two of them actually make a higher profit when they are both producing than when the smelter is closed. And here, were the jam maker to have the right to clean air and hence could demand the smelter to close, the smelter makes enough to propose a deal to compensate the jam maker, and stay in operation. Although the jam maker can increase his profit by $7,000 shutting down the smelter, the smelter can earn $10,000 staying open. So the smelter can offer some deal of more than $7,000 but less than $10,000 for permission to stay open and continue to pollute (i.e., a price such that both benefit).

It is useful to use a different notation to discuss these examples. We can show the "value of the game" to each of the two enterprises, and of a joint agreement. On line 1, we see that the value of the jam-making enterprise, noted as $v(J)$, is $25,000, and for the smelter, $v(S)$ is $4,000. On the other hand, the value of them having an agreement $v(JS)$, which in this case is the smelter shutting down, totals $v(JS) = \$32,000$. Similarly, the situation on line 2 can be written as $v(J) = \$25,000$, $v(S) = \$10k$, and $v(JS)$, an agreement giving the jam maker compensation, is worth $35,000. On both lines a Pareto optimal deal can be reached which makes the two parties better off. Once a deal is reached, there is no way it pays for one of the two parties to defect since neither could guarantee itself a better outcome.[1] In other words, any such deal is in what we have identified as the core (page 99).

So we can see precisely what Coase asserts: the parties will be able to reach a deal to their mutual benefit without the introduction of governmental policy (other than the legal policies and institutions that enforce any contract and property rights). Even were there serious costs to reaching a bargained solution, one might conclude that instead of regulating, the government ought merely to subsidize the negotiations, so as to decrease

---

[1] The value of what we might call the "grand coalition" of everyone cooperating can always yield a Pareto optimal outcome, since if the best cooperative outcome is for each to go their own way, that can be accommodated.

TABLE 11. *Values of Coalitions – No Core*

Values of Coalitions	
Of One Person	**Of Larger Coalitions**
$v(i) = 0$	$v(i,j) = 9$
$v(j) = 0$	$V(j,k) = 9$
$v(k) = 0$	$V(i,k) = 9$
	$V(i,j,k) = 12$

the cost of bargaining and negotiation. The rest should be up to private negotiations between the parties. The distribution of property rights need not be of concern in solving the problems of externalities, but rather can be handled as a separate aspect of governmental policy. Once set, the Pareto optimal outcomes will be reached. The stakes in this discussion are large: if Coase is right, the regulatory role of government is vastly diminished.

Considerable testing of this theory was done, with some of the best being done in the laboratory.[2] But in 1981 Aivazian and Callen found that the theory was not general; it only held in a "special case" when there were outcomes in the core; it did not hold when the core was empty. Recall that if an outcome is in the core no coalition is likely to form to upset the outcome as none could be sure of doing better. Such an outcome would have payoffs that guarantee all the coalitions more than they can be sure of getting if they pull out. The core is empty when no such outcome exists. To see how this argument unfolds, we need more than two parties to the problem. Let us consider a three-person case.

Call the three people i, j, and k. Assume that if any two get together they can gain a benefit of 9, while the value of all of them, the grand coalition (see Footnote 1), coming together is 12. The values are depicted in Table 11. Note that in this context, although the grand coalition outcome is Pareto optimal, it is not stable. Consider, for example, the coalition of i and j. They could guarantee themselves 9. But this is true for any pair. Each pair could get 9 were they to pull out of a three-way agreement. So why should any pair settle for less than 9? But there isn't enough value in the grand coalition to satisfy all pairs. Neither is any two-party coalition stable: the party left out has 3 to offer to split to be allowed back in to a three-person coalition with an uneven division of payoffs. But there is still

[2] See Harrison and McKee, 1985 as well as Hoffman and Spitzer, 1982 and 1986. All of these tests were done with situations that had a non-empty core.

TABLE 12. *Instability of Agreements with No Core*

Coalitions and Their Values	Possible Payoffs to Players		
	a	b	c
v(ab)=9	4.5	4.5	0
v(abc)=12	6	5	1
v(bc)=9	0	5.5	3.5
v(ac)=9	3	0	6
v(ab)=9	4.5	4.5	0

not enough value available in the grand coalition to prevent another destabilization of the agreement. No particular two-person coalition dominates and no stable bargain exists. The value of the grand coalition just isn't sufficient to make it stable and hence there are no possible results in the core; the core is empty. (One possible pattern of cycles is illustrated in Table 12.) As is, this game doesn't have a stable Paretian outcome nor even a cycle sure to stay in the Pareto set: the core is empty.[3]

The non-existence of a stable outcome can be divorced from the optimality question. If there were an outcome in the core, it would necessarily be Pareto optimal (the grand coalition can always achieve an optimal outcome – see Footnote 1). But we can have cycles among Paretian outcomes as would be the case were we to have a better value to playing the game alone.[4] So, for example, we can modify the value of each of the participants in Table 11 so that any 2 person coalition is also worth 12. Then the two-party and grand coalitions outcomes would all be Pareto optimal. But none are stable. Any two-person coalition that breaks away can grab 12 for itself, leaving nothing for the outsider, who can then bargain to destabilize the formed coalition. But the real problem for society occurs when the Pareto optimal outcome isn't stable and other non-optimal results are arrived at via cycles. Under those circumstances, if we don't regulate properly, we are not likely to get optimality. So not only do we need property rights, such as for clean air, but, in contrast, with Coase we need them to be carefully allocated for socially acceptable results to

---

[3] Were the value of the grand coalition more than 13.5, each party could get more than 4.5 and outcomes would exist such that no group would have an incentive to leave the grand coalition.

[4] This is illustrated in the divide the dollar example in Table 20, p. 141.

occur.[5] We cannot rely on the forces of bargaining among the parties to reach good results.

An unpublished experimental study by Blake, Guyton, and Leventhal (1994) indicates the problem is serious. They ran experiments with the values shown in Table 11 when the core was empty and with a value of 7 for the two-party coalitions to generate a non-empty core situation. When the core was empty, a high proportion (55 percent) of outcomes were suboptimal yielding a total payout of $9 rather than the available $12.

The conclusion is stark: more generally,

WHEN WE FACE EXTERNALITIES, ONLY WHEN A PARETIAN BARGAIN IS IN EQUILI-
BRIUM CAN WE EXPECT INDIVIDUAL RATIONAL BEHAVIORAL OUTCOMES TO
GENERATE OPTIMALITY.

Aivazian and Callen

Further, this implies a lemma not usually considered by those who borrowed Coase to support free market anarchist prescriptions:

FACED WITH EXTERNALITIES, GOVERNMENTAL ACTION IS AS LIKELY TO BE NECES-
SARY TO ACHIEVE GOOD SOCIAL OUTCOMES AS NOT.

And so, faced with what appears to be a virtually inescapable need for government, we now consider some of the implications of our previous arguments for the design characteristics of governmental institutions.

POLITICAL LEADERSHIP: MONOPOLY AND COMPETITION

As articulated in Part I of this book, politics is important precisely because it is about the satisfying of shared interests or, as we have also phrased it, about the obtaining of public goods (see definition, page 27). Recall that public goods have two properties: if one person gets the good, so do others and the individuals share the item. The non-exclusion property implies the possibility of free-riding. The property that the good is shared means that when larger numbers of persons receive the good, additional units of the good are not needed for each additional person getting it: no more of it is needed (although, this can be modified when there is "crowding" – see page 28). This is to be contrasted with the provision of private goods in a market.

[5] A good example of such a case is contained in Mueller (2003, p. 30).

In markets it is a safe bet that firms providing private goods, where increased consumption requires increased production, are eventually going to run into increasing marginal costs. Eventually, they get too big to remain cost competitive. Then competitors can enter their markets and produce and sell virtually the same private good for less. The important lesson to take from this is that normal competition in markets for private goods is over market shares, not elimination of a competitor. There is usually room for numerous suppliers.

In the case of pure public goods when there is no crowding the story is very different. The political organizer will be supplying a public good program to a group (say: flood control to residents in a river valley). There may be alternative views and programs available, but it isn't likely that flood control measures (e.g., channelizing a stream) need to be enlarged because of a modest increase in the valley's population (and hence in the number of consumers of the public good). This leads to the proposition:

IN MOST PUBLIC GOOD SITUATIONS THE SUPPLIER IS A NATURAL MONOPOLIST.
(Frohlich, Oppenheimer and, Young, 1971)

And from this, we have the corollary:

COMPETITION AMONG WOULD-BE SUPPLIERS OF PUBLIC GOODS IS ABOUT REPLACEMENT RATHER THAN MARKET SHARE.
(Frohlich, Oppenheimer, and Young, 1971)

Since there is a problem of free-riding, the supplier can't rely on a pricing mechanism to pay for the good. As was discussed in Chapter 1, there usually have to be incentives for people to pay for the good independent of the public good itself. As we all have experienced, political processes be what they may, these are usually in the form of taxes. Hence we see, without surprise, that great wealth can be amassed by political leaders even when the general population is neither affluent nor well served.

Often, but certainly not always, the replacement struggle requires resources that are collected by differentiating oneself as a supplier with a substitute program. Such program differentiation will be either about the nature of the public goods, or how the programs are to be paid for. But instrumentally, the differentiation is often done to raise resources to compete to replace the leadership. As we indicated above (see page 29), there is a relationship between the size of the group, the profitability of leadership, and the seriousness of competition. Given that political competition is usually a winner-take-all struggle of replacement, and that the resources available are potentially enormous, the competition is far more consequential to the competitors than standard economic competition is.

The consequences of this are that political competitors have enormous resources and enormous stakes to "battle it out." In other words, political competitions can be incredibly costly to the population. It follows that:

The first requirement of any decent political system is to ensure political succession not be contested in a manner that jeopardizes the welfare of the general population.

Such a requirement is very difficult to engineer. Hobbes (1651) noticed this years ago and argued a stable political system with agreed-upon rules of power transfer (e.g., a monarchy or a democracy) is required for civilization to bear any of its fruits. He noted that times without such peaceful succession implied a life that is "solitary, poor, nasty, brutish, and short." The fratricidal wars implicit and explicit in Shakespearean, Greek, and other classical dramas reflect much of human history and attest to the intuitive accuracy of his observation.

Civil strife is an underlying threat in politics but we can do something about it. Proper design of political institutions and processes requires a most careful analysis of the incentives generated by the arrangements. This is essential to minimize the chance for political violence from competition over the spoils of political power. One ingredient to decrease the chance of violence is to ensure that losing power does not involve great material or security losses by the individual and his family. By ensuring that the general rewards for leadership service are not totally cut off when that person loses power, we decrease the cost of losing, and hence, the value of violence in political competition. Also proposing rules for succession (e.g., hereditary, or electoral) that are not based on violence and allowing dissenting positions to be considered in political competitions that don't use violence to win, ensure that it becomes less attractive to use violence in such competitions. Indeed, a strong minimalist argument for democracy by Przeworski (1999) claims that nonviolent succession is the real benefit of democracy. Although helpful, democracy can't ensure a peaceful politics, as we can see in the history of secessionist movements and other violent events in democracies.

TETHERING POLITICAL LEADERS

If free-market anarchism fails and politics is necessary, is democracy the only prophylactic to pure tyranny? Mancur Olson (1993, and McGuire and Olson, 1996) developed a useful response to the question. He notes that there is a natural limit to the rapacity of all thieves, whether they are political or private in character. So, for example, consider the bandit. She may steal all there is to steal, and leave everyone in abject poverty. But this means that she must seek out new targets each time. Hence, a bandit with no forethought must become a roving thief. But if the bandit sets up lodging in the land from which she wishes to extract her riches, her demands may begin to moderate. For now she will want to leave enough to extract her riches over time. She will not, for example, kill all the farmers and steal their cattle to send to market. Rather, she will prefer that they continue to have productive farms from which she can extract booty time and again. So a sedentary bandit is better for a village than a roving one.

From this one can see that the inhabitants would be happy to have a sedentary bandit take root, were she to protect them from her roving competitors. Further, if her tenure is going to be long, she will be interested in the development of public infrastructure products (roads, dams, irrigation, markets, public health matters) that allow the villagers to be more productive.[6] Indeed, the tyrant has her interests quite in sync with those of our villagers, until it comes to taxes. She will like to take away as much she can without so changing the villagers' incentives to produce that it diminishes her overall purse. The governor will balance her extractions or taxes such that any revenues she gains from increasing taxes is offset by a loss in productivity of the citizenry. But there is another difference between the interests of the citizens and those of the governor. The governor has a problem of tenure. Her interest in the productivity of the citizens is tempered by her time horizon. So, if the villagers allow her heir to become her legitimate successor as rapacious landlord, she would have a longer-term interest in meeting their needs. The perspective is interesting for a number of reasons. First, it leads us to the conclusion:

NON-DEMOCRATIC GOVERNMENT BY SELF-INTERESTED RULERS CAN LEAD TO A PROSPEROUS CITIZENRY. FOR CIVILIZATION TO THRIVE, DEMOCRACY IS NOT NEC-ESSARY BUT GOVERNMENT MUST HAVE AN INCENTIVE FOR THE POPULATION TO THRIVE.

(Olson, 1993)

---

[6] Sened (1997) develops the argument further, showing that property and other rights would be extended to citizens under specific conditions in order to improve the income of the entrepreneurial political – bandit leader.

The notion that a single person can act as the ruler is not going to be a realistic simplification in all but the smallest human societies. A coalition is required to govern and to put down competitors. And here we can begin to see some of the problems with non-democratic governments. Imagine that there are N persons in the village, and a ruling coalition of the bandit and her gang of loyalists. Were the ruler setting her policies to gain all of the profit from the village, she would invest enough in public projects to maximize her profit. If, on the other hand, she is sharing them with her henchmen (say they get half to divide among themselves), then her policies will change. For now, she only gets half the benefits of the projects. So she has a reduced incentive to support the productivity of the citizens as a whole. Indeed, the larger her coalition's share of the profits, the lower will be hers and the less would be the value of the public infrastructure projects to the ruler.

We can generalize this. Indeed, identify her taxes as a percentage of the GDP: say 50 percent. Then to increase her revenue by $1 she needs a $2 increase of the GDP. If only the leader gets the taxes, she increases taxes until she reduces the GDP by more than $2 for the next tax dollar she is to receive. Imagine now that she is sharing the booty with her gang. They get half, but she sets the policies. Now she personally gets fifty cents for a $2 decrease in the GDP. She will continue to increase taxes until the last dollar causes more than a $4 drop in GDP.

INCREASED COSTS OF A NON-DEMOCRATIC RULER'S COALITION INCREASES THE RULER'S RAPACIOUSNESS AND HURTS THE WELL-BEING OF THE CITIZENS.

(Olson, 1993)

Now compare this with a democratic rule of the village. Assuming as a start that it will be ruled by a majority, we can see that the ruling coalition will (on average) get at least half of the benefits of the project. Indeed,

THE LARGER THE DEMOCRATIC (MAJORITARIAN) COALITION THAT RULES, THE MORE THEIR INCENTIVES WILL COINCIDE WITH THOSE OF THE CITIZENRY.

(Olson, 1993)

We can see that political leaders are very likely to have interests quite distinct from those of the people. Clearly the more general problem of keeping the political leadership tethered to the interests of the citizens isn't an easy problem. And with rational ignorance of the citizens to help them, it is all too easy, and efficient, for special interest groups to make it worthwhile for politicians to ensure that policies are bent in the interest group's direction: that policies yield special profits and privileges for special individuals.[7] How then are we to analyze this problem of the citizens trying to keep the "hired" politicians on target so as to get the populace's collective interests met?

The Constituent-Beneficiary-Agent Problem

Given the seriousness of the stakes of political competition, and that public revenues are collected, in the main, quite separately from the population's evaluation of the public goods being supplied, the principal-agent problem will be severe. After all, with revenues quite independent of the desires of the group members, without carefully designed institutions, contestants for power need not have their eye on their obligations to the members of the group. Indeed, the disconnect may be so great that the justification for the agents' enshrinement in power becomes divorced from the welfare of their principals: the general citizenry.

In using the principal-agent model in political contexts, it is useful to distinguish between three classes of persons:

- those who make policy (the agents, politicians, or leaders);
- those who determine the tenure of the politicians (the principals, or voters, or constituents);
- and those who receive the benefits of the policy: the beneficiaries.

Much of the 'support' for democracy is premised on the notion that political agents can be controlled: their actions can be controlled to conform to the interests of their constituents. Here I investigate some of the problems that exist in these relationships in general rather than in democracies (reserving democratic contexts for Chapter 7).[8]

The complications that arise in the principal-agent problem stem from both the nature of the actors (the constituents, the beneficiaries, and the

---

[7] The benefits that are sought after are referred to as **rents**, and much of the activity of politicians and special interest groups can be described rent-seeking. This form of corruption occurs in all political systems but some institutional arrangements are more likely to be fertile grounds for it to spread than others. We focus on this in subsequent pages. See, for example, the section on checks and balances, beginning on page 161.

[8] Note that we have already discussed some things that affect this relationship: the general ignorance of the public and the reluctance of citizens to reveal their evaluation of public goods (see p. 41) will make holding political leadership accountable more difficult. Also (as we will discuss in Part IV), there are no easy mechanisms to interpret "group interest" without some ability to make interpersonal comparisons of welfare. Similarly, various arrangements such as special majority rules can make it more difficult to get anything like the group's interests met. In this chapter we examine these relationships further.

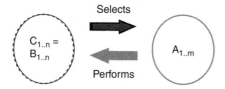

FIGURE 35. The simplified constituent-beneficiary-agent problem when constituents ($C_{1..n}$) are also the beneficiaries ($B_{1..n}$).

agents) and their relations with one another. For this reason, and to emphasize the complications, I will refer to this control problem of the political leaders as the constituent-beneficiary-agent problem. A good starting point probably is to consider a simple case: when the beneficiaries are identical to the constituents of the leaders or agents (see Figure 35). Then, in many ways the problem looks like the traditional principal-agent problem.

But even this simple case is more complicated than the standard principal-agent problem. Political contexts have properties that create additional relevant details.

First, actors such as principals and agents are usually not single individuals but rather groups of individuals. Typically, one doesn't select *the* agent but rather only a member of a *team* of agents, $A_{1..m}$ in the figure, (as in an election of a member in a legislature). The agent, in other words, is usually a group, or even a whole governmental system. This complicates the tethering of an agent to the principle of a principal. After all, with multiple agents working as a team, it is more difficult to tell who is responsible for the team's veering from the principal's interests. But what of the principals? They are often also a group, and then free-riding and rational ignorance enlarge the scope of the control problem. Further, they are not likely to be of a like mind. Some of those principles want agents to construct wider streets, while others want wider sidewalks. So the principal-agent model needs elaboration to fit politics. This is implicitly portrayed in Figure 35.

And when the agents are sitting in multiple structures (such as legislatures and executives), other problems ensue. Who among the team of agents is responsible for the under-performance of the agency will be difficult to ascertain. Agents are usually organized with a division of labor, as when structures are specialized. This generates a problem related to the *Liberal Paradox* (see page 165). Under these conditions, achieving Pareto optimality may be elusive as each agent exercises responsibility over only part of a problem. We will consider some of these related complications separately later in the next chapter.

But there is also a second general problem that needs addressing. The "principal" is often two distinct groups: constituents and beneficiaries. Recall, we refer to those who select the agents and determine whether the agent will continue to serve, as the agent's constituency. The second group are those who are affected by the agent's behavior: the beneficiaries. Ideally, there would be a tight relation between these two groups. But in the real world, unlike in the above models, they can be quite distinct.

In some cases this is by design: prisons, for example. The administrators of prisons have two classes of beneficiaries: the citizenry as a whole, and the prisoners. Indeed institutions such as prisons are designed so that some of the beneficiaries of the policies are purposely *not* the constituents. We design prisons so that the administrator is responsive to the judicial system or to the state government, and *not* to the prisoners. This is so even when the policy is for the benefit of the prisoner (as in the case of prisoner medical policy). But this disconnect often has repercussions: unsatisfactory policy outcomes. These problems are rarely followed up with salutary changes in the institutions and conditions, in part because prisoners' complaints have little clout in the setting of the rewards of the agents (or prison administrators). The people who decide the incentives (i.e., the tenure, salary, promotion, and budget) of the prison administrators are totally separate from the inmates. So why should the agent (the prison administration) even consider itself responsive to the needs of the prisoners beyond ensuring that no public scandal be created? Although some would argue this is all well and good in prisons, similar structural disconnects generate problems in other sorts of institutions such as nursing homes, homeless shelters, and day care centers.

The more general cause is to be understood as the separation of the beneficiaries from the principals or constituency of the agents. When agents' constituencies are divorced from the beneficiaries problems of responsiveness ensue. For example, consider institutions where the population is incompetent to demand better services. These include nursing homes, hospitals, mental hospitals, and foster care. In mid-twentieth century America, the problems were so bad in state mental hospitals that federal courts forbade states to prescribe long-term involuntary treatment for patients.

When the beneficiaries are distinct from the constituents the asymmetric information problem of the typical principal-agent problem is increased. For when the beneficiary is not the constituent, or principal, another

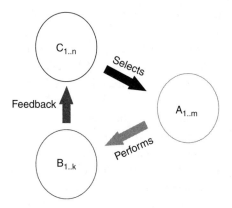

FIGURE 36. The typical political / policy problem where the constituents aren't necessarily the beneficiaries (here showing a case of no overlap).

information link is required. The constituent is required to pay attention to the agent's effects on the beneficiary and the beneficiary must have a strong positive tie to the constituent. Although in some very basic human relations we expect that a strong fiduciary relationship exists and is sufficient to overcome this problem, more generally, constituents may not have the interests of the beneficiaries in mind.

An example of a situation with strong fiduciary ties would be day care. These strong relations are expected to lead to natural corrections of wayward agents or administrators in "day-care" situations. Parents are expected to go to considerable lengths to stay informed as to what is going on in the day care centers their children attend. But when the fiduciary relationship erodes, there is no reason to expect that control by constituents, even well-informed ones, leads to policies that are in the interests of the individuals who are primary targets of the policies. In many institutions, the interests of the policy beneficiaries have no effect on the rewards going to the agents delivering the policy. So I would suggest political problems are best thought about as the enhanced principal-agent problem, as depicted in Figure 36.[9] We can conclude:

BETTER OUTCOMES FOR BENEFICIARIES REQUIRE THAT THEIR INTERESTS IMPACT THE REWARD STREAM OF AGENTS.

[9] Actually, with public goods most are beneficiaries, and the groups (i.e., circles) have substantial overlap.

Methods for implementing policy improvements when beneficiaries are not the constituents can sometimes be instituted easily. For example, one can institute a well-funded ombudsman's office that has the clout to bring policy needs to the agents and who has a role as one of the agent's constituents. Without that, even the notion of Pareto optimality is ambiguous and makes little sense. For if all the constituents are made better off, it need not be that the beneficiaries will be helped. In general, there is no simple solution to the principal-agent problem other than developing structures that reward the agent for doing right by the principal, defined as both constituents and beneficiaries.

Credible Commitment

Most of the problem of holding leaders (agents) accountable can be understood in another way: as a problem of commitment. Commitments are like IOUs or contracts for future behavior. We all make commitments, but some commitments are more credible than others. When a teenager drives the family car on a Friday night to a party and states a commitment not to drink, the commitment may, or may not, be credible. How can we analyze whether a commitment is credible? Credible commitment problems come up when exchanges take place over time (e.g., I pay you now for a future action) and when there is a degree of conflict of interest over your future performance. Figure 37 illustrates the problem with what is called a *game tree*.

Such a tree starts at the top, with one player (**A**) making a decision, followed by the next player (**B**). The tree in Figure 37 depicts a simple two-person prisoner dilemma game without simultaneous moves. Consider the possibility of an agreement that **B** will cooperate if **A** does. But if **A** cooperates, **B** is at her left-hand decision point in the

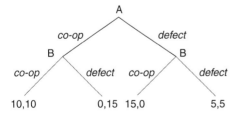

FIGURE 37. Credible commitment illustrated with a 2-person prisoner dilemma game.

game tree. **B** can choose to cooperate and get a payoff worth 10, or not, worth 15. Without any enforcement behind the agreement what is to assure **A** that **B** will deliver? Why should **A** presume that she won't be played as a sucker?

We can use the concept of rollback, or backward induction (see Footnote 26 of Chapter 1) to solve this game. Contemplating her first move, **A** can ask, "Were I to cooperate, **B** would have two choices: defect or cooperate. If I cooperate (putting **B** in the left branches of the tree), **B** would have an incentive to defect as she could get 15 instead of 10. And so, cooperation by me would lead to my getting 0. Further, even if **B** promised not to defect, when she got to the point of responding, it would pay her to defect. So I should expect 0. Now what if I defect? Then **B** will also defect, and I will get 5. Since 5 is better than 0, I ought to defect now."

In markets, these problems are usually covered by contract law. But contract law rarely rarely applies to political promises. For example, what is to ensure that a pay-as-you-go[10] retirement system will be around when current wage earners are retiring?[11] In politics, the credible commitment problem is compounded by the uncertain tenure of political leaders, their division of labor, and the instability of any coalition representing constituents' interests. Institutional designs that try to overcome this problem by making policy stability an increased priority necessarily imply a decrease in institutional responsiveness. Note Rogowski's (1999) conclusion:

INSTITUTIONAL DESIGN TO INCREASE COMMITMENT TO POLICY DECISIONS IMPLIES A DECREASE IN POLITICAL RESPONSIVENESS.

Responsiveness and commitment are inversely related, and how best to balance the two values will depend on the type of policy one is considering. One must design institutions differently in different policy spheres. Thus, for example, commitment has to be built in to long-term projects such as retirement schemes and infrastructure projects. In other cases, responsiveness to new preference or financial constraints, for example, might be more important, and institutions need to reflect that.

---

[10] Pay-as-you-go means that current wage earners' taxes are paying for current retirees' benefits. No money is accrued in their own accounts.

[11] Thomson (1992) describes in some detail a case where the commitment failed, and the future beneficiaries were not repaid for their support of current beneficiaries.

REGIME CHANGE

In a book of some brilliance, Carles Boix (2003) outlines a theory of democratization. Boix identifies and tests a model of how one gets regime change to a democracy from political agitation of the citizenry. The variables that he focuses on are the initial degree of equality in the society, and the mobility of wealth. Boix begins with a simple model: a society in which there is a rich class (that rules) and a poor class with a non-democratic right-wing authoritarian regime. It excludes the poor (a majority) from a role in the making of social choices. This requires repression, with repression costs borne by the wealthy. The size of these costs depend on the capability of the poor to engage in collective action and the degree of equality in the society.

Two alternative regimes come to mind. The first is a democracy, where, in the simplest story all would vote, with the median voter ruling the day. The median voter is poor, not rich. And so, if we think of politics as the fight for who gets what, the rich have to fear the democratic government taking their wealth and distributing it to the populace as a whole. You might think that the rich could trade their protective regime for a promise of low taxes. But if we go back to our notion of rollback (see Footnote 26 of Chapter 1 and Figure 37) and credible commitment, we can understand that the party representing the poor can't make a credible commitment or promise to not impose taxes once they gain power. Hence, the rich can't trust the promises made by negotiators: the rich must expect the tax rate to be set to maximize the payout to the median voter (a poor person). The struggle would seem to go on.

But the more equal the distribution of wealth before the political struggle for regime change, the less is at stake. Further, wealth is not homogenous, it is held in different forms. Some forms of wealth can be easily shipped abroad (financial assets, money, etc.) while some cannot (land, mines, etc.). High taxes can cause mobile forms of wealth to be shipped abroad. The mobility of the country's capital sets limits on how high taxes can go: capital that is moved abroad yield no tax receipts. And so the actual mobility of capital puts a cap on taxes, and hence, on the stakes that democratization has for the rich.

DEMOCRACY IS EASIER TO ACHIEVE FROM A POLITICAL STRUGGLE INVOLVING REGIME CHANGE WHEN CAPITAL IS MOBILE AND THE SOCIETY IS RELATIVELY EGALITARIAN.

(Boix)

In a nutshell, three factors increase the chance for democracy: first, mobility of capital; second, higher costs of repression; and third, the initial degree of equality in the society. Each of these makes it more likely that the plutocrats will agree to a democratic government without a civil war. Boix is able to develop the model further, with more than two classes, and more complicated sorts of regimes. But the basic story remains. What he doesn't tell us is how it comes about that sometimes the victory goes to the oppressed – as in the histories of the Eastern European countries that struggled against the Communists and which was discussed above as a cascade (see page 77), or as in the American civil rights movement (see Chong, 1991).

IN CONCLUSION

The hoped-for control of political leaders is a generic problem for all citizens. Even without specifying institutional rules, general problems of governance are identifiable. These require that we go beyond the simpler principal-agent problems developed by economists. Applying the principles to a specific situation requires substantial detailed knowledge: what are the relations between the constituents and the beneficiaries; is capital really mobile, etc. But the generalizations appear to hold. For example, if capital isn't mobile and inequality is high, then moves to democratize will be costly.

Most generally, when the rulers don't have an incentive to take the population's welfare into account they will ignore the population's welfare. This will be true in all regimes, democratic and non-democratic. And even though there are many reasons to desire democratization, vast improvements may be possible without it. But when the citizens' needs are long ignored or left unsatisfied it is clear that a redesign of the institutions is called for. And in the design of institutions, the lesson is clear: we need to design incentives to generate the results we wish. Incentives must place the power with the populace, those who are the rightful beneficiaries and who must therefore become the constituents of the rulers.

But how to design institutions that can and will deliver results over the long arc of history is problematic. And it is to consider some of these problems that we now turn.

CHAPTER 7

A Few Institutional Pitfalls

As argued in Chapter 6, governments, with their political institutions and behaviors called politics, are necessary for society as we know it. But good public policy requires responsiveness to some collective interests, some understanding of the notion of social welfare: a concept that we will delve into in the next section. But even without that understanding, we can see that the proper design of political institutions and processes requires careful analysis of the multiple values one is trying to satisfy and some sense that one can make justifiable tradeoffs between these multiple values while staying responsive to the needs of the citizens.

To control and design a more responsive government we must consider how its structural characteristics create or block incentives of the political system to achieve these values. To do this, we turn again to the notion of a veto player (Tsebelis, 2002), a type of actor that is created by the design of political institutions. Veto players are part of all political systems and their nature will bring us to examine Sen's (1970) Liberal Paradox and the observation that veto players must have the incentives and possibilities to get us beyond the status quo.

DESIGNING INSTITUTIONS TO GET RESPONSIBLE GOVERNMENT: CHECKS AND BALANCES

History is littered with attempts to design better political institutions to improve government. Many individuals have tried to get around problems inherent in political behavior. We have inherited some of their efforts as knowledge claims – some of which are enshrined in the democratic structures of the United States and elsewhere. For example, the idea that checks and balances will help keep politicians responsible and responsive to the needs of the citizens. Checks and balances have also been argued to help wrest the government from majoritarian factions. Obviously, they have other effects as well. They affect the goals of responsiveness, commitment, and the possibility of meeting the interests of the citizenry.

Checks and Balances and Veto Players

Governments are collective enterprises, with many actors. Different governments are organized in quite different fashions. Even democracies are varied in how they are organized. So, for example, there are parliamentary and presidential systems, centralized and federated systems. One way to compare all these sorts of systems is to consider what it takes to get things changed (perhaps in specific policy areas): who has to "sign off" for policy to take effect. This inquiry generates a "list" of all those who have a veto over a change (in general or regarding a particular policy). Such a list of veto players can help us understand the likely outcomes of any political system. Some on this list may be individuals (e.g., an official, a president, etc.); others may be a collective (e.g., the senate). For change, unanimous agreement of this group is required. Recall (see Footnote 5 of Chapter 5), that any group of players can be thought of as having a Pareto set. If they all must agree to a change, we could expect them to achieve an outcome in their Pareto set by their decision-making processes. But note that being in their Pareto set does not mean that those people who are not veto players aren't hurt. Nor does it mean that being in the Pareto set of the veto players implies that we are in the Pareto set of the larger group of the citizenry not members of the set of veto players.

This set of veto players helps determine the properties of the outcomes. If the veto players are very diverse and representative of the populace, the hull of ideal points (i.e., the Pareto set) will be larger, and fewer possibilities for movement of the status quo will exist.[1] But often these veto players are institutionally placed individuals who have to compete to hold on to their positions. And it is the occupant of the position that has veto power. In this case, we might wish to amend the list so that it contains both the veto points (e.g., the governor) and, parenthetically, the occupant who would be identified as the veto player of the moment.

---

[1] Unanimity of the veto players leads to their Pareto set but also prevents movement within it.

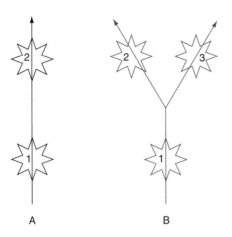

A   B

FIGURE 38. Two different systems of veto points.

Systems differ greatly not only by the number and diversity of their veto points, but also by their structure. Veto points can be structured in parallel or in series. Consider, for example, the two systems displayed in Figure 38. They each have two veto points that must be gone through. In system A the veto points are in series: one must get approval of actor 1 and then actor 2. In system B one needs actor 1 and then either 2 or 3. There are alternative second veto points in system B constituting alternative or parallel paths. Only one of the two need be gone down (Dixit, 2003). If those challenging the status quo may choose the path they take, the difference can be substantial in terms of outcomes.

In system A, the proposer of change (P) would make a proposal. For it to be acceptable, P's proposal would have to improve both veto players. The veto players will only accept a change to the status quo that would be in the lens created by the intersections and indifference curves. Normally, they could be expected to agree to a point on their contract curve, within that ellipse but perhaps with skill, P can push it closer to her ideal point (the zone cross-hatched).

In system B, 2 and 3 are competing for the power of determining the outcome. The proposer, P, has a choice of which gate to go through. Compare system A (Figure 39) and B (Figure 40).

Here we see how things change if P needs to satisfy player 1 and then only either 2 or 3. Here, in Figure 40, we put a new player, 3, closer to[2] P.

---

[2] Of course if player 3 is further from P than player 2, then it could be that P's situation is not changed. P would prefer to utilize the path through 2 to secure the change.

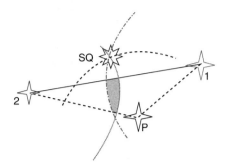

FIGURE 39. Outcome prediction with two veto players.

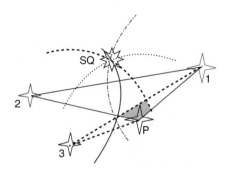

FIGURE 40. Outcome prediction when the second veto players have to compete.

Again, we shade in the possible contract zone: this time between P and 1 and 3. The likely outcome is obviously more advantageous to P; P's prospects are much improved.

Imagine a second scenario. Let the outcome be primarily of concern to the proposer. But rewards are to be bestowed to the veto players that enable the proposal to become policy. Consider the two political structures illustrated in Figure 38 (A and B). They imply a different division of the spoils. How the competition affects the distribution can be seen from some experimental results.

In a rather frequently run experiment called the **_Ultimatum Experiment_** (Roth 1995), two players are to divide up a sum of money. One player (the proposer) makes an offer, and the other (the decider) must decide whether to accept or not. The veto players are the deciders in the situations described here and depicted in Figure 38. If the offer is not accepted, then no one receives any money (the status quo). Brit Grosskopf (1998) ran ultimatum experiments with one proposer and three deciders: in parallel. Any one of them could accept the proposal. The deciders were competing. The proposers' demands were significantly higher when the deciders competed. In 2003 she ran experiments in which the number of proposers was increased. Each made offers to a single decider who then could select one or no offers: the proposers were competing. The offers made were far more favorable to the decider.

Note that in terms of the constituent-beneficiary-agent problem, the veto players are agents and the value of their offices are diminished by the existence of alternative paths for the changing of policy. In system A each can demand a great deal, perhaps leaving **P** not much value for moving the status quo. The two veto players are likely to be able to get an equal share. But if the proponent for change can make an offer to either of the two second veto players, as in system B, the proponent can go through the gate with the cheapest toll: veto players 2 and 3 have to compete.

THE CHANCE OF OBTAINING RESPONSIVE POLICY CHANGES IS GREATLY IMPROVED WHEN CITIZENS (BENEFICIARIES) CAN PROPOSE CHANGES IN ALTERNATIVE FORUMS.

Multiple veto players often stem from a division of labor that has been deliberately inserted into the political process putatively either to increase expertise or to ensure checks and balances. In the United States, it is often the case that specialized legislative committees write portions of legislation, and have a veto role in the development of policy. A similar story can be told about policy development in the executive branches of many governments. Specialized agencies and departments each have a special role in the writing of rules. How are we to analyze the role of these veto players in the development of public policy?

Specialization and Division of Labor and Veto Players

Amartya Sen developed a theorem in the early years of the social choice literature called the Liberal Paradox: it is relevant to the analysis of veto players. Sen notes that liberalism requires at least that each person has some basic rights to choose over some issue such as sleeping on one's belly without the interference of others. The **_Liberal Paradox_** is the demonstration that the exercise of these rights can conflict with the attaining of Pareto optimality. The conditions that lead to the conflict in the Liberal Paradox occur when each actor cares more about the other's choice than they do about their own choice. Note this is a property identified with prisoner dilemma games (see Footnote 16 of Chapter 1).

Specialization and division of labor leads to independent decision making about aspects of public policy, as do veto players. Indeed veto players are precisely defined by their rights to ensure the status quo is maintained, so we can see that the lessons of the Liberal Paradox may be relevant to analyzing political and policy-making institutions.[3]

The Liberal Paradox

I use Sen's own example (Sen, 1970b) to illustrate the Liberal Paradox: assume that there are two persons, one of whom is quite lewd, and the other, quite prudish. To keep things simple, we shall call them Lewd and Prude. They plan on going for a weekend in the country and are staying at a B&B. In its library they discover only one book they haven't read: DH Lawrence's *Lady Chatterley's Lover*. Now both Lewd and Prude have the right to read, or not read, the book. Prude would prefer that no one read it ('*n*' in Tables 13 and 14). Prude prefers that he read it himself, '*p*' in the tables, than for his partner, Lewd to read it ('*l*' in the tables). Lewd would prefer that Prude take in the joys available from such a read but would prefer reading it herself than having no one read it.

Now the notion of minimal liberty means that each person is decisive about the things he is at liberty to choose. In Sen's example, Lewd is decisive over whether she reads the book or not (and hence over the pair *l* and *n*). Similarly, Prude is decisive over whether he reads the book or not (and hence over the pair *p* and *n*). Prude cares more about Lewd's behavior than he does his own (Lewd's reading the book would be Prude's worst outcome). Similarly, Lewd finds it of greater import that Prude read it than

TABLE 13. *Liberal Paradox: Preferences over the 3 Outcomes*

Prude: (decisive *n, p*)	Lewd: (decisive *n, l*)
n	p
p	l
l	n

---

[3] Gary Miller (1992) first noted the application of the Liberal Paradox to the problem of division of labor.

TABLE 14. *The Cyclic Nature of Outcomes in a Liberal Paradox Situation*

Reasoning for the Choice	Outcome
Pareto and both prefer *p* to *l*	p
Prude is decisive over *p*, *n* and prefers *n*	n
Lewd is decisive over *l*, *n* and she prefers *l*	l

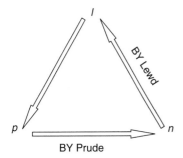

FIGURE 41. The cycle in the LP

that she does herself. In other words, for both, the externality of his partner's behavior is of greater value than the internality from his own behavior.[4] And this leads to a cyclic pattern of decision making, as depicted in Figure 41 for the reasons shown in Table 14. In other words:

WHEN INDIVIDUALS HAVE RIGHTS AND WHEN THEIR BEHAVIOR IS OF GREATER IMPORTANCE TO OTHERS THAN TO THEMSELVES, AND THEIR PREFERENCES ARE IN CONFLICT, PARETO OPTIMALITY MAY BE SACRIFICED.

(Sen, 1970b)

Division of Labor in Policy Formation

How then is the Liberal Paradox problem relevant to the division of labor in policy formation processes? To make this leap a bit more intuitive, let us change the situation a bit. In the above two-person example, there was an overlapping outcome that either could veto, yet neither could secure unilaterally: *n*, no one reads the book. In many situations when there is a division of labor, each actor specializes in getting something of the whole project done. They are decisive with regard to getting an aspect of the

---

[4] Sen referred to these sorts of preferences as "nosey preferences."

TABLE 15. *Liberty Game Form*

Row's Options	Options to Column	
	C	D
A	A,C	A,D
B	B,C	B,D

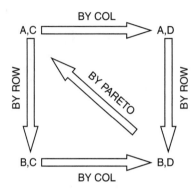

FIGURE 42. Liberal Paradox and prisoner dilemma cycles

project defined and completed. This can be easily depicted in a table with two actors, as in Table 15: Row and Column. Row can do (choose) either A or B, and Column can similarly choose or do C or D.[5]

What is going on if we add the preferences underlying the Liberal Paradox? In those cases, each player was concerned more about the choice of the other player than about his own choice: Row, for example, finds the difference between AC and AD matters more than that either between AC and BC or AD and BD. Adding the conflict between these freely chosen outcomes of the individuals and their preferences over the outcomes AC and BD, we can get a conflict with Pareto optimality. This is displayed in Figure 42. As was discussed previously, this conflict between the rational choice of individuals and the suboptimality of the resulting social choice can be understood as the defining property of the prisoner dilemma game.

In other words, underlying a prisoner dilemma game is a type of Liberal Paradox and in such a game, given the conjectured preferences, there is

---

[5] In this form, we have a game without specified preferences. As such it is known as a **game form**.

always an underlying cycle, as depicted in Figure 42. All we need to add to the mix to generate a prisoner dilemma from the game form in Table 15 is that B and D were dominant strategies, that each was more affected by the choice of the others than by his own choice, and that they had conflicting preferences with regard to the options that their partner could decide – precisely the ingredients for a Liberal Paradox.

So what we can see is that the properties of the Liberal Paradox are inherent in the prisoner dilemma game. But the Liberal Paradox is giving us a different lens to view the political landscape. Just as in the Liberal Paradox, in the two-person prisoner dilemma there is a conflict that can be overcome by a trade. Since both care more about what the other does than her own choice, they could "trade" places and make the choices for the other person, and both would do better.[6] Indeed, Schwartz's (1981) general instability theorem (see below, page 209) is all about these sorts of events: arguing that whenever an outcome requires a trade to occur, there must be an underlying cycle of preferences over the outcomes.

The employment of a division of labor in legislative committees and bureaucracies can lead to precisely these sorts of problems. The many aspects of policy, decided by many different committees, lead to aggregate policy which is often the sum of these separately authored parts, and these can easily be Pareto suboptimal. Hammond and Miller (1985) first noticed that the use of experts and expert committees for partial policy design easily lead to problems that look like the Liberal Paradox.[7]

And underlying much of the art of politics is the notion of trading to get things done. Having multiple institutional actors (rather than individuals) taking charge for parts of the bill only makes those trades more difficult to happen. Take the typical bill trying to get through the United States Congress. It is assigned to a number of committees in the house and the senate. The committees are composed of members who are particularly concerned with the substantive domains of their committee's work. By their actions, any one of the committees may be able to kill a bill: each becomes a veto player. And special interest groups, even small ones, can reward committee members for their work on these committees. These rewards then facilitate decisions that are in line with those of the interest

---

[6] Indeed, experiments were run where the game that was played was an n-person prisoner dilemma but the players didn't know which payoffs they would get. This yields a game of pure cooperation, and that was the result. See page 49 (Frohlich and Oppenheimer, 1996 and Frohlich, 1992).

[7] Miller (1992) gives us interesting examples from the history of the Ford Motor Company.

group, even when the diffused interest of the majority outweighs the narrow interests of the minority.

Other members of the public may be quite concerned with how the committees decide things, but they are unable to enter into the trade because of their lack of information and organization. When this is the case, and the outsiders don't have the same preferences as those on the committee, we have the makings of a Liberal Paradox/prisoner dilemma. And as we saw earlier, such conflict can easily lead to a less than optimal outcome.

LOCALISM AND ITS LIMITS

In the previous section, we found that obtaining Pareto optimality can be threatened by individual liberties. This conflict between liberty and community group interest was discussed as a consequence of the division of labor in legislative and executive contexts. It showed up as Liberal Paradox problems and prisoner dilemma games. But this conflict between liberty and community welfare can crop up in other ways, too, and with regard to values other than Pareto optimality. Consider the difficulties of defining a good boundary for a government that provides services in the context of modern metropolitan governance and problems of breakaway localities. The problem is more complicated than we might presume. When we consider the boundaries of government we go beyond the original formulation of the constituent-beneficiary-agent problem. Boundaries determine membership in both the constituent and beneficiary groups: rules of inclusion and exclusion.

The boundary issue occurs, logically, prior to the evaluation of responsiveness. For to whom is the government to be responsive? Not only are there many possible majorities, there are many possible boundaries. And we must wonder, "Responsive to whom?" It is obviously not enough to answer, "Responsive to the majority!" Broadening one's normative concerns beyond Pareto optimality means that we may have an even more difficult time specifying the answer to this question. Consider the problem of localism: keeping governmental authority as close to the beneficiary group as possible.

Pork Barrel Politics

When we don't have localism, we have few incentives for efficiency. Let's take the extreme case: a legislature with one house, where each member comes from a different district. To get a local public good project funded in one district, one would need to get majority support. But each district's projects only benefit the people in that district. So only the representative of that district would support it. One could trade projects to get a majority. If each project costs $X and there are n equal districts, then we could expect at least $[(n/2) +1]$ projects costing $$[(n/2) +1]$ X. With n districts, each would pay a share of the total, even if they got no benefits.[8] So, the following happens (see Buchanan and Tullock, 1962; Buchanan, 1965; Weingast, 1979, 1994; Shepsle and Weingast 1981; Bickers and Stein, 1994):

1. Some districts (those not in the winning coalition) won't get benefits (projects) commensurate with their share of the taxes used to pay for the projects in other districts.
2. Assuming only enough districts receive projects to get a majority in the legislature, each district pays less than the full cost of a project: actually, a bit more than half the cost, given the assumptions.
3. Faced with the reduced costs, locals will support projects that they wouldn't want were they to have to pay full fare.

So there are good reasons to want the local government to be responsible for choosing, and paying for, its own local projects. One would want the boundaries of the tax district to more or less be coterminous with that of the beneficiary group.

Localism, as a conclusion, would seem obvious: assuming no broader externalities, we would want the beneficiaries of a public good to be the group that decides whether to deliver it and how they are going to pay for it (Olson, 1969). We would want the governmental structures to be designed with sufficient incentives to ensure that those who are to receive the public benefits, and who are to pay for them, have jurisdiction. Further, as may appear obvious, but is often disregarded in politics, when the benefits are local, save for efforts to generate distributive justice, all decision making and funding should be local (Olson, 1969). When one decides to build a new highway in Topeka or an urban transit system in Chicago, the benefits are usually concentrated in those locales. It makes little sense for the funding of those systems to include taxpayers in Texas, California, or New Hampshire. As Olson pointed out, "If the benefits are local and the

---

[8] Obviously, the benefitting district has an intense interest in the project, and the costs, being widely distributed, are diffuse and less intensely felt. The problem here is similar to the one described regarding broad and narrow interests.

taxes national, even a collective good which brings gains much greater than its costs will still create more losers than gainers" (op. cit., 482). More generally,

WHEN THE GOVERNMENTAL BOUNDARIES DON'T MATCH THE BOUNDARIES OF THE BENEFIT GROUP FOR THE PUBLIC GOODS BEING SUPPLIED, ONE CAN EXPECT A PARETO SUBOPTIMAL OUTCOME.

(Olson, 1969).

We cannot have a separate government for each public good with a unique boundary, but the basic idea is simple. If one has a federal, or confederated, political structure, the functions of the governments should be allocated tasks less on principal than on the boundaries of the main beneficiaries. As technology, externalities, and structure change the nature of benefit groups, the programs that states, provinces, and localities should be responsible for should change. As public goods change, boundaries should shift. Indeed, we can expect that even the populations or memberships of the localities will change with the public goods they supply. But this raises a problem needing further analysis. Should groups be able to break off from more central authority to authorize their own local programs? What might be the effects of such changes on the remaining population? Here we are concerned with more than Pareto optimality. We must consider fairness.[9] Let us examine why.

Too Much Democracy, Too Much Freedom?

A conflict can arise between localism and fairness. In the first part of this volume we noted other problems that stem from liberty: free-riding can swamp the otherwise good intentions of group members to contribute toward a collective effort. But the problem of individual liberty undercutting a collective pattern goes beyond simple prisoner dilemma games and social dilemmas.

As an example, consider a large metropolitan area governed centrally. Everyone in the area gets the same sorts of programs. (Of course there can be neighborhood variation, but assume taxing and legislating is via a central authority.) Tiebout, 1956, argued that everyone in such a jurisdiction could be made better off if the neighborhoods could split off from the central government and set up their own, more local, jurisdictions. This would enable individuals to choose the programs they want more locally,

---

[9] The nature of fairness is a major subject of Chapter 8.

and could lead to individuals changing where they wanted to live. In the new situation, those with children who wanted excellent schools would demand that their tax dollars be spent on schools. Those without children may prefer other amenities such as better public transportation, parks, or even just lower taxes. Different jurisdictions would be oriented toward these different groups. And the people would sort themselves out accordingly: "Voting with their feet," we might say. Indeed, many modern cities have allowed precisely this sort of localism by having a myriad of independent and differentiated suburbs.

It would seem to follow that everyone would be better off were the neighborhoods given the right to pull out from the central government and the variety occurred – after all, just as in markets, people have varieties of tastes regarding the policies they prefer. Tiebout saw that more choice leads to a greater match between individual preferences and the social programs delivered by jurisdictions. He saw the issue as one of simple efficiency – who could be hurt by the separating out into preference classes? It seemed to be a Pareto improving idea.

But as the idea took root, others began to notice problems. First was Hirschman (1970), who noted that the exit of some may leave others in a worse position. There may be costs that the jurisdiction must bear, and an exodus could also decrease the political clout of those remaining to get their voices heard.

But others (Miller, 1981 and Ellickson, 1973) raised a second important concern: fairness in distribution. Tiebout's mechanism for revealing and responding to the varieties of tastes in the population has redistributive consequences which are capable of yielding grossly unfair consequences in heterogeneous environments.

How do these redistributive consequences come about? Which community you will want to join depends as much on your tastes as on your budget constraint or your financial abilities. Obviously, in a democracy the tastes and finances of the others in the community help determine the outcomes, and hence, the amount of your tax bill. Which community is worth joining depends upon the tax base of the community, and hence, what you get for your money. The poor are less desirable in a jurisdiction because they can't pay as much. With crowding (and with the collective supply of private goods such as education) their presence adds to the cost and they may not pay their freight. That is, their participation in the programs may need to be subsidized. They will prefer to be in jurisdictions with higher benefits, as long as they are subsidized. But, if left in their own jurisdiction, without subsidies, they vote only for public goods they can afford with the taxes they can collect. This will be in line with their tastes – as constrained by their budgets.

This lets us understand the distributive consequences of Tiebout's proposal. The wealthiest neighborhood will leave a jurisdiction to pay for higher-cost public goods but without the added cost incurred by the program also going to the (even slightly) less fortunate. They prefer to be paying a tax bill for their own goods, without paying subsidies for services that benefit other poorer neighborhoods. Pulling out of the jurisdiction the wealthy neighborhood now leaves the poor without the subsidies. Those poorer residents who stayed, now don't ask the city to build that extra amenity or park; the residual less wealthy no longer would vote for that. Given their newly reduced tax base, they turn to other concerns. And the tax bills in the new wealthy jurisdiction are now higher than they are left with, so the poor are not likely to move there, given their constrained budgets. But the newly somewhat impoverished (by the loss of the wealthiest residents) city is not stabilized. The next wealthiest neighborhood will be ready to pull out for exactly the same reason.

The prediction is clear. There is a core to the voting-by-the-feet game: a unique, yet stable, outcome. The city will break up into sub jurisdictions segregated by income. And this is what we find in many modern urban areas. This secondary redistributive effect complicates the relationship between the constituency and the beneficiary groups. For example, imagine a metro area with one large school system. If a wealthy area pulls out and takes its resources out of the budget, the wealthy émigrés can improve the welfare of their children. And others lose. In terms of overall social fabric, if the idea is to ensure that all have security in getting their basic needs met, then the liberty to pull out threatens the less fortunate from meeting their needs. This is a cost that must be considered in one's design of political institutions. Or:

ALLOWING SUBGROUPS OF BENEFICIARIES TO SET UP A LOCAL AUTHORITY TO IMPROVE THE DELIVERY OF PUBLIC GOODS FOR THEMSELVES WILL USUALLY HAVE REDISTRIBUTIVE CONSEQUENCES THAT CONFLICT WITH NOTIONS OF FAIRNESS.

(Ellickson, 1973; Miller, 1981)

The beneficiary group in the original school system was the entire metro area population. Changing a locality's schools changes the distributive characteristics of the program. Since these can't be disentangled in the real world of policy, the issue is how to change situations from the status quo so that the "losers" are properly compensated. Such compensation issues are difficult to solve. Shifts of a group from one jurisdiction to another must be done with a careful eye not only to who gains, but also to who loses and how their compensation is to be determined, and how and when it is to be paid.[10]

Overall, we are faced with the difficulties of satisfying often conflicting values: in this case, efficiency, fairness, and liberties. The argument that localism can be expected to lead to income segregation is yet another illustration of the difficulty in aggregating values in a sensible and straight-forward fashion. As such, it is another perspective on the problems that were investigated by Arrow (see the discussion in Chapter 8) and Sen (see the discussion of his Liberal Paradox, page. 165). Because we can't reduce our normative principals to a simple and achievable monism we are faced with conflicts. Given our interests in satisfying multiple values, all discussions of institutional design become more complicated.

In politics, because there are teams of agents and hoards of constituents design of institutions must take care to ensure that agents can be held responsible and that their actions are highly visible. One design feature much touted to overcome these difficulties is the notion of checks and balances. But checks and balances ensure that most of the time no one group of agents can be held responsible for something not getting done, and responsiveness to the needs of policy beneficiaries is likely to suffer.

Who is to decide whether the government is responsive or not? And more precisely, to whom ought the government be responsive? As argued earlier, once we have noted that there are many possible majorities, it is not enough to answer, "Responsive to the majority!" Broadening one's normative concerns beyond Pareto optimality to include distributive justice, for example, means that we will have a more difficult time specifying the answer to this question. And this is what we have seen manifest in the problem of localism.

RESPONSIVE TO WHOM?

If we have difficulties in deciding the proper relation between efficiency and fairness in political jurisdictional problems (where should one government's jurisdiction end and the next one's begin), such issues will spill

[10] Federalism is yet another way in which functions are split across institutions. Like other divisions of labor it will have the benefits and problems of conflict with Pareto optimality that were identified in the section of the Liberal Paradox, as well as some of the problems we attributed to 'localism" in this section.

over into questions of franchise, turnout, and voting. After all, if a rich neighborhood can improve its welfare by pulling out of a metro area, it can similarly gain if the turnout for metro elections is highly skewed in its favor. And if jurisdictional questions are part of the mix, so is the extent of the constituency, or more basically, the franchise within any jurisdiction. Who votes determines the boundary between the constituency and the beneficiary group.

Turnout and Social Justice

Limitations on voting rights or enfranchisement come in many forms. The difficulties in establishing one's credentials to vote (in the United States this comes in the form of voter registration hurdles, and more recently, voter identification rules), the distribution of polling places, the timing of elections (on holidays or on work days), and the like. Automatic registration as a voter is a standard that rules in most modern democracies. Indeed, the United States (where, it must be noted, elections are governed separately in each of the states) stands out as an exception in this manner in that there are multiple and varied hurdles placed in the way of voting in the different states. Indeed, turnout for the pivotal Florida vote in the 2000 presidential election was clearly affected by the earlier decision to purge the voter registration rolls of those who had been convicted of crimes in other states. Those voters had to register anew in order to gain the right to vote.[11]

But even if there are neither discriminatory laws nor regulations that prevent equitable turnout, turnout may be an important determinant of policy decisions. When differential turnout is the determinant of the electoral outcomes, candidates are going to ensure that they appeal to sustain the turnout of their "likely" supporters. They need the reluctant supporter to show up by being sufficiently riled up to go to the polls. This can polarize the electoral appeals. To see this, return to the discussion of Figure 14 (page 105) showing how alienation contributes to diverging platforms. Further, money raised for such contests will be used to generate messages to mobilize the turnout of likely supporters. And so, perhaps surprisingly, laws penalizing non-voting (as in Australia) have the effect of moderating

---

[11] Florida required those who 1) were convicted of felonies in other states, and 2) subsequently restored their rights by said states), and 3) wished to vote, to request clemency and a restoration of their rights, from Governor Bush. Such a process is slow and was, in any case, left to Bush's discretion. (Palast, 2002)

the appeals to the voters. Subsequently, alienation contributes less to the polarization of platforms.[12] Or, we can note:

COMPULSORY VOTING LEADS TO LESS POLARIZATION OF PLATFORMS.

Less polarization of platforms need not lead to fairer outcomes. But it does increase the chance that the appeals are made toward the center of the electorate. Further, the universalizing of the franchise, and the actual voters, ensures that the median voter is more reflective of the median opinion in the population. As such it leads to a reinforcement of some notions of fairness that accrued to the moderating effect of democratic rules. This can be stated as a corollary:

Compulsory voting leads to platforms that, as a set, better reflect the values of the population as a whole.

In any case, restrictions on the franchise impose differential costs on the voters and thus lead to some legitimate voters being excluded. These restrictions are often touted as measures to prevent vote fraud. But, at least in the United States, studies show that vote fraud is a statistically marginal problem. The efforts to restrict the franchise are surely deliberately designed to minimize the power of selected segments of the electorate so as to favor some political factions and outcomes over others. As such, they violate fundamental underlying legitimating notions of democracy such as "one man, one vote."

In opposition to the suggestion for compulsory voting in the United States one hears three major arguments, each of which can be answered, to a degree:

1) "Forcing people to vote" is a violation of their freedoms. What has been found is that a rather modest tax savings is sufficient to motivate people to the polls. Showing up at the polls and actually voting are two different things. But by giving people the opportunity to cast a blank ballot (i.e., "none of the above") in protest, one obviates the notion that the individual has been forced to vote.

2) Those people who aren't motivated to go to the polls are not likely to have preferences between the candidates. This may be so, but facilitating their casting a blank vote will increase the probability that candidates will modify their platforms so as to attract the

---

[12] This has been the experience of, among other countries, Australia, which adopted a small tax break for those who went to the polls (even if they voted "no preference" in the contests).

support of these alienated voters. The motivational cost of such appeals will be less since the voters are going to the polls in any case.

And finally,

3) Those who aren't motivated to go to the polls but go to avoid the tax are less likely to be informed and so cast less informed ballots. This may well be so. But one must note that we already have found that the voters' information level is not high. By knowing that they will go to the polls, some of the individuals may increase their consumption of political information.

In any case, it is clear that there are both positive and negative arguments to be considered in this debate. Its importance, however, should be clear. To the extent that voting is the key to governmental responsiveness in a democracy, excluding individuals from the voting public increases the chance that the government will overlook their needs and desires. Indeed, this is the main political reason for excluding those individuals in the first place.

Money in Electoral Competitions

As we are here concerned with "responsive to whom?" a word must be inserted on the role of money in determining responsiveness. The outcomes of political competitions can be distorted by more than discriminatory voting rules. For if candidates need votes, and their appeals to get votes cost money, they must try to get the money to appeal for votes. How the costs of expensive political campaigns are borne determines how some in the electorate can extract favorable treatment for their preferences in exchange for their financial backing. Not all the donors need be members of the electorate. In our capitalist democratic systems collective actors such as corporations, unions, and other organizations will have far more capacity to put money on the table than will individuals, even though they are not part of the electorate. Private funding of elections ensures that the wealthy are more likely to be well represented than the poor. When campaigns are fought and displayed, at least partially, in private media spaces that must be paid for, money is related directly to problems of responsiveness. If we are concerned with the fairness of outcomes in our public policies, we must also be concerned with these potential distorting factors to the political process.

Problematic Policy Arenas

Incentives to keep the government responsive are to be weighed against the ability of the government to make commitments over time so that proper follow through for its policies can be assured. Rational ignorance, free-riding, and multiple agents lead to a lack of specific responsibility for failures. Therefore, special effort must be made to ensure that voters can attribute praise and blame properly. This means that when responsibility for policy is very diffuse (as when there are many veto players) the design of the system may prevent voters from holding the parties responsible for missing the mark.

There is no "ought" from an "is." And certainly there is no "ought" if there is no "can." We shall see in Chapter 8, Arrow and subsequent research have identified considerable roadblocks to what can be expected from any democratic organization. Yet, there is much that can be achieved by better design of our democratic institutions. As democrats we are interested in responsiveness of governments to the needs of citizens, be they voting or not. The lesson is clear: we judge our political system by its accomplishments: the freedom it ensures for its citizens, the vibrancy of the economy that it engenders, the efficiency of the solutions to social problems it puts in place, and the justice of the society that ensues. There may be no simple paths to better political outcomes, but there are clear signs of worse political design.

If democracy is to live up to its promise, voters must be able to hold politicians accountable for their actions. A system of checks and balances that is too complicated undermines that. The benefits of any system of checks and balances and veto players (such as the assurance of commitment) must be balanced with its effect on decreasing voters' ability to send clear signals and holding the political agents responsible. Such disempowerment must be thought about as an important quality to be avoided in the designing of a democratic system. If the voters are to deliver directional signals to their agents, the governors, the voters must be able to discern the separate directions of the governors they vote for. In democracies, this is eased by parliamentary government and disciplined political parties.

Nothing threatens all these relations more severely than a general disconnect between constituents and beneficiaries. When these are sufficiently distinct the principal-agent problem will be most acute. Is it then surprising that the agents (politicians) continually try to prevent some from voting and hence prevent them from continuing their membership in the constituency group?

Of course, there are policy arenas in which there is a necessary and unbridgeable gulf between constituents and beneficiaries. Two examples come to mind: intergenerational policy such as global warming, and foreign policy such as foreign aid. In such cases the voters and citizens of today have a fiduciary relationship with those others who are the supposed beneficiaries of the policy. Such fiduciary relations are most difficult to engineer successfully within our current conception of democratic political institutions.

The lack of institutional innovation to balance any long-term needs of future generations with the desires of current citizens has not begun to be addressed. Such problems as environmental sustainability are particularly difficult to "get right" in a democratic context. Without some massive constraints on individual preferences (as might occur through a real change in our own consciousness) political responsiveness tilts against the future. If some sort of "representation of the future" were to be built in to the policy process, it is likely that it would be one more veto player that would have to be satisfied in the development of public policy.

This lack of representation of some beneficiaries is related to, but quite distinct from, the problems of externalities. Consider, for example, the spill-over of domestic policies into international arenas. Within the international community people have tried to structure international participatory institutions to give representation to those who are not in the centers of world power and yet who suffer from the decisions made there. But, as we can understand, these institutions have not been overly successful. The autonomy of the nation-state has prevented the major powers from having to take into account the needs of those citizens of other countries affected by their policies.

There are no simple answers to how to ensure better policy in these sorts of policy arenas. But we should be thinking about institutional design questions now, so as to be able to develop better outcomes in the future.

FOR FURTHER READING

On the Tethering of Political Leaders

Desai, Anita (1991), "India: The Seed of Destruction," *The New York Review of Books*, v. **XXXVIII**, No. 12 (June 27, 1991). pp. 3–4. This is an interesting piece on the development of bribery and its role in Indian politics. It highlights how these rewards to leaders determine public policy.

Frohlich, Norman, Joe A. Oppenheimer, and Oran R. Young (1971), *Political Leadership and the Supply of Collective Goods*. Princeton, New Jersey: Princeton University Press. We analyze the political structure of competition over public goods and introduce the notion of entrepreneurship as the solution to collective goods provision problems.

Kinzer, Stephen (2001), "Nicaragua: A Country Without Heroes." *New York Review of Books*, v. **xlviii**, no. 12 (July 19,2001): 31–33. This piece gives a view of the old Sandinistas as just being politicians who want to hold onto office to get rewards.

Kitman, Marvin, *George Washington's Expense Account*. New York: Grove Press. Kitman writes an insightful and humorous annotation of the actual and shocking expense account George Washington handed in to be reimbursed for his services during the American Revolution.

Michels, Robert (1915), *Political Parties*. Hearst's International Library. Repubished in 1959 by Dover Publications: New York. This classic is a sociological work focusing on early twentieth-century socialist parties. He argues that the development of oligarchy is a natural outgrowth of democracy.

Remnick, David (1992), "Dons of the Don," *New York Review of Books*, v. **XXXIX**, No. 13 (July 16): pp. 45–50. This short essay gives a detailed account of the entrepreneurial, "on the take" "mobster" behavior of the USSR post-Stalin leadership.

Riordon, William L. (1994), *Plunkitt of Tammany Hall*. Boston: Bedford Books of St. Martin's Press. Riordon recorded this set of frank interviews of a New York politician at the start of the twentieth century. It gives a clear description of the relation between electoral politics and corruption.

Wagner, Richard (1966), "Pressure Groups and Political Entrepreneurs: A Review Article." *Public Choice*. 1, No. 1, 161–170. Wagner introduced the notion of entrepreneurship to the solution of collective goods provision problems in this book review.

On the Principal-Agent Relation

Alt, James and David Dreyer Lassen (2003), The Political Economy of Institutions and Corruption in American States. *Journal of Theoretical Politics* **15**(3): 341–365. They formulate hypotheses regarding the effect of institutions on the prevalence of political corruption in American states. They use both survey data and data on convictions to examine them empirically.

Cox, Gary W. and Mathew D. McCubbins (1999), "The Institutional Determinants of Economic Policy Outcomes," in Stephan Haggard, ed. *Presidents, Parliaments, and Policy*, Cambridge: Cambridge University Press: 21–63. Like Rogowski (see below), they argue that macro aspects of democratic political institutions make a difference in the principal-agent relationship, and hence in such properties of the political processes as "ability to commit."

Moe, Terry (1984), "The New Economics of Organization." *American Journal of Political Science*, v. **28** (November): 739–777. Moe gives a very useful overview of rational choice applied to public and private organizations. He focuses on property rights, transactions costs, rent seeking, free-riding, and monitoring principal-agent problems. He includes a good bibliography.

Olson, Mancur (1982), *The Rise and Decline of Nations: Economic Growth, Stagflation, & Social Rigidities*. New Haven: Yale Universty Press. Olson argues that social stability leads to proliferation of narrow interest groups and develops nine propositions concerning how such groups fight for narrow policy gains to redistribute income in their favor. By so doing they distort incentives in manners that lead to slow economic growth rates and inefficiency.

Riker, William H. (1982), *Liberalism Against Populism A Confrontation Between the Theory of Democracy and the Theory of Social Choice*. Prospect Heights, IL: Waveland Press. Riker argues that democracy can only punish the incumbents for bad performance. He writes that there is no justification for developing a positive interpretation of an electoral victory as a policy mandate.

Rogowski, Ronald (1999), "Institutions as Constraints on Strategic Choice," in David A. Lake and Robert Powell, eds., *Strategic Choice and International Relations*. Princeton, New Jersey: Princeton University Press: 115–135. Like Cox and McCubbins, Rogowski argues that macro aspects of democratic political institutions make a difference in the principal-agent relationship, and hence in such outcomes of political processes as the 'ability to commit," "free trade," and so on.

On Institutional Design

Buchanan, James and Gordon Tullock (1962), *The Calculus of Consent*. Ann Arbor, Michigan: University of Michigan Press. In this classic, they develop the notion that one judges institutional design by the relative costs and benefits that individuals can expect. They argue for both majority rule and unanimity.

Hammond, Thomas H. and Gary J. Miller, "A Social Choice Perspective on Expertise and Authority in Bureaucracy." *American Journal of Political Science*, vol 29, No. 1, Feb. 1985: pp. 1–28. They argue that bureaucratic control could be seen as a form of Sen's Liberal Paradox. This gives them a social choice interpretation of bureaus. They show that giving way to expertise is a form of decentralization which leads to the liberal paradox.

Hirschman, A.O. (1970), Exit Voice and Loyalty, Cambridge, Mass: Harvard University Press. Hirschman explores how voice and exit combine to generate pressures for quality improvement, and bankruptcy, of government and other institutions. The argument is very provocative and suggestive for issues of migration and efficiency of markets and polities.

Lijphart, Arend (1999), *Patterns of Democracy: Government Forms and Performance in Thirty-Six Countries*. New Haven: Yale University Press. This is a careful study of the performance of various forms of democratic government with a statistical examination to see which forms support which sorts of policies and outcome.

Rae D.W. (1969), "Decision Rules and Individual Values in Constitutional Choice." *American Political Science Review* 63, (March): 40–56. Continuing the efforts of Buchanan and Tullock, Rae examines what constitutional rules are best from the point of view of the individual. He argues for majority rule, saying that it maximizes the expected value of the benefits from a set of group decisions when you don't have any *a priori* reason to think you will lose more often than win.

On Regime Change

Douglas North and Barry Weingast (1989) "Constitutions and Commitment: The Evolution of Institutional Governing Public Choice in Seventeenth-Century England," *Journal of Economic History*, v. **49**, 4 (Dec): 803–32. This is an alternative view to that of Boix regarding the development of democracy. They argue that democracy is consolidated by pacts among elites. Looking at the history of England, they argue that the imposition of constraints on the king in the seventeenth century worked because the system was "self-enforcing." This line of argument is developed further in Weingast (1997), "The Political Foundations of Democracy and the Rule of Law." American Political Science Review, V. 91, No 2 (June): 245–263.

PART IV

SOCIAL JUSTICE, CHOICE, AND WELFARE

The many hurdles identified in earlier sections of this volume project a tone of pessimism regarding politics. Without formal political institutions, collective interests are unlikely to be properly addressed. But even with formal institutions, given the manipulations, preference cycles (as discussed in Chapter 5), and more, the achievement of collective interests, appears always threatened. Now it is time to clarify "collective interests." One objective of political analysis is to identify the relationship between social choice and social well-being (or as it is commonly called, social welfare). To this point, all we have identified are some difficulties in this relation. We have some positive work to do.

What are collective interests? As we will find in Chapter 8, in trying to conceptualize collective interests, one runs into severe problems. Is this only because preference cycles make interpretation of results difficult? Can this be avoided by bypassing majority rule? Although we may desire to design institutions to help us hit the target of social well-being, Kenneth Arrow (1963), has shown there will be no easy method to even identify the target. If, as many economists think, individual well-being is to be conceptualized as the satisfaction of one's preferences, and social welfare is to be understood as the aggregation of individual well-being, Arrow identifies enormous roadblocks to any easy understanding of social welfare. His argument is the main focus of the first part of Chapter 8.

In Chapter 8 we also explore the political nature of social welfare and some of its necessary properties in democracies. I develop the notion of a democratic obligation to social welfare and social justice. This feeds into implications of Arrow's work. Arrow showed the difficulties both in defining social welfare in terms of individual welfare, and in aggregating individual choices to reflect group desires. Indeed, any notion of a simple, sensible social choice method as the "natural translation" of a bunch of measures of individual welfare is shown to be quixotic.

On the other hand, Arrow's arguments are built on the classic presumption that one can't compare one person's well-being to that of another. That starting point implies a very messy underbelly to the concept of the "people's interests." It leads one to wonder what alternative starting points may be employed to get better leverage. Arrow's arguments regarding the difficulties of aggregating individual well-being are also applicable to problems of meaningful vote aggregation. Discussing this leads us to consider, in Chapter 9, how a variety of voting rules measure up to the job of sensible vote aggregation. But regardless of how individual choices are translated to social choice, the central normative question is how to evaluate the *quality* of social choice.

In light of the challenge of Arrow's argument, we follow the advice of Amartya Sen and go beyond the presumption of noncomparability of individual well-being to make sense of collective interest. But, saying that we *must* make interpersonal comparisons doesn't tell us *how* to do it. To answer the "how" question, in Chapter 10 I make further presumptions about the nature of individual welfare. These enable us to compare well-being across people.[1] But even after that bold step, we still must link those comparisons to conceptualize aggregate welfare. To do this, I employ modern social justice theory and report on experimental studies regarding social justice. We find a basis for interpersonal comparison of well-being nested within those theories of social justice. The theories help us justify some interpersonal comparisons of individual welfare.

Adopting reasoning from social justice theory lets us identify the properties to focus on so as to get beyond the theory of preference satisfaction that forms the basis of Pareto optimality.[2] Those properties support a different definition of social welfare, well-being, or collective interest: one that focuses on the basic needs of individuals. This notion of social welfare is related to the justification of democracy. It yields a partial answer as to what is social welfare, and how we can measure "better" and "worse." I utilize this perspective to construct a metric of

---

[1] Such presumptions were the step taken by classical utilitarians such as Priestly, Mill, and Bentham when they advocated the greatest good to the greatest number, and presumed that this could be discovered by addition.

[2] The work in this chapter reflects my work done with Norman Frohlich.

performance for modern, economically developed, democratic regimes. From this I conjecture some of the constitutional properties that could lead to better performance of these states. The metric is incomplete, but in conformity with the observation of Sen (1999a, p. 254). As he put it: "It can also be argued that judgments of 'social justice' do not really call for a tremendous fine-tuning precision ... Rather what is needed is a working agreement on some basic matters of identifiably intense injustice or unfairness."

Until now, we have mainly identified and collected law-like propositions and knowledge claims. In this section that will be continued. But the reader may feel uneasy with some of these claims, as they are at times built on normative presumptions. Hopefully, I will help the reader over these difficulties.

The field of inquiry discussed in this section can be thought of as containing two problems of aggregation and a political dream or hope of relating them.

THE TWO PROBLEMS OF AGGREGATION

Consider, first, the problems of aggregation. The problem of social or group choice is that of aggregating individual choices (votes) into a collective choice (see Chapter 9). Similarly, the problem of social welfare is that of translating the well-being of individuals into social welfare. The great hope of democratic politics is to design mechanisms that securely link social choice to social welfare. This is displayed in Figure 43. There, I depict a central normative problem of democratic politics as the hope, or perhaps dream, that one can get from individual choices to group choices, that is, to outcomes, that reflect social welfare.

Economists, who see individual preference satisfaction as inextricably related to individual well-being, tie the tops of the two vertical lines together. Institutions that satisfy more individual preferences increase the well-being of individuals. Markets are then extolled as institutions well designed to satisfy preferences. Another way of viewing markets is that they distribute "to each according to how much he benefits others who have the resources for benefitting those who benefit them" (Nozick, 1974: 158). Ignoring the economic injustices that might exist, divergence at the bottom of the diagram would then have to do with imperfections in preference aggregation and would be strictly a question of identifying impossibilities (as in Arrow's theorem) that need to be minimized via the development of better institutions and voting rules.

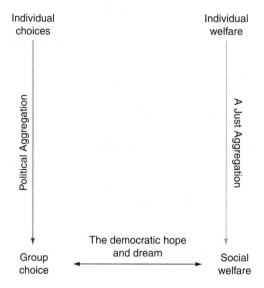

FIGURE 43. Social choice and social welfare problems and their political relationship.

You have already spent some time on the problem of aggregating individual choices to yield sensible group choices. Since individual choice was explained in terms of individual preferences we solved some problems by restricting preferences in a group to a one dimensional "spatial" context. But the relation to social welfare is more complicated than mere sensible aggregation of votes. In most cases, votes count equally. This holds even when the preference that one voter has for alternative A over B is substantively much less "important" than the preference of another voter on the issue. Your preference or choice equals mine even if the changes in your well-being and mine are clearly unequally affected by the issue. As discussed in Chapter 9, some voting schemes (voting by veto, approval voting, point voting, etc.) are developed to be more responsive to differences in intensities. But they are also limited in their ability to handle the differing impact problem.

Indeed, the traditional manner of handling individual preferences does not let us compare my potential loss to your potential gains. But in everyday life, we do make such comparisons. Consider a concrete situation: Jim and Robert are neighbors. A local transportation issue has come up concerning a bus stop that sits between their houses. Jim wants it moved to another block because he doesn't like the noise and sight of the stopped bus across from his house. Robert likes the convenience that the stop offers him in riding the bus. A vote is taken and Jim votes for moving the stop; Robert votes against. The comparative welfare content underlying these preferences is irrelevant to the aggregation of votes into choice. But such content could differ wildly and could change behavior, as in this altered illustration. Assume Robert is severely handicapped and the stop is his only access to transportation. Voting to determine the collective choice might be democratic, but the outcome could be morally undesirable: moving the stop so Jim gains better scenery denies Robert access to transportation.

All I have done is added some welfare detail to the preference story. Preferences always have such detail in their foundations. Our abstractions consider preferences without content. Hence, they gave noncomparable "ordinal" information: Robert preferred the stop to no stop, Jim had the inverse preference. As such they conveyed no interpersonal welfare information. In contrast, in the second example, Jim may be thinking that "Robert's need for the stop outweighs my desire to move it." This implies the value or welfare differences underlying preferences *can* be interpersonally compared. Such a conclusion indicates two things: first, we can both get beyond our own self-interest and be sensitive to each other's needs. Jim might come to prefer to keep the stop so as to maintain Robert's access. Preferences can be other-regarding. Second, to make comparisons with others sensible, we would want sufficient good[3] information to be communicated as a framework of the aggregation process. Any good political process must be sensitive to these nuances.

If welfare information needs to be communicated along with preference reports, discussion or other more complex communication structures ought to precede any voting or collective choice mechanism. This has implications for the design of political structures so as to tie choice to societal well-being. For these interpersonal judgements to affect the problems of defining social welfare properly, the substantive details behind the judgements must be communicated. To illustrate, for a hospital to have a sensible triage policy, its medical staff must agree on what takes precedence. Information regarding the severity of the patient's status, with regard to the details of the triage policy, must be communicated. Those details then lead to an intersubjective agreement of the triage evaluations.[4]

---

[3] Recall the difficulties of getting individuals to reveal their true preferences regarding public goods (see Footnote 15, Chapter 1).

[4] Sayre-McCord (1988) has an interesting discussion of the role of subjective but interpersonal communication in ethics.

Is this intersubjective agreement on the judgements of well-being purely cultural? Or is there something more universal going on? Universal or not, any intersubjective agreement threatens the Pareto justifying notion that we can make no interpersonal comparisons of welfare. After all, we *do* often change our judgments (and behavior) because of the impact we perceive we have on others, including those whose personal welfare doesn't impact our own. Were we not to allow any such interpersonal comparisons, we would diminish our understanding of humanity. This leaves us with the following law:

Any acceptable conception of social well-being requires that individuals' welfare be comparable.

(Sen, 2002)

Hence, sensible notions of social welfare reflect these sorts of interpersonal comparisons of welfare. If interpersonal comparisons can go beyond a purely cultural justification, and are based on a firmer footing, then any notion of social welfare ought to reflect the interpersonal welfare comparisons that we are cognitively capable of observing, feeling, and understanding. We cannot deprive a theory of social well-being the very content that we use to make evaluative judgments. Our understanding and values regarding one another's well-being must figure into any acceptable notions of social welfare.

THE GREAT POLITICAL HOPE

The need to make interpersonal comparisons of well-being the link between group choices and social welfare cannot be easily satisfied. A purely mechanical system of electoral and voting institutions (as in casting and counting decentralized votes) can't forge that link. That is the lesson of the combined works of Arrow and Sen. To move to interpersonal comparisons one must have nonmechanical sorts of information exchanges: ones that reveal the well-being information behind preferences. A considerable portion of Chapter 8 develops Arrow's proof that this link can't be easily forged without interpersonal comparison of well-being. By showing impossibility, Arrow's conclusion reflects that his assumptions are too strong to be descriptive of any extant democratic institutions. As pointed out by Sen (2002) in his Nobel Prize acceptance speech, much of the lack of fit of Arrow's (impossible) conditions and the real world can be overcome by noting that we are aggregating something richer than the classical notion of individual preferences. We need to analyze the relationship between a fuller characterization of preferences and the possibility of improved social welfare.

In any case, for politics to serve social welfare, welfare content must be added to preferences in aggregation. Further, we must recognize processes that facilitate taking these comparative claims into account. The two processes of aggregation (that of individual well-being and of individual choices) may then hopefully be related so that the corresponding products, choice and welfare, have some possibility of connecting. It is only then that we can explore the nature of social welfare and individual preferences in order to show the relationship between particular political processes and institutions and the achievement of a better society.

CHAPTER 8

The General Problem of Collective Welfare and Choice

To combine the discussion of collective welfare and collective choice in one chapter is to admit an aspirational bias: we would like collective choice to promote collective welfare. Trying to answer, "What should be the collective outcome?" directly links to the question, "What is in the interest of the group?" (Lest anyone think this question of little import, reflect on the number of wars that have been fought, and their associated number of deaths, based on the claim that they were in a nation's interest.) So the two topics, collective choice and collective interest, are intimately related: if there were no question of the "interest of the group" there would be little reason to consider collective choice. Further, as demonstrated by Kenneth Arrow, the two topics share problems of analysis.

SETTING UP THE PROBLEM

At the heart of both the welfare and choice problems lies the difficulty of aggregation. In one case it is aggregating the well-beings of a collection of individuals into a notion of collective well-being, and in the other it is the aggregation of individual decisions into a binding group decision. As noted in the discussion of Figure 43 (page 188), one main justification of democratic political institutions involves the presumed positive relation between the welfare of the citizens, the outcomes they would choose, and the welfare of the group. Thus, the two subjects, social choice and social welfare, are inexorably intertwined for democrats. Substantial empirical research (see page 92) has shown numerous positive indicators of democracy's superiority, but understanding why democracy 'works" runs into difficulties.

So, though we know democracy does pretty well, without a fuller understanding of why, the problem of designing better institutions is left unsupported. We need a better understanding of how *individual* choices and well-being relate to *social* welfare in order to design better democracies. This chapter lays some of the foundations to take on this problem.

Begin with two conceptual foundations, the first of which you may find obvious: social welfare relates, at least in part, to some "aggregation of the welfare of individuals."[1] Second, a society's understanding of social welfare relates to what its population believes political institutions ought to do: the legitimizing premises of its political arrangements. When those arrangements are democratic, collective choice reflects the decentralized individual decisions expressed in actions such as votes. Why do we value such procedures? In part because voting gives a specific sort of bent to what ought to be done: a tie to a specific sort of notion of social welfare.

Social Welfare and Democracy: Politically Empowering a Notion of the Good

Any political regime gains legitimacy by its implicit support of *some* conception of the good and how the citizens are to come to know that conception. Liberal democracy is no exception. Its core set of principles regarding individual rights and liberties reflects its justificatory premises. For liberal democratic institutions the individual is the principal legitimate arbiter of what constitutes her own welfare.

How does this conception relate to a democratic understanding of the welfare of a group? Democracy requires that political decisions are made by (or in a republican, indirect democracy, are seriously informed by) the people via some procedure of aggregating preferences, as in the form of voting choices.[2] Those citizens' choices are presumed to be tied to the individuals' own well-being. By reflecting those citizens' choices, the community's choice is thought to have a good chance of reflecting the community's interests. For voters' choices to have any significance, the

---

[1] The idea is that the group interest is wrapped up in the interests of the concrete individuals that make up the group. It is an implication of methodological individualism (Schumpeter, 1909).

[2] These procedures may be quite complex, direct or indirect, and so on. It is only important that the individuals' decisions are arrived at freely, and that the agenda options are open to free debate and amendment.

voters are presumed to know their own welfare status.[3] This implies an important epistemological proposition about the individual's good in a democracy:

No-one, in general, is in a better position than the individual, to gain direct knowledge of what is good for herself based on observation, discussion, consultation, and inward reflection.

(Hayek, 1960)

This is not to say that the individual necessarily knows what will support her well-being. But she has a greater interest in getting that knowledge than anyone else. In legitimating those judgments, the democratic process reinforces the normative assumption that individual welfare constitutes a major component of the good. If the good is knowable at all, it is the individual's right to seek it for herself or to delegate the authority to someone whom she reasonably believes has better tools to determine it (her doctor, her financial advisor, her representative in the legislature, etc.). Democracy's welding of social choice to the direct or indirect aggregation of citizens' choices aims to tie the social good to some function or reflection of those citizens' decisions (or those of their elected representatives).[4] More succinctly,

In a democracy the social good is inextricably wound up with the well-being of the citizenry.

As such, it is a function of each citizen's estimation of what is good for herself, and her judgment as to what is good for the group.

[3] More is actually required. For example, one's current welfare status is mainly based on what has already happened: how incumbents have performed to date. How does this relate to votes, which hypothetically govern future behavior? Evidence shows that retrospective voting (voting on past performance) can generate future outcomes that are responsive to the preferences of voters. See Collier, et al. (1987).

[4] This is not a simple matter. The "social choice" literature (Arrow, 1963; Sen, 1970) presents problems for this perspective. Unavoidable cyclical majorities, or the surrender of other desirable properties of democracy, make normative interpretation of citizens' collective decisions problematic. Presumptions of probabilistic decision making on the part of representatives or voters permits a partial reintegration of standard arguments regarding social welfare and individual choice (see Mueller, 2003; Coughlin, 1988). Other paths are opened by Miller (1983) who argues that one ought to conceptualize the relation between social choice and social good not in terms of any one decision but rather by the trajectories of the policy paths. Sen (1966) pointed out that a general restriction of values (similar to, but less restrictive than, single-peaked preferences) held by the citizenry would alleviate the problem. Later, Arrow (1977) himself argued that a shared conception of some forms of justice can circumvent the social choice problem. Frohlich and Oppenheimer (1999) build on this notion.

Few welfare implications can be directly known by virtually everyone, though we usually presume groups have a collective understanding of commonly shared experiences. Examples that come to mind include the value of nurturing a child, of fear of hunger, and so on. Some things with this property of near universal understanding are the everyday components of an individual's welfare – they are a part of the human condition.[5] They require neither expert knowledge (such as is required to establish the existence of subatomic particles or microscopic carcinoma) nor divine revelation. It is the voter as every-man, or an elected representative, that has access to them. This epistemological presumption forms the basis of what we will call a "realist" ontology. And it implies:

Individual welfare is given an implicit moral status in democracies: it is good.

The justificatory structure of democracy is built (at least in large part) upon this, in that individual welfare is assumed to be directly reflective of the voters' considered choices.

Let us be clear. This process of social aggregation via votes authorizes each citizen to evaluate her own welfare. By legitimating the vote, the state empowers the individual.[6] The vote is the reflection, at least in part, of the individual's expression of her own welfare. But it is also a demarcation of her welfare's relationship to the larger fabric of social welfare. That votes are counted in a decision process reinforces and legitimates a certain underlying conception of this notion of the social good.

Now, differences of opinion regarding the social good are to be expected, and can lead to political disputes. The epistemological presuppositions inherent in democratic thought do not demand that knowledge is acquired by all or that, given a certain level of information, all individuals

---

[5] A second moral ontology is available to democrats: the concept of the social will, as understood and argued for by Rousseau. In Rousseau's formulation, all are able to perceive it if they only put on the right lenses. It relates to the main idea behind the Condorcet Jury theorem (see Mueller, 2003 for a discussion of the Condorcet jury theorem): that the voters are helping each other collectively to arrive at the "correct" or "right" outcome. But in light of Arrow's (1963, p. 81+), and, derivatively, Riker's (1982) arguments, some would see the connection of democratic procedures to "the right outcomes," as an oxymoron: a chimera of ill-formed argument. It can, however, be partially resuscitated by probabilistic decision models (see footnote 10) or shared values (Frohlich and Oppenheimer, 2007; Sen 1999a, Chap. 11). Perhaps I don't need to take a position in this debate.

[6] This is a bit of an overstatement. Empowerment is limited by the structure of the agenda and the resources made available beyond the vote, in order to persuade, cajole, and so on, others. And if there is considerable asymmetry in the holdings of resources for communication, it may well be that individuals are given neither sufficient information to know their "real welfare" interests nor sufficient resources to protect these interests.

will agree on anything at any point in time. Individuals in one subcommunity may wish a different conception of the social good to prevail, or may wish to permit or restrict activities in a manner more in keeping with their own desires, customs, and accepted life plans. Also, an individual in a particular community may dissent from such prevailing norms within that community.[7]

What is ensured by the properties of democratic liberalism is that the individual who is not in agreement with (or is oppressed by) the social mores associated with her community and its conception of the social good has options. She may speak, organize, and attempt to acquire notions of the social good that she finds more congenial. By voting and other political actions, she may seek to have changes explicitly adopted by the society. Failing that, she may seek adjudication of a potential dispute between herself and her cultural community to allow her to pursue her personal view of her welfare. And the individual is free to leave the subgroup and become a member of another community. Democracy leaves open public discussion on the fit of its agreed conception of the social good and individual welfare, although it in no way guarantees consensus or any other specific outcome.

It is useful here to summarize the ties we have identified in liberal democracies:

1. Social welfare is a function of individual well-being.
2. Individual well-being is known best by the individual herself.
3. Individuals are rational, and act to make themselves better off.
4. Voting can be expected to reflect the expected welfare improvement of the citizenry.

With this understanding of the foundations of social welfare as resting on the well-being of the citizenry, we can see that in democracies the notion of social welfare is certainly strongly constrained by and tied to the well-being of individuals.

But now to Arrow. Arrow points out that the processes of democracy can **not** be assured to produce more social welfare as here understood. Arrow's fundamental argument is that without making stronger assumptions about what constitutes individual well-being, we have insufficient, and even contradictory, elements in our concept of social welfare. Political scientists have interpreted his arguments to be mainly about voting rather than social welfare, but here we shall emphasize his other concern: social

---

[7] See the interesting work on exit by Hirschman in *Exit Voice and Loyalty* (1970).

welfare. About this, he concludes that the "democratic" conception of social welfare isn't coherent without further input.

Arrow's Argument

After World War II, Kenneth Arrow was working at the Rand Corporation. He was asked to figure out the best placement of submarines in the Pacific Ocean, given the increasing hostilities between the United States and the USSR. To calculate how each party might place its submarines rationally, Arrow needed to know what the national interests of both the Soviets and the Americans. He found the notion of national interest puzzling. He could conceptualize the USSR's interest as that of Stalin. But how was he to conceptualize the aggregate interest of the people of the United States?

He believed that social welfare should determine whether one alternative was better for the group than another. Starting with the principle, generally accepted by economists, that we can't compare the welfare of one person to that of another, all he had to work with were the preferences of the individuals: how the individuals ranked the possibilities. Such a preference ranking would be a proxy for individual well-being. He came up with a minimal set of characteristics to be satisfied by any notion of social welfare.[8] But then, he showed that these characteristics were impossible to be satisfied: they were contradictory.

To understand the analysis, imagine starting with a set of individuals, each with her own personal needs and welfare. The first task is to pick policies[9] by comparing pairs of them with an eye to choosing the one that is the best, or those tied for best. Arrow began by identifying minimal criteria that would constrain our choice (see Table 16) and then showing they don't work: are contradictory. Begin by examining his criteria.

First, Pareto optimality (we refer to this as **P**, see page 35). Were one policy better for some, and not worse for anyone, when compared to a second policy, we could refer to that policy as weakly Pareto dominating the second policy. Any Pareto-dominated policy is to be rejected as not in the group's interest; it is associated with lower social welfare. Any policy that makes someone better off and hurts no one is better for the group, and is to be preferred.

---

[8] Others had tried to nail down social welfare (see Bergson, 1938).

[9] Actually, for Arrow, alternative policies were understood as complete alternative "states of the world." Thus choices were conceptualized as being made between these alternative states of the world.

TABLE 16. *Arrow's Proposed Desirable Characteristics for a Conception of Social Welfare*

Desired Condition	Description
P – Pareto	If everyone is better off, so is the community.
N – Non Dictator	The community's welfare is not to be determined by the welfare status of only one individual.
T – Transitivity	If A makes the community better off than B, and B better off than C, then A makes the community better off than C.
I – Independence	In judging the worth of any two outcomes only the well-being of the individuals from those outcomes matter.
U – Universal	All pairs of logically possible welfare distributions can be compared.

Second, the group's choice of policy should not just reflect the welfare of any one individual. This is called *nondictatorship*. I refer to this as **N**. It reflects the notion that no one person's well-being ought to determine the evaluation of the options for the group. That would be tantamount to dictatorship, and we would want to rule that out.

Third, the selection process should be capable of generating an ordering of the options being evaluated. This means, among other things, that the ranking of the options should be transitive (referred to as **T**, see page 16). In other words, if policy **A** is better than **B**, and **B** is better than **C**, **A** must be better than **C**. The justification here is that for us to say one policy is best requires that we are able to rank the policies in an orderly fashion.

Fourth, when we consider any two policies, **A** and **B**, their ranking as a pair should only depend on the rankings of those two policies: their pairwise ranking is to be *independent* (referred to as **I**) of the ranking of other options. Then, if **A** is considered better than **B**, for the group, we ought to be able to say this is so regardless of the existence of other policies that are to be ranked.

Fifth, we should be able to use this system to compare any two policies, regardless of how the available options impact the people. In other words, the concept of social welfare must be capable of motivating a judgement of comparative community well-being for any pair of distributions of well-being among the individuals concerned. Call this *universalism*, **U**: social welfare is to be applicable universally regardless of the distribution of welfare.[10] We will see that in the proof, this last property, U, lets us construct outcomes to be compared so we can uncover the potential tensions between the other conditions.

Conflicting Requirements

But now we can foresee the undoing of these demands, for tensions exist between these criteria. We can illustrate the difficulties by focusing on one sort of conflict: satisfying I and T simultaneously. To see the conflict, consider these properties of relations in another context: the relative heights of mountains. Assume the ranking of any two mountains should only be determined by their heights, and not by the heights of any third peak (I). This implies that the height of Stony Man Mountain should not affect the ranking of Mount Marcy and Mount McKinley. Now what happens when we also insist on T? Consider the implications of T in that context: assume we have two pairwise observations – McKinley is higher than Marcy, and Marcy is higher than Stony Man. Transitivity requires that McKinley is higher than Stony Man; the height of Marcy is no longer irrelevant in the comparative judgement regarding McKinley and Stony Man. But there seems to be no problem here.

The relative heights of McKinley and Stony Man was determined via Marcy and **not independent** of it. The two comparisons of Marcy relative to Stony Man and McKinley enabled us to reach the judgement that McKinley is higher than Stony Man. Satisfying T could conflict with satisfying I. What makes this conflict "no problem" in the mountain story is that the relationship "HIGHER THAN" *is necessarily* transitive: not by stipulation, but by its nature. So although we may have reached the McKinley-Stony Man judgement via transitivity, it will not conflict with "facts."

Now contrast the rankings of mountain heights with another relationship that isn't necessarily transitive, such as "CAN BEAT" in basketball. If Maryland can beat Missouri, and Missouri can beat Texas, we can't imply that Maryland can beat Texas. That pairwise comparison must be decided by the abilities of Texas relative to Maryland. Finally, consider "BETTER FOR THE GROUP" rather than HIGHER THAN. Like CAN BEAT, it *may* be transitive, but if so, it isn't so obvious. Note that if the notion BETTER FOR THE GROUP is also to be determined by the relative well-beings of the individuals in the group, then these two constraints, I and T,

---

[10] We could, instead, place restrictions on the distribution of impact of the policies that are being considered. This is what we did in the two chapters dealing with spatial analysis where we imposed single-peakedness as a property of preferences.

place some serious constraints on how these well-beings must relate both to one another and to the notion of BETTER FOR THE GROUP. Note that the implication is that we will have to see if our substantive notion of BETTER FOR THE GROUP can be capable of supporting the conditions we are placing on it.

We can get a further sense of the difficulties for the conception of BETTER FOR THE GROUP. Here we are trying to see what is better when each individual has different well-being associated with each of the alternatives. So, in considering social welfare, we are not talking about the height of any one mountain, but rather evaluating the height of a collection of peaks (or individual states of well-being): some higher, some lower. We then are judging whether one collection, as a whole, is higher than another. Second, although the height of any one of the mountain peaks is actually independent of the height of any other one, this needn't be so for the well-beings of individuals in a group. The well-being of my family, my neighbors, my friends, may well affect my own well-being.[11]

Arrow's (modified[12]) Theorem: No system of evaluation that sticks to these criteria (**P, N, T, I,** and **U**), can be developed as a consistent welfare metric. Of course, the argument stems from the conditions Arrow specified. But because these are relatively innocuous and in keeping with our notions of what it means to be in a group's interest, it makes the conclusion – that there is a conflict between them – all the more serious. Indeed,

WITHOUT INTERPERSONAL COMPARISONS, WE WILL BE UNABLE TO DO MORE THAN SEEK PARETO OPTIMALITY WHEN DECIDING WHAT IS BETTER FOR THE GROUP.[13]

(Arrow, 1963; Sen, 1970)

---

[11] This interaction violates a technical property called additive separability which is assumed in most modern consequentialist theories. Such an assumption rules out all synergies and team interdependencies among members of society, and as such is perniciously wrong (Oppenheimer, 2002). See Hamada (1973) for a discussion of the assumption's implications, also discussed in Sen (1973).

[12] I say modified because Amartya Sen (1970) showed that unanimity (i.e., Pareto) does work as a limited welfare criterion. Unanimity, however, gives us no way to compare outcomes that can only be reached with some persons being made worse off. So imagine a market economy that leaves some very badly off. A Pareto criterion would find a change consisting of a tax on the wealthy to help the poor to be of equal value to a change consisting of a tax on the poor to help the wealthy.

[13] In Chapter 10, I argue that we can make interpersonal comparisons of welfare. This means that such an impoverishment of our normative claims, based on exclusion of interpersonal comparisons, is unjustified. I also specify the basis for those comparative evaluations of individual welfare.

Proof of Arrow's Theorem

For those who don't know Arrow's impossibility theorem, I now sketch a proof of the theorem: showing a contradiction between the five desirable traits (**P, N, T, I,** and **U**) of their contradictory conception of social welfare.

The proof is aided by defining a *decisive group*. A subgroup of any community will be called decisive, G_d, with

respect to two alternatives if the community is said to be better off when one of those alternatives would make all the members of G_d better off were it chosen, even though all the other community members would be better off with the other alternative.

P, or Pareto optimality, implies that if the well-being of everyone in the group is improved then the welfare of the group is improved. Thus, the community as a whole is decisive. If the notion of social welfare conforms to **P,** there is necessarily a *decisive* group. Because of **P,** every community has at least one decisive subgroup: itself. There could be other subgroups that are decisive over particular pairs of alternatives. For example, were there a conception of social welfare that whatever made the royal family better off would make the society better off, the royal family group would be decisive. Of course, we would then need to ensure that the other conditions are met, and that, for example, the decisive group is not made up of just one person, violating **N.** Arrow showed that no notion of social welfare could be found that was consistent with the five conditions.

The proof will proceed as follows: first, I prove that since there is a decisive group over a single pair of alternatives, satisfying the five conditions requires (implies) that this same decisive group must be decisive first for *one*, and then for *all,other* alternatives.[14] I then show that the smallest decisive group – and there must be a smallest one – consists of only one individual. In other words, to satisfy the other conditions, we have to give up **N,** or nondictatorship. No conception of social welfare can conform to the five criteria Arrow put forward: they are contradictory. Here is a sketch of the proof.

[14] What follows mirrors, with minor modifications, the logical structure of the proof presented in Mueller (2003). Other proofs of the theorem could show the conditions are contradictory by insisting on another starting point, and leaving different criteria violated.

TABLE 17. *The Group Decisive for A, B Is Decisive for All Alternatives*

	Well-being of those		
Rank	in G_d(A,B)	All Others	Evaluative Conclusion and Justification
1	X	B	A>B by G_d(A,B)
			X>A by P & X>B by T. Hence G_d(X,B).
2	A	Y	B>Y by P
3	B	X	X>Y by T hence G_d (X,Y)
4	Y	A	

A Decisive Group over a Pair of Outcomes Is Decisive over All Pairs of Outcomes

By P, if everyone in the group is better off with policy A than policy B, then the group is better off with policy A than with B. Now let's see why any group decisive over one pair of outcomes is decisive over all pairs, given the other four desired conditions. Of course, not all decisive groups need be the whole group (think of a majority in a majoritarian system).

So there is necessarily a decisive group: the group as a whole. It is decisive over any pair. Perhaps it is intuitive that the group as a whole would be decisive always (see Footnote 12). But what about other decisive groups? How does coupling N, T, I, and U with P imply that any decisive group must be decisive over all policy pairs? To see this, begin by specifying our decisive group, as decisive over **A,B**: which I write as G_d(**A,B**). The situation is depicted in Table 17. The second column shows that everyone in G_d(**A,B**) would be better off with **A** than with **B**. The next column shows all the others would be worse off with **A** than with **B**. By definition of being decisive, **A** is evaluated as better for the society than **B**.

In the table, we actually display the ranking of two other outcomes: **X** and **Y**.[15] Option **X** has two properties. First, *everyone* is better off with **X** than with **A**: hence, by P, it must be the case that the community is better off with **X** than with **A**. Second, since our notion of social welfare is to conform to transitivity, **T**, and since **X** is better than **A**, and **A** is better than **B**, it follows that **X** is to be judged better than **B** for the community. But, only the members of G_d(**A,B**), the decisive group, are better off by **X** to **B**.

[15] Throughout the proof, we rely on universalism. It insures that we can compare *any* patterns of individual well-being to each other and reach a conclusion as to which, if either, of the two options generate more social welfare. So we select patterns of well-being that are convenient for our argument: ones that show the conflict between the qualities we have insisted upon.

Although we established this judgement by using transitivity it must be that, by **I**, only the well-being of the individuals with respect to **X** and **B** can determine the ranking of **X** with respect to **B**. Since this is required, examine the distribution of well-being in the community. Only members of G_d are better off with **X** than with **B**, yet the community is judged better off with **X** than with **B**. Thus, being decisive between a pair of alternatives (**A,B**) implies that the group will be decisive between any other **X** and **B**. We have thus established that given the requirements of **U**, **T**, **I**, and **P**, if $G_d(A,B)$, then $G_d(X,B)$.

Repeating this sort of argument will allow us to establish that any group decisive over one pair must be decisive over all pairs of policies. The next steps in the argument are outlined in column 4 of Table 17. So the subgroup $G_d(A,B)$ – decisive over one pair – is shown to be decisive over every pair or $G_d(X,Y)$ as long as we insist on satisfying the requirements of **U**, **T**, **I**, and **P**.

The Smallest Decisive Group Can Contain No More than a Single Individual

Using the same counterintuitive "tricks," I establish that if we insist on **T**, **I**, **U**, and **P**, the decisive group turns out to be a decisive individual, a conclusion that violates **N**. So insisting on a decisive group that is smaller than the whole community implies that there would have to be a dictator.

Now, how big is the smallest decisive set? Since there is a decisive set, there *must be* a smallest one, call it $G^*_d(X,Y)$, or G^*_d. There must be *someone* in that set, so let us identify one of those members of G^*_d as *i*. There may be others in G^*_d, but *i* certainly is in it (see Table 18).

In Table 18, the community's relative welfare regarding **X** and **Y** are determined by the decisive group, G^*_d. Everyone in G^*_d is better off with

TABLE 18. *The Decisive Group Is One Individual*

Rank	Well-being of those not in G^*_d	in $G^*_d(X,Y)$		Evaluative Conclusion and Justification
		i	All Others	
1	Y	X	Z	X>Y by G^*_d
2	Z	Y	X	not Z>Y by minimal G^*_d
3	X	Z	Y	X>Z by T

X (see the third and fourth columns). So **X** is judged to make the community better off than **Y**, even though those not in G^*_d are better off in **Y**. Now consider a third outcome, **Z**. We pick a **Z** that only is better than **Y** for those members of G^*_d who are distinct from i. Since G^*_d was the smallest decisive group, G^*_d without i can't be decisive. So it can't be that the welfare of the community is considered better with **Z** than with **Y**: **Y** is at least as good as **Z**. But **X** makes the community better off than **Y** and **Y** can't be worse than **Z**, then by transitivity **X** is better for the community than **Z**. But only i is better off with **X** than with **Z**. Hence, i gets her way in spite of everyone else being worse off.

So i alone is decisive; i must be the smallest decisive set. There can be no one else in G^*_d. This violates **N**. We conclude: any social welfare evaluation rule that supports our presumption that one can't make interpersonal comparisons of welfare can only generate evaluations of outcomes (beyond Pareto optimality) if it violates one or more of the five desired properties listed in Table 16.

Discussion of Arrow and Impossibility

Arrow's theorem is telling us something about collective welfare. His finding puts limitations on conceptions of collective interest and social welfare. It shows that we can't get beyond Pareto (i.e. that the decisive group is the whole community) if we don't make comparisons of individual welfare. Of course, to argue that we should make such comparisons does not tell us *how* to, or even whether we can, do it. But Arrow also has substantial implications for the work of political scientists who are concerned with the performance and design of democratic political institutions. Let's look at both of these threads before moving on.

The Result and the Notion of Group Interest

Arrow showed that *any* rule other than unanimity, or Pareto, that purports to aggregate the well-being of the members of a collective to arrive at a social welfare judgement will be fraught with difficulties. To get around this one must do one or more of the following: restrict the sorts of options considered, restrict the underlying pattern of individual welfare implications of those options (as when we considered the single-peaked preferences), or one must admit of interpersonal comparisons of well-being. Otherwise, it will be futile to generate a social welfare judgement on the basis of the well-being of the individuals that will be normatively attractive (i.e. conform to the other properties in Table 16).

Technically, Arrow established a contradiction between some desirable properties of social welfare when individuals' well-being can't be compared. At first many attacked the specific conditions used in his proof of the contradiction, but these attacks led to discoveries of similar theorems (well reviewed in Plott, 1976). Since his discovery in the late 1940s a vast literature has accumulated establishing that the findings are robust.

What to sacrifice (no interpersonal comparison or some of the five normative premises) is not answered by Arrow's analysis. These alternatives are implicitly considered in the discussion in the next section on collective choice. For example, the observation that there is tension between T and I can be partially overcome by relaxing T or I. But don't get the wrong impression, any weaker property of T that maintains some semblance of the common sense meaning of "better for the group" generates a weaker ability to order the outcomes. With weaker notions of ordering (relaxing T), the minimal size of the decisive group is no longer precisely one. Instead one gets conflicts with larger groups, such notions as an oligarchy (see Plott, 1976). Dropping I allows one to generate more flexible rules of voting (such as the Borda count, see page 213), but doesn't help us clarify what social welfare might be.

The deeper conclusion is that the quest for a social welfare function that contains an ordering metric reflecting "better for the group" is nonsensical without further consideration of the content of what "better for the group" means. And any fuller consideration of group interest is inexorably linked to interpersonal comparisons of individual welfare. This insight will lead us into a broader inquiry of distributive justice which we delve into in Chapter 10.

The Result and Normative Properties of Collective Choice

Arrow's theorem has as much to do with group choice as with social welfare. By replacing the notion of individual well-being with the notion of individual preference, we shift away from the concern of aggregating individual well-being to social welfare toward the aggregation of individual choices to a collective choice. This moves us from the world of social welfare to the world of voting. In this second interpretation, Arrow's theorem concerns the futility of choice mechanisms, constitutions, and voting rules to abide by all the properties in Table 16. Now in one interpretation in the voting context the theorem is finding that there are preference cycles (as discussed in Chapter 5, and violating T), and that these choice cycles are only broken arbitrarily. This stems from demanding

TABLE 19. *Preferences Supporting a Voting
Cycle with Majority Rule*

Rank	*i*	*j*	*K*
1st	A	B	C
2nd	B	C	D
3rd	C	D	A
4th	D	A	B

the same properties (**P, N, T, I,** and **U**) and hitting the same barriers of impossibility.[16]

So for example, the problem of "decision cycles" is a problem of violating **T**. In the case of majority rule these cycles can be generated by patterns of preferences of the sort displayed in Table 19. There a group of people (*i, j, k*) using majority rule would choose from among the four options (**A, B, C, D**) with preferences as shown in the table. Imagine they have a decision system that requires they consider their options in a pairwise fashion, where defeated motions cannot be reintroduced. The winner of each contest (the one that gets a majority) survives to "go against" the next undefeated option until only one option is left: the winner. Note immediately that with the preferences in the table, each of the options can lose: there is a majority that prefers some specific other outcome to each of the options: two voters (*i* and *k*) prefer **A** over **B**, *i* and *j* prefer **B** over **C**, all prefer **C** over **D**, and *j* and *k* prefer **D** over **A**.[17]

This sort of cycle has pernicious potential. The winning motion could be anything. What is chosen will be determined by something beyond preference; perhaps the order of the vote, or the structure of the agenda in a legislature. The latter would usually be a strategic choice controlled in part by a committee chairperson, or a party leader. So using the preferences in Table 19 as an example, with sufficient manipulation or bad luck, even **D**, the only Pareto suboptimal outcome could be chosen by the group, even

[16] We have seen that by confining the preferences in the group to those that support a dimension with single-peaked preferences (in violation of **U**) sensible outcomes can be generated with majority rule. Violating others of these conditions also brings relief. See the discussion on voting rules in Chapter 9.

[17] Condorcet identified cyclical preferences as a problem of majoritarian voting. In the next chapter I explore some of the ideas for alternative voting rules to try to ameliorate the underlying difficulties.

though the voters *unanimously* prefer C to D.[18] To see this, imagine a system in which defeated options are removed from further consideration and there is pairwise voting. For such a system to lead to an outcome of D, the agenda would have to be structured so that C is defeated by B. And then the survivor, B, would have to be paired against A. A could eliminate B, and D would be left to defeat A. And from what we have seen, in multidimensional cases, there will, in general, be the possibility of cyclic outcomes. In any case, it ought to be clear, in such a case:

1. There is no "stable" outcome.
2. The outcomes cycle.
3. Without further information, "winning" or "losing" carries no normative weight.

As argued in Chapter 5, not all combined preference patterns lead to cycles. So we could examine sets of preferences to see if they support a cycle, or not. One might wonder, what is the likelihood that a preference set supports a cycle? There have been many attempts to answer this second question and the results could be read ambiguously, but I believe the real message is not ambiguous.

We might assume preferences to be distributed "randomly" among the population and then ask what is the probability of a cycle? With three persons and three issues, it isn't very big. Only 12 of 216 (5.6 percent) possible "strong" preference rankings of the outcomes[19] support a cycle. So if preferences for three outcomes are randomly distributed among three voters, there is only a 5.6 percent chance of a cyclic outcome. Maintaining the presumption of random mixes of preferences, increasing the number of voters or outcomes increases the chance of a majority preference cycle greatly (Riker, 1982, p. 122).

But random mixes of preferences is a bizarre starting point. Take, for example, alternative patterns of dividing a dollar among three persons. If each person has purely selfish interests he might vote for a bigger share of the dollar over a smaller one. In such purely distributive problems (in general), proposals would cycle. An example is in Table 20 where, with majority rule, each proposal (represented by the payoffs on a line) beats the preceding one.[20] As we can see from the table, the selected outcomes

---

[18] In other words, even a Pareto-suboptimal outcome can be in a cycle.

[19] A strong preference is one without ties. Each person has six such orderings: x>y>z; x>z>y, and so on. And the total number of combinations possible is then 216 (6x6x6).

[20] This is strongly related to (i.e., can also be proved from) the theorem that there is no "core" (see p. 99) in any game purely about redistribution (see Luce and Raiffa, 1957).

TABLE 20. *Distributive Proposals that Cycle*

Possible Divisions of a $1 Among Three People		
i	j	k
1/3	1/3	1/3
1/2	1/2	0
0	2/3	1/4
1/3	1/3	1/3
2/5	0	1/2

support a cycle; no outcome is stable. A cycle can even include outcomes that are "inefficient," as in the third and fifth lines, where the total doesn't even add up to the whole dollar. More generally:

WHERE EACH VOTER IS FREE TO PROPOSE NEW ALTERNATIVES, PURELY DISTRIBUTIVE ISSUES CYCLE IF THE JUDGEMENTS ARE BASED ON SIMPLE SELF-INTEREST.

This means that the outcome would be determined by other factors, such as agenda control.

Were Harold Lasswell (1935) right, and politics was about "Who Gets What, When, and How," we might have started this volume deriving this conclusion. But politics is about many things, and in legislative matters they often involve trades between representatives: "I'll support your bill, if you'll support mine." But such vote swapping and log-rolling can be only effective in changing a losing outcome to one which wins when underlying it is a similar cyclic preference pattern. In general:

EFFECTIVE VOTE-TRADING REQUIRES AN UNDERLYING CYCLIC PREFERENCE PATTERN.

(Schwartz, 1981)

More generally, when there are cyclic preferences underlying a collective choice, and that appears to be quite often, we can conclude:

POLITICAL OUTCOMES ARE NOT EXPLICABLE BY THE PREFERENCES OF THE VOTERS AND THE VOTING RULES ALONE. RATHER EXPLANATION REQUIRES CONSIDERATION OF THE STRATEGIES VOTERS CHOOSE, ALONG WITH THE RULES OF THE POLITICAL INSTITUTIONS THAT GOVERN THE AGENDA.

These are the sorts of conclusions brought to us by the examination of Arrow's theorem when it is applied to the world of voting. But by showing that we can't gain all the desired properties he laid out, Arrow is begging the question of whether we can specify a worthy set of achievable values and engineer systems of collective choice that can help us secure the democratic dream of tying social welfare to social choice. That is the subject of the next two chapters.

CHAPTER 9

Voting Rules

Democratic collective choice, as we have noted, is about aggregating disparate choices made by individuals so as to determine which outcomes will be selected by and for a group. How these individual choices are aggregated, and hence how the outcome is chosen, is defined by what we call voting rules. All of us know about a few different voting rules: majority rule, special majority rule (e.g., 2/3 majoritarian rules), and simple plurality rule (the item with the most votes wins, whether a majority or not). From the arguments by Kenneth Arrow and the work of other social choice theorists, we know that we won't be able to obtain all the properties that we might desire from any such "decision system." Real-world political arrangements must be a compromise.

Here, rather than examining many different voting rules to identify and compare their properties, I will develop a comparison of a handful of systems. Of course we shall examine what each precisely demands to declare a winner. We will also specify some desireable properties so we can compare the rules in terms of their likelihood of delivering "good results." Perhaps the reader should keep in mind that most times (as described in Chapter 4), not selecting a winner doesn't mean all sides lose: rather, usually, this maintains the status quo. We begin by considering the nature of one of the most ubiquitously utilized voting procedures: majority rule. Analyzing it gives us an idea of the achievable.

DEFINING THE ACHIEVABLE

Majority Rule When There Are but Two Alternatives

Consider a simplified group choice problem: a group is to make a choice of one from a pair of alternatives (say X and Y). Each voter either prefers X to Y, the reverse, or is indifferent between them. Kenneth May (1952) showed, in what is usually referred to as May's Theorem, that majority rule is the *only* decision rule that, when applied to voting on a pair of alternatives, has the following four desirable characteristics:

1. Decisive: It is always capable of concluding that either one or the other is chosen, or they are tied.
2. Anonymity: The outcome does not depend upon *who* cast which vote.
3. Neutrality: The outcome is independent of the labeling of the alternatives and only dependent upon the pattern of preferences over the alternatives by the individual voters.
4. Positive Responsiveness: If one individual changes her mind and becomes more supportive of an alternative (say X) and no one else changes their vote, then if X was tied previously, it would now win and if it won earlier, it would still do so.

Issues of *transitivity* are avoided by requiring that we only are worried about making decisions among one pair of options. We also rule out Arrow's problems of *independence* by the frame of the problem: translating only preferences over X and Y to a group choice between the pair.

But note that we can't be too greedy: if we want these four conditions, then only majority rule is available. As noted, majority rule doesn't perform as simply with more than two alternatives. Further, majority rule includes no incentive to develop moderate alternatives. The very threat of a "tyranny of the majority" is often used to rally support for reform of voting rules.

More than Two Alternatives

Having more than two alternatives complicates many things. And it is this more complicated scenario that has led to the development of multiple voting rules. Most of the rules that have been developed act like majority rule if there are only two alternatives. But when there are more than two alternatives, a number of other properties of the rules can become salient. For example, with numerous alternatives, different voting rules require more or less information from the individual voter. And recall that these voters are often wilfully and woefully ignorant (see the discussion of rational ignorance in Chapter 3).

What a voter needs to know to cast a vote is ambiguous. For example, to cast a full and effective ballot in a plurality system, you might think one need only know what outcome is her favorite and cast a vote for it. Certainly, voting for someone with a plurality voting rule can't hurt the chances of the selected individual winning. But what if there were a few candidates, and the voter's most preferred candidate were a sure loser in the polls (e.g., Ralph Nader in the Gore/Bush 2000 presidential election in Florida)? Then, the voter might find her second or third candidate worthy of support, since one of them might have a chance and could block what the voter might believe to be a heinous alternative. With two candidates, this doesn't come up. But how much information the voter needs to have to cast a maximally effective ballot clearly varies when there are more than two alternatives.

And precisely what information is needed varies by voting rules. For example, there are a bunch of rules, usually referred to as "ranking rules," that require more than one choice by the voter. Consider the eponymous ***Borda count.***[1]

Borda's proposal was put forward to get around the problem of voting cycles that Condorcet discovered and we described in Chapter 5. His suggestion was for each voter to rank the alternative outcomes. Each ranking would receive a score and the scores derived from each voter's ballot would be added up. To illustrate, if there were four alternatives, each voter would rank the four, and points would be allocated as follows: 3 for a first-place ranking, 2 for a second-place ranking, and 1 for a third-place ranking. Then the points each alternative received from each voter are added together. The alternative with the highest score wins. Such a system would obviously prevent cycles. But to make a full and informed choice on the ballot, the voter needs to know not only her first choice, but her rank-order preference for all choices.

From the discussion of Arrow, we know that all voting rules, including the Borda count, must violate some of the desired characteristics of aggregation. Borda violates Arrow's condition I.[2] Since the score each outcome

---

[1] This was proposed by the mathematician and engineer, Jean-Charles de Borda, who was one of Condorcet's (see Footnote 2, Chapter 4) colleagues analyzing problems of governance prior to the French Revolution.

[2] Recall that I, or independence, requires that the pairwise ranking of alternatives, for the group, does not depend upon the existence (or non-existence) of other policies that are to be ranked.

TABLE 21. *The Borda Count Violates Independence*

Points	i	j	k	Total Scores
	I. A Two-way Contest between A and B: A Wins			
1	A	B	A	A = 2 (wins)
0	B	A	B	B = 1
	II. A Four-way Contest between A, B, C and D: B Wins			
3	A	B	A	A = 6
2	B	C	B	B = 7 (wins)
1	C	D	C	C = 4
0	D	A	D	D = 1

receives from a Borda count depends upon its ranking, the relative ranking of A and B could be effected by other alternatives. Table 21 gives an illustration to demonstrate the problem. In the table, we consider three voters, *i*, *j*, and *k*, who are to decide among four alternatives using the Borda count. To begin with, note that if they were only considering the two alternatives, A and B, A would beat B. This is shown in the top portion of the table.

Now expand the contest to a four-way struggle, introducing two other alternatives, C, and D as in the next section of the table. Each member of the group is assumed to maintain their same preferences with regard to A and B. But now, given the full preferences of the three individuals over A and B as well as two other alternatives, C, and D, we can see that the group would choose B over A. This is a clear violation of I. Just as in the plurality race with Nader, Gore, and Bush, the outcome can be "manipulated" by putting in more or fewer alternatives. With plurality, the alternatives can "split the vote," while with the Borda count, and other ranking procedures, changing the number of alternatives can alter the relative scores.[3]

Parallel to May's theorem (page 212), Peyton Young (1974) identified the unique positive properties that define the Borda count. Three of the five conditions are similar to three of those used by May to characterize majority rule. The five are:

[3] It is of interest to note that violating I may have different gravitas when it is a property for a voting rule and when it is a property for a notion of social welfare. It is hard to understand what we might mean by "better" when we are comparing possible outcomes and our "measuring tool" gives different results between two items when we introduce a third. This might not be considered so "serious" a normative matter in a voting rule.

1. Ability to define the set of best outcomes (choice set): Similar to May's decisiveness but extended to situations where we may have a number of best alternatives.
2. Neutrality: As in May's theorem, the outcome is independent of the labeling of the alternatives and only depends upon the pattern of preferences over the alternatives by the individual voters.
3. Cancellation: Similar to May's anonymity condition, ensuring that the voters' identities don't matter.
4. Faithfulness: Were there but one voter, the rule would choose the voter's most preferred option.
5. Consistency: If two groups, voting separately over the same options, were each to select the same option for their group, then, were the votes combined into a single electorate, the outcome chosen would be that same option.

Again, we can gain some very specific, desirable properties with the adoption of a particular rule. But other properties can also be compared. For example, the upshot of each voter giving weight to her second and further choices also implies that Borda, like other ranking systems, also contains a reduced threat of a tyranny of the majority. But we can also see that the attractive qualities of the Borda count depend upon the properties of the agenda control system in the polity. Without a "good" system of control of the items on the agenda, one can introduce items strategically, and hence subvert the positive properties of Borda.

Another Property We Might Hope For: Condorcet Efficiency

We have already shown that there are times when there are voting cycles when no one alternative can beat all others. But when there is no cycle, and one outcome can beat all the others, we might expect, and desire, that our voting rule would pick the outcome that can beat all the others. Such an alternative is referred to as a Condorcet winner (see Footnote 2, Chapter 4). But under just the right conditions, all voting rules that don't require a pairwise voting tournament can fail at this.

For example, take a plurality rule, with a number of alternatives on the agenda. An example is shown in Table 22 where a simple plurality rule does not choose the Condorcet winner. The obvious plurality winner is **Y** (it is the only alternative to get more than one first-place vote). But **Z** is the Condorcet winner (it beats **X** 4-to-1 and **W** and **Y** 3-to-2). Plurality rules, although particularly bad at this, aren't the only ones that can't reliably

TABLE 22. *Condorcet Criteria*

Rank	Voters				
	i	*j*	*k*	*l*	*m*
1	W	X	Y	Z	Y
2	Z	W	Z	X	Z
3	Y	Z	X	Y	X
4	X	Y	W	W	W

select Condorcet winners. Indeed, no rule can ensure that a Condorcet winner, if one exists, will be selected under all profiles of voter preferences except pairwise voting. We might hope our arrangements pick a Condorcet winner when it exists, at least most of the time. As such we can propose a desired property of a voting rule: that it is Condorcet efficient. In other words, we would prefer one rule over another, all else equal, if it led to Condorcet winners being chosen a higher percentage of times. We refer to the relative performance on this criteria as **Condorcet efficiency**. One of the more Condorcet-efficient rules is the Borda count (see Cervone, et al.). Note that here the Borda count would give Z, the Condorcet winner, the maximum score (10).

This allows us to consider the relative Condorcet efficiency of the rules that we have already talked about. To do that, we would need to presume various bits of information: the number of voters and alternatives and the distribution of preferences over the alternatives. Usually random distribution of preferences is presumed for such comparisons.[4] Results would obviously vary with the number of options that are on the agenda: when there are two items, all the voting rules choose the Condorcet winner. With more than two alternatives, plurality is particularly poor in its selection of winners and its efficiency falls off quite steeply with increasing agenda items.[5]

More Relaxed Systems

Given the problems with demanding too much from the voter and the difficulties that majoritarian and plurality rules have, a number of attempts have been made to design alternative procedures. Two stand

[4] See Table 7.4 in Mueller (2003), p. 150 for an example of such calculations.
[5] Other evaluative criteria are also considered in Mueller, 2003.

out in terms of their spirit of consensus-building without asking very much of the voter: voting by veto (Mueller, 1978) and approval voting (Brams and Fishburn, 1978). Both of these are developed to get around some of the problems that were discovered in traditional voting systems. They are less susceptible to manipulation, and can quite easily ensure that the outcome chosen is likely to be a Paretian improvement.

Voting by Veto

In this two-stage system, to make collective choices each voter gets to propose an alternative to the status quo and then, when all the alternatives are "on the table," each voter gets to veto one alternative. The order of voting is generated randomly and it matters: someone else who votes before you do may veto your least desired outcome, the one you would have vetoed. That would allow you to veto another item you do not like. Since the number of alternatives will be one more than the number of voters (the status quo is always one of the items in the agenda) there will be one survivor. This sort of voting rule is not likely to work in large groups where it would be difficult to get a sequence of voting specified and implemented. But in small committees the procedure has some nice properties. Each voter would be best served by trying to place a "reasonable" proposal on the agenda, since the more people who dislike it, the more likely it would be to be vetoed. Given the randomized order of voting, what is vetoed, and hence the result, is probabilistic. The chance of an outcome's survival depends upon how many others view it more favorably than its alternatives. Hence, voters will tend to put forward alternatives to the status quo that others will like. This is intuitive but also easily shown by considering a specific example, given in Table 23.

TABLE 23. *Voting by Veto and Moderation in Choice*

Proposals	Voters' Preference Orderings		
	i	*j*	*k*
p^1	First	Fourth	Third
p^2	Third	First	Fourth
p^3	Second	Second	First
Sq	Fourth	Third	Second

There, each player is likely to propose something he prefers to the status quo.[6] In the example, we might presume that p^1 has been proposed by i, p^2 by j, and p^3 by k. Presumably, each voter plans to veto his worst choice. In this example, those worst outcomes are different for each voter so each voter will eliminate a different one. For example, p^2 is certain to be vetoed by voter k if no one else has already vetoed it. Indeed, any proposal considered worse than the status quo by everyone except the proposer will be vetoed. The others are then more likely to be viable alternatives that survive. Which will actually be the chosen alternative? Voter i will certainly veto the status quo, voter k will take out p^2, and voter j will eliminate p^1. In this case, we have a Pareto improvement. Voting by veto ensured that those items that were worst for each player were eliminated. The system tends to select outcomes that are ranked highly in the voters' preferences. Any proposal that really hurts a number of voters is quite surely eliminated. Here we see directly the relationship between agenda formation (which possibilities will be proposed) and the rule of selection. It is the very possibility of the voters' vetoes that generates proposals' with "nice" properties.

We can see more of the voting rule's properties by considering a distributive issue. Imagine that the committee of three are to divide a certain amount among themselves. Then any proposal that leaves little or nothing to a particular member is likely to be eliminated by that member. Another less desirable property can be readily seen by focusing on redistributive issues. Imagine 3 persons of quite equal wealth. They decide to use voting by veto to decide on how to distribute their wealth. If two of the three voters form a coalition, they can ensure that the third will be hurt. For example, let the proposals be a status quo (no redistribution), p^1 and p^2; similarly, divide k's wealth more or less equally between i and j. Let k's proposal, p^3, be divide the wealth equally. Then we know i and j can get their way to grab k's wealth. But any voting rule may lead to this sort of conundrum if agenda items are not constrained by such principles as property rights.

Voting by veto puts emphasis on what you surely *don't* want. A similar motivation is behind a more positive proposal: approval voting. But approval voting asks voters to cast positive votes, rather than negative votes.

---

[6] Only likely because we can imagine circumstances as follows: one voter loves the status quo – it is her most preferred outcome. But others can be predicted to veto the status quo and, hence, she may propose her second best.

Approval Voting

In approval voting, each voter can be faced with a set of k alternatives. The voter then casts up to k votes: one for each of the items that she would approve. In this case, the voter has a similar motive to vote against (by not casting an approval vote for) the things she dislikes. The item which most people approve of gets passed. In this sense, it demands less of the voter than the Borda count system. Rather than demanding a full ranking of all the alternatives, the approval vote system merely requires that the voters know what is acceptable and what is not.

As such, it is hard to predict the Condorcet efficiency of approval voting. Consider, for example, the situation depicted in Table 22. If each of the voters only find her first choice acceptable, then Y would be accepted and the Condorcet winner, Z, would be rejected. However, assuming a randomized threshold for the voters, approval voting does adequately on this score, but not as well as rank voting methods such as the Borda count.

The lesson to take away is that we can't design rules without problems, but we can distinguish between rules that are more or less Condorcet efficient, that are more or less likely to choose compromise outcomes, and are more or less likely to privilege the status quo. Or,

THE CHOICE OF VOTING RULES WILL MAKE A SUBSTANTIAL DIFFERENCE IN THE QUALITY, RESPONSIVENESS, AND STABILITY OF THE OUTCOMES THAT THE GROUP CHOOSES.

THE ROLE OF DISCUSSION AND DELIBERATION

All formal voting systems have implicit some notion of interpersonal comparisons: a setting of equality of importance for yea and nay votes in majoritarian systems; equality of rank in ranking systems; equality of the notion of acceptability and non-acceptability in both approval voting and voting by veto, and so on. Such an interpersonal accounting, either explicit or implicit, is required for any aggregation. But once we are in real-life situations, and preferences refer to real differences in real gains and losses to individuals, votes do not usually capture enough information to give certainty to the hope that the winning side is the best for the society.

Discussion and deliberation give weight to some of the substance that lies behind the preferences and hence improves collective decision making. Most public decisions are made by votes cast in an environment of public deliberation and disputation. Such communication inevitably is multifaceted. Public discussion involves both articulating one's positions and having others hear those positions. It involves sharing both the discussion space and the content of the discussion. It is hard to see how interests are to be responded to unless individuals can signal these interests to others. Markets and votes are but two methods. And usually, prior to either market transactions, or votes, discussion is the precursor of decision making.

Discussion itself is liable to alter the sorts of items that are on the agenda as well as the positions that are taken by the individuals involved. David Miller (1991) has argued persuasively[7] that one can expect preferences to change by deliberation. These changes are likely to reduce the risk of cyclic preferences. For example, in smaller groups such as legislative committees, or even legislatures, issues of redistribution may be hard to discuss publicly from a purely self-interested point of view. Instead, the disputants are likely to adopt a more impartial point of view. By restricting the extent of self-interested discussion, deliberation can cut down on cycles and foster the adoption of less extreme outcomes. Deliberation may even generate more single-peaked one-dimensional issues as discussion may lead to a separating out of subsidiary issues (dimensions). This could lead to an increased tendency of median voter outcomes. And if each dimension is decided separately, it could tend to the median in each dimension winning.

This more nuanced conception of democratic decision making contrasts with the social choice conception of democracy as the simple aggregation of fixed individual preferences. The deliberative conception of democracy is of a process of open discussion leading to an agreed judgement on policy. Social choice theory has identified problems – the arbitrariness of outcome choice given voting rules, the vulnerability of choice to strategic consider-ations – which are often held to undermine the democratic ideal of respon-siveness of social choice to the needs of group members. Deliberative democracy may reduce the vulnerability of actual liberal democratic systems by inducing a shared understanding of the dimensions of conflict. Hence, the process of discussion may produce policy preferences that are single-peaked; and within a deliberative setting it may even be possible to vary the decision rule according to the nature of the issue to be decided. As such, Miller's conception of deliberative democracy is quite attractive.

But not every instance of deliberation would result in a consensus, nor even in a less contentious decision. Votes would still be required, and the problems of social choice will still crop up. Miller points to two major advantages of a deliberative model (p. 83): first, preferences that are purely self-interested will tend to be eliminated by public debate, since they will

----

[7] See also Dryzek and List (2002), and Knight and Johnson (1994).

have to be justified rationally. And second, discussion tends to activate norms by "inducing participants to think of themselves as forming a certain kind of group."

Miller's insights don't suggest discussion is a panacea. He develops no way to get around debates where there are fundamental or moral imperative differences, such as those over abortion or gay marriage, where participants tend to polarize either to one side or another, and rational argument has no swaying effect.[8] But he certainly is correct that discussion is an element that we need to consider further when we look at the properties of political systems. Indeed, the fruitful discussion requires meeting some conditions.[9] Claims of needs, depravation, and injustice involve complicated statements regarding situations of individuals in particular contexts and circumstances. Such claims can only be made, heard, and evaluated with open communication and discussion. As originally argued (see page 186), to get to a more serious evaluation of social welfare we must go beyond the notion of no interpersonal comparison of welfare and value. Any interpersonal comparisons require that we consider those of our values that go beyond simple self-interest. If we are concerned of deprivations and injustices borne by others it must be that we are not self-interested but other-regarding. To reflect such other-regarding feelings, we need to consider social welfare as more than a simple aggregation of some non-interactive individual well-being and think of the quality of the social fabric that connects all of us. Discovering the impact of possible outcomes on this more complicated notion of welfare requires a deep commitment to communication[10] if we are to get to a basis for interpersonal comparison and, hence, beyond the barriers reflected in Kenneth Arrow's seminally negative findings.

IN CONCLUSION

In the spirit of some institutionalists in political science, I might have pursued a more complete comparison of voting rules to identify the

---

[8] See Skitka and Houston (2001) for interesting insights into these cases.

[9] Jurrgen Habermas has developed a conception of both democracy and justice by putting verbal communication at the center of his analysis. See his 1996 collection of essays for an introduction.

[10] Given the previous discussion of preference revelation, one must ask how important honesty is in communication. Substantial work has been done on this (and the associated role of "cheap talk") in the literature of "signaling games." To pursue this would lead us astray, but see Kreps (1990) for a basic discussion.

desirable qualities and limitations each system has.[11] At this point, we have mentioned two formal criteria, Pareto optimality and Condorcet efficiency, in the way of benchmarks to apply to any comparative analysis. In addition, different rules impose different demands upon voters in how much they must report about their preferences. We have also noted that discussion can perhaps ameliorate some of the problems that are inherent in some cyclic preference situations. We have also considered the decrease in the threat of the tyranny of the majority that ranking and approval systems can generate.

It should be clear now that what counts as appropriate rules will depend upon setting: the size and nature of the body. Legislatures and committees are quite different than electorates. Legislative committees have endogenously morphing agendas and discussions. Elections involve fixed agenda items. These differences matter greatly in selecting sensible rules for aggregating votes. We found, for example, some rules, such as voting by veto, are truly not sensible in large groups.

And if voting rules must be thought about in their contexts, so, too, should the nature of discussion. We must ask, what is the incentive for honesty, compromise, and other values, in the context of the discussion. We have all experienced situations in which discussion has led to more, rather than less, extremist positions being articulated: just think of American talk radio.

Finally, nothing can prevent voting from taking a nasty turn. As pointed out in the voting by veto example, voters can gang up and hurt a losing coalition. Side constraints, or rights, such as property rights, must limit the content of collective choice in order to ensure that politics doesn't become a losing game for segments of the population that are vulnerable.

But pursuing the formal properties of voting rules leaves out the substantive nature of a recognizable, and acceptable, conception of social welfare. If the goal of governments in democratic societies is the well-being of its citizens, then we must be concerned in the identity of this aggregate and its relation to the rules of collective choice. Therefore, rather than focus further on the cataloguing of comparisons of rules, I turn to identify the substantive nature of social welfare in democracies.

---

[11] Such comparisons are available elsewhere, as in Shepsle and Bonchek, 1997, and in Wikipedia's article "Voting Systems."

CHAPTER 10

Social Welfare and Social Justice: A Partial Integration

A sensible notion of social welfare does not come without some sort of interpersonally comparable well-being. On the other hand, collective choice rules can be designed to improve the chance that a democracy achieves good things for its citizens. But without being more specific in stipulating what constitutes social welfare, our measuring rod for identifying "good things" disappears just when we would wish to use it. Further, merely noting that interpersonal comparisons of individual well-being are needed to gain traction over social welfare doesn't tell us *how* to make the comparisons. Without more details, how can we tie our notions of collective choice to social welfare? How are we to get around the problems Arrow identified? That is the focus of this chapter.

TO AGGREGATE OR NOT TO AGGREGATE: A FALSE DILEMMA

Arrow's negative finding stems from his insistence that what is being aggregated are either individual preferences or something very similar to that: an indicator of well-being with ordinal properties of consistency but no basis for interpersonal comparisons. This is a relatively unfortunate, if realistic, assessment of the problem of social choice. After all, voting rules only aggregate some shadow of the rankings of proposals by voters in some way. To make a social choice, the rules aggregate very limited individual information. Any conception of social welfare must utilize a more complex mix of inputs than voting rules utilize.

A great body of political and ethical theory is devoted to the problem of what are the right goals for governments. One substantial subset of these, "consequentialist" theories (see Footnote 14, Chapter 1), argues the goals are to enhance the well-being of the citizens. But the problem of aggregation bedevils them. How to aggregate the well-being of two different people? The classical answer, by such utilitarians as Mill and Bentham, to "add their happiness together," is unacceptable. Not only can't we add these items, but the substance underlying the concept of happiness is not comparable: we can't measure the happiness in an individual and compare it quantitatively to that of another.[1]

On the other hand, we can't just throw up our hands and give up on aggregation. That would be tantamount either to giving up the challenge and declaring social welfare to be an incoherent concept, or to putting forward a notion of social welfare built on something entirely different, such as the glory of the state or its stability. Many popular indicators of social welfare, such as economic performance, individual liberties, procedural fairness, political responsiveness, or the securing of just deserts also require aggregation. To illustrate, let us take as an indicator of social welfare "procedural fairness."

We can have procedural fairness at the bureau of motor vehicles – everyone must stand in line, mail their forms in for processing, or go online to renew their driver's license. But we may have more limited procedural fairness when it comes to having access to appealing a court decision. So, for example, there may be no lawyer available to the poorer persons in the society. Hence procedural fairness (and any of the other "indicator") must be aggregated both across types (court, motor vehicle administration) and across affected persons. Since we are concerned with social welfare in general, clearly we can't avoid aggregation. Nor is the structure of social welfare to be viewed as a simple quantity, such as the length of a piece of thread. It is obviously a tapestry, to be judged by its overall quality.

WHO IS TO SPECIFY WHAT TO AGGREGATE?

Where, then, are we to look for the stuff to aggregate? And once we find it, how are we to proceed? On this there may be many answers. I have already indicated that each regime may give quite distinct answers to such a question. Perhaps we must be more permissive and note that a democracy is all about letting its own population define its own goals. Every

---

[1] The current efforts to measure the happiness of citizens of different countries around the world belie this to some degree (Veenhoven, 2009).

democratic group must express itself and its own needs and desires. Such a view, that the notion of social welfare will emerge *endogenously* from the preferences and political institutions of the society, is, at first blush, attractive to a democrat.[2] But it is also problematic.

Given that democratic institutions partially determine the outcomes that can be obtained, to justify a particular endogenous notion of social welfare one has to assume a starting point for the political process. If the starting point is an historic accident, then, the outcome merely would reflect all sorts of inequities that existed prior to and at the beginning of the decision process. And why should such happenstances privilege a particular definition of social welfare, or even its path of development? And must we begin with a fair procedure for a group to define its own notion of social welfare? Unless we have a fixed and justified criterion for fair, we prejudice the outcome by the definition of fair. Indeed, the method of selecting a concept of social welfare will certainly help determine the outcome of the debate. To simply kowtow to democratic predispositions and leave each society to define social welfare for itself means that social welfare remains a relativized concept.

An alternative is to tie some minimal conditions to notions of social welfare and give them a prioritization in the scheme of things. This is, for example, what is done in the American political system, where our constitution limits the possibilities of governmental action. Such side constraints prioritize human liberties such as those specified in the Bill of Rights above the government's solving of the everyday political problems of the society. In an analogous fashion, what is being proposed is that some elements of social welfare be prioritized as more fundamental than others. They would help measure social achievement and what is needed much as a triage system helps us understand how to evaluate the operating of a hospital: the timely and successful handling of a patient's broken finger has a lesser priority than the handling of another's heart attack.

The trick, then, is to identify those elements which ought to be foundational elements of any measure of social welfare in a democracy. Such fundamental elements would not prevent each society from establishing its own goals, but rather would specify those goals that are fundamental to all democracies and give them a status lexicographically prior[3] to other goals that might well further improve the well-being of the members of the society.

---

[2] Endogeneity as the way out is put forward in Schotter (1990).
[3] A lexicographic ordering is dictionary-like. All the things in category "A" come before those in category "B".

LOOKING TO SOCIAL JUSTICE TO FIND SOCIAL WELFARE

What elements must serve as the spine of social welfare? I propose that to find them, we search the theories of social justice. Of course, such theories are not all in agreement and hence it might appear that I am about to cherry-pick a conception of social welfare to satisfy my own predilections. But this is not the case. Konow (2003) identifies three main classes of theories of social justice: those that begin with a presumption of impartial reasoning; those that are concerned with effort, reward, and just deserts; and those that are concerned with the maximization of an aggregate, such as the utilitarians.

The centrality of impartiality in any notion of fairness and justice can't be overemphasized. To arrive at any judicious measure of justice one must skim off the self-interested partiality from one's judgements. Indeed, my major criticism of anchoring one's notion of social welfare in the legislative definition arrived at democratically (see the previous section) was based on this.

Of course, there is more than one way to take an impartial point of view. Institutionally one can imagine impartial experts (judges), outside observers or arbitrators, or individuals just adopting a stance of empathy to gain impartiality prior to evaluating their options. And these different procedures may yield differing outcomes. On the other hand, even similar procedures can lead to differing conclusions.

So, for example, Rawls (1971) and Harsanyi (1953), Economics Nobel laureate in 1994, reach fundamentally differing conclusions in trying to discover fairness in distribution; yet they utilize a very similar impartial point of view. Both presume individuals are to decide on a distributive rule from a vantage point that deprives them of their own interests. Rawls argues that under such conditions individuals would adopt a rule to maximize the well-being of the worst off in the group. Harsanyi, using virtually the same mechanism, concludes individuals would want to maximize their expected value and hence choose policies that maximize the average well-being of members of the society.

Others, such as Hayek (1960) and Nozick (1974), opposing such impartial reasoning as starting points, put their emphasis on just deserts for productive effort. Presuming the just deserts position to be antithetical to those of Rawls and Harsanyi, Nozick argues that any call for a patterned distribution would prove to be unstable. Once impartial reasoning gave way to real world life, self-interest would kick in, and the support for the impartially reasoned choice would collapse. Instead, rewards for productivity plus fairness in property transfers (as ensured by a system of property rights, markets, gifts, and so on) would ensure that the system yielded fair results. Although some exceptions were made to subsidize those who had to be included in the group (for reasons of geography, etc.), public goods were generally to be obtained via membership in clubs and associations in which one paid for what one got.

These two approaches to the understanding of social justice have, however, developed into a less confrontational melding of ideas. This came about serendipitously from research developed from the dialogue regarding interpersonal comparisons of well-being and the plurality of ideas as to what might occur from impartial reasoning regarding justice. For years economists have devalued the notion of using social welfare as a metric (Hausman, 2008) with arguments resting on two axioms: 1) We cannot compare the happiness of two individuals; and 2) Each individual is sufficiently unique that we must give up seeking a substantive definition of welfare. We must revert, they say, to preference satisfaction. As Hausman puts it:

There are many theories of well-being, and the prevailing view among economists themselves has shifted from hedonism (which takes the good to be a mental state such as pleasure or happiness) to the view that welfare is the satisfaction of preferences. Unlike hedonism, taking welfare to be the satisfaction of preference specifies how to find out what is good for a person rather than committing itself to any substantive view of a person's good.

We then are not to judge whether the satisfaction of one preference is more desirable than that of another. Again, Hausman:

Because the preference satisfaction view of welfare makes it questionable whether one can make interpersonal welfare comparisons, few economists defend a utilitarian view of policy as maximizing total or average welfare. (Harsanyi is one exception; for another, see Ng 1983.) Economists have instead explored the possibility of making welfare evaluations of economic processes, institutions, outcomes, and policies without making interpersonal comparisons.

But philosophers weren't all convinced; Rawls's view was clear: we can identify the worst off, and know when her conditions were ameliorated. There is a long history of argumentation regarding the non-comparability of the welfare between persons. Many of these arguments carry great weight. These arguments establish both the difficulties of making comparisons and the justifications of requiring actions that favour one person over another. But those arguments lose their force when confronted with most cases of great depravation regarding basic needs.

A WELFARE FLOOR TO GUARANTEE BASIC NEEDS

A notion of obligation to meet the needs of citizens supports the development of a useful metric for interpersonal comparisons of well-being. The reasons for this are straightforward and are justified both theoretically and empirically.

Sen (1973, 1992) argues that the metric we use in interpersonal comparisons comes from empathy. Many casual observations of reputed differences in well-being do not grab your attention. But people everywhere are especially attentive to observations of those who can't get their basic needs met. It may be nice, and welfare-enhancing for you, gentle reader, to get a fine new cotton shirt to replace the faded one you still often wear. But you are likely to agree the change in welfare from such an addition to your wardrobe does not rival that which would obtain were the shirt to go to a person who has never had a new shirt and seems currently to have none at all. Satisfying the basic needs of an individual so that she can survive and function versus satisfying less basic desires generally sets up an unusually easy comparison. Supporting individuals' basic needs facilitates adjudicating between satisfying individual preferences and increasing social welfare. You realize this by hypothetically placing yourself in their shoes and considering your evaluation of the difference that the shirt would make to you were you but in the other's circumstances.

At times, empathy fails. And then other forms of impartial reasoning can be used to check for the claim that we *know* that "basic needs" must be given a special status. Sen (2009) adds that impartial outside observers bring further understanding and light to disputes regarding what is really needed, or what is right, or fair. Prejudices may make empathy more difficult or even inoperable. Hence, an impartial outsider with other experiences, from another society without those prejudices, might be needed to supplement simple empathy. In any case, meeting basic needs or necessities, when they are identified, is compellingly different than preference satisfaction.

Toward a Theory of Social Justice

In many ways, John Rawls (1971) reinserted the problem of social welfare into our political lexicon by linking it to social justice. He asserted that social justice rested on fairness, and linked fairness with impartiality. But

Rawls developed a more complicated path of impartial reasoning: a thought experiment that he believed justified that social welfare should be judged in terms of the welfare of the least fortunate. Rawls imagined representative individuals charged with choosing, "from behind a veil of ignorance" (and hence, stripped of their interests), a way of developing a foundational law for an as yet unknown society which they were to inhabit. The law, he argued, would include basic political and economic rights. Those would include an understanding prioritizing economic distribution.

Ignorance of what roles were to exist in the new society, and which roles the individuals would occupy in the society, leads each to associate her lot impartially with those of all others in the society. This, Rawls argued, channels rational self-interest in the direction of justice and fairness. As such, the result of such reasoning would be a foundational theory of social justice. Borrowing from game theoretic arguments, Rawls presumed individuals would choose a policy that would want to maximize their welfare were they to receive their worst possible outcome. People would select a principle that would maximize the welfare of the worst off individual in the society. He called this notion the "difference principle."

But we might conjecture that an individual's concern with the worst off individual would be motivated by the substance of her deprivation, rather than by her rank. After all, there is a cost to all such policies: maximizing the benefits to the worst off must have some negative consequences for others. However, Rawls' emphasis on the welfare of the poorest allowed him to skirt the issue of "preferences" altogether by classifying certain goods (called "primary goods") as warranting "special" consideration. He did not explicitly focus on "needs," but they seem implicit in his discussion.

Rawls' argument can be reformulated as stemming from two premises: one normative, and one positive:

The Normative Premise: Exercising impartial reasoning will generate fairness which is at the root of justice.

The Positive Premise: Stripped of self-interest and cultural backgrounds, people using impartial reasoning all will have the same preferences and behavior. Therefore, they will be able to decide things with unanimity.

These premises were then used to generate five conjectures.

1. Individuals would always wish, and be able to, negotiate a unanimous foundational agreement before entering an unknown society.
2. In that agreement, individuals will first ensure individual liberties and as long as there is at least moderate scarcity; they would also

unanimously agree to a redistributive contract rather than enter the new unknown environment and start living in it as one of a multitude.

3. This contract would always be the same.
4. The contract would always maximize the welfare of the worst off (the difference principle).
5. The contract would be a stable framework for subsequent details once the individuals were living in this new environment and were no longer behind a veil of ignorance.

Others (Braybrooke, 1987; Doyle and Gough, 1991) have taken a different, but related, tack. They argue that any fair response leads to ensuring that basic needs of all members of society are met.

Sen (1993, 2009) has built a theory quite parallel to a basic needs approach but one which goes further. In a sense he personalizes, and extends, the notion of needs. This extension is reinterpreted by him as capabilities. Capabilities are the individual's abilities "to do things he or she has reason to value" (Sen, 2009, p. 231). Basic needs would have to be satisfied before we can expect an individual to have the abilities to accomplish other things beyond existence that they have reason to value. As such, capabilities reflect the personal conditions of the individual, as well as her talents, resources, and goals. Given that in all societies numerous individuals are left not having the means to meet their basic needs, Sen would have to agree to focus on needs as a prioritized subset of capabilities. A needs orientation is fundamental to the more general problem of capabilities. By focusing on capabilities, however, he is also shifting the spotlight from resources to individuals and their requirements. Doing so expands the social welfare and justice stories and gives them a more human development focus. In any case, his basic orientation to capabilities is strongly related to needs. Any capability notion underlying social welfare and social justice requires that all individuals are able to meet their basic needs.

Further, democracy, based on the philosophical justification of the individual knowing her own good, is legitimated at least partially by its performance on the basis of basic needs.

These very bold conjectures invited empirical tests.

Empirical Support

Rawls' five purely theoretical conjectures regarding distributive matters are, in the main, surprisingly backed up by data. We (Frohlich and

Oppenheimer, 1990, 1992) ran experiments to test four of Rawls' five conjectures. We didn't test number 2: the conjectured priority of liberty. The experiments were replicated by others around the world (in Japan, Australia, the Philippines, Poland, Canada, and the United States). The results were almost always the same. Universally, people want to establish fundamental rules under which to live and earn a living. All experimental groups drafted and agreed on those rules unanimously. Three out of the four tested Rawlsian conjectures held up surprisingly well. But conjecture number 4 (the difference principle) was totally contradicted by evidence: people did not want to maximize the well-being of the worst off. They wanted to set a floor, and tax those above the floor to ensure that everyone could have a minimum. Discussions among the subjects in the hundreds of groups in the experiments also showed surprising consensus. Everywhere people believed in rewarding good work; they wanted any system to allow for just deserts. They wanted to give people incentives to work and produce. But they demanded a decent floor for people to live. These notions constituted, in the conversations, their notions of fairness for a foundational rule for a society in which they wanted to live. And this was the rule they agreed upon.

The fifth conjecture (the stability of the contract), though supported, was supported in an interestingly nuanced fashion. Since all groups picked very similar support and tax structures, we ran a version of the experiment that replicated the first part of the experiment until the group's moment of choice. Then, rather than allowing the group to choose, we imposed the expected choice as an outcome. The subjects in both conditions (where the group chose their contract and where we imposed the contract) then worked and earned money. Those who were insufficiently productive to support themselves at or above the minimal level stipulated by the contract received income subsidies paid for by taxes imposed on the others.

When the groups chose their contracts, the subsidized, less productive workers, were grateful and loyal. As such they worked harder and over time became more productive, thereby leading to decreasing tax burdens for the others. In other words, authorship by the group of their own rules enabled the groups to overcome the moral hazards[4] of redistributive programs. Over time, under these conditions, all members of the group showed high and increasing support for the contracts they had chosen. However, when similar contracts were imposed on the groups, the less

---

[4] Incentives generating a threat of such shirking behavior are known as a "*moral hazard*" and are an inevitable side effect of any insurance program.

productive did not make an effort to increase their productivity. Rather the less productive found that they could earn the minimum and could continue to do so, even with decreased productivity. So, when the contract was imposed, over time, taxes needed to support the less productive did not diminish. Under these conditions, the taxpayers first resented the regime, but over time, even they became supportive of the contract.

Brock (1994, 2005, 2005a) has usefully reinterpreted and applied these empirical results wherein people demand a floor. She argues that as the result of empathic impartial reasoning people demand the satisfying of the basic needs of everyone.

This notion, that people universally desire that basic needs are taken care of, and then demand compensation for work and risk-taking, by profits or just deserts, is duplicated in numerous other studies quite independent of the Rawlsian program (see, for example, Konow, 1996 and 1997).[5] In general, then, it appears that there is a species-wide demand for a distributive order for society to ensure minimum basic needs can be met. What that minimum ought to be will vary with the group's wealth, environment, and so on. Further, any more detailed definition of that minimum would have to include some personalized assessment of what constitutes needs, much as Sen argues. Wheelchairs for invalids illustrations the need for personalization. But the conclusion is clear: set a floor to meet basic needs. In other words:

PEOPLE WANT A FLOOR OF SUPPORT SO ALL MAY BE ABLE TO MEET THEIR BASIC NEEDS.

(Frohlich and Oppenheimer, 1990 and 1992)[6]

It is useful to note that this social insurance role is reflected in human politics everywhere. It has been an ingredient in the political mix of many societies over time. For example, Isaac Schapera (1956) reports extensively on the politics of tribal societies. He finds a great deal of variation. Not in all tribes, for example, does the tribal chief or council enforce rules of theft and so on. But, as he notes,

---

[5] Similar motivations have been identified in the political behavior in other primates. For example Frans de Waal (1982, 1991), a prominent primatologist, found that among chimpanzees, the alpha male is likely to face increasing opposition and can be deposed if the females find that he delivers insufficient protection to the females and the young.
[6] Note that Rawls only deals with social justice within a community. Similarly, our experiments did not take a "global" perspective. See Brock, 2009 for the extension to this wider problem.

One important duty only he [the chief] personally can fulfill . . . . [h]e is always the wealthiest man in his tribe. But he does not use his wealth merely for domestic purposes . . . . He places cattle on loan with many of his subjects, supports destitute widows and orphans, sometimes sends food to sick people and newly-confined mothers, and in times of famine distributes corn from his granaries or, if the need is great, sends men to purchase supplies from his neighbours. 'The chief is the wife of the tribe', say the Tswana, i.e. he looks after the needs of his subjects, and Zulu refer to him as 'the breast of the nation', i.e. the source from which all draw sustenance; . . . he is often greeted as 'mother of the people' or 'mother of orphans.' One quality always expected of him is generosity, and should he fail in this respect he soon becomes unpopular (p. 76).

How similar this is to the basic advice of Plunkitt of Tammany Hall (Riordon, 1994). In his talk "To Hold Your District, Study Human Nature and Act Accordin'!" he puts it,

What tells in holdin' your grip on your district is to go right down among the poor families and help them in the different ways they need help. I've got a regular system for this. If there is a fire . . . for example, any hour of the day or night, I'm usually there with some of my election district captains as soon as the fire engines. If a family is burned out I don't ask whether they are Republicans or Democrats, and I don't refer them to the Charity Organization Society, which would investigate their case in a month or two and decide they were worthy of help about the time they are dead from starvation. I just get quarters for them, buy clothes for them if their clothes were burned up, and fix them up till they get things runnin' again. It's philanthropy, but it's politics, too – mighty good politics (p. 64).

If basic needs are the substance, what then is necessity? It would seem necessity is made up of the minimal assets required to survive and function adequately in the socially required roles in one's society. These roles usually include those needed to be a good citizen, to be a productive member of the economy, and to be a responsible member of one's community and family. Hence, in different societies, different items would constitute necessities. Literacy and numeracy are likely needed to make the judgements expected of a citizen in a modern democracy. If so, then education sufficient to give one those skills would be looked upon as a basic need. But what role does politics play in ensuring the citizen has adequate opportunity to obtain these necessities? Clearly this is another question that must be on our agenda.

Back to Politics[7]
Now combine our understanding of the nature of democratic government with the universally held value of ensuring the meeting of basic needs of

---

[7] Much of what follows in this chapter stems from Oppenheimer et al., 2010.

those in society. It need not be the government that takes on the burdens of satisfying the material needs of the populace. What arrangements there are for this will vary. And people have other values: a vacation, a solid education for their children, a comfortable retirement, that all get in the way of their expression of their preference for a welfare floor.

But ultimately it will be the political institutions of government that will be held responsible if those systems that supply basic needs are found wanting by a visible and sizeable proportion of the population, and the needs of the people are not sustained.[8] In other words:

DEMOCRATIC GOVERNMENTS ARE IN PART LEGITIMATED BY MEETING THEIR CUSTODIAL OBLIGATIONS TO THEIR CITIZENS.

And from this we can develop a corollary of importance:

Democratic governments have an obligation to ensure conditions are met so the basic needs of their citizenry can be satisfied.

This means that to a degree, democratic governments ought to be judged by their citizens in terms of the sustenance of the needy. But there are other constraints. People care about such things as liberties, opportunities, just deserts, and so on. And individuals can be fooled. After all, they can be expected to be rationally ignorant, and hence open to manipulation via propagandistic claims. But we would expect that in a democracy there will be continual[9] and relentless pressure to develop a social safety net that is not porous. The more mobility that exists in the society, the truer this will be since people will be better able to imagine themselves as downwardly mobile. We now have a template to judge the performance of the governments in the developed democratic societies of the world. And it is to this that we now turn.

MEETING NEEDS: A MEASURE OF DEMOCRATIC
SUCCESS

Given that meeting basic needs is one of the primary functions of democracies, it is of no small interest to examine whether real-world democracies perform that function, and if so, how well. To do this we would need a measure of what constitutes basic needs. For groups of people to meet their needs over time, they must have the freedom to organize themselves

---

[8] This assumes that the society is wealthy enough to meet those needs.
[9] Continual, but not necessarily continuous. (see Frohlich and Oppenheimer, 2007).

politically. If nothing else, this gives a solid justification for liberal political orders. As noted, the premises of democracy include the equality of each individual's weight in voting in elections. They also include equal protection of citizens' rights by the government. These act as basic constraints on any evaluation of the performance of democratic governments (Nozick, 1974). Of course, no social welfare metric will become essential as an indicator of the quality of democratic *performance* until a democracy is the stable form of government. And there will always be other indicators of performance including the protection of liberties, the keeping of social stability, and a state's ability to muster an appropriate defense of itself in the face of threats encountered.

But we can evaluate how well democratic states meet the democratic promise that citizens can get their basic needs met. To do so we need only identify the content of basic needs and develop a scale of basic need satisfaction. There are many types of democracies in countries of widely varying economic and social development. Some of those, such as India, have insufficient economic capacity to solve the basic needs problems of the citizenry. Some are quite new (e.g., Korea, Israel, Taiwan) and hence perhaps without the citizens' expectations for their social welfare performance. So I put forward a metric only to be applied to the established, developed democracies. I look only at those with a continuous record of meeting the sorts of side constraints mentioned above for more than a number of decades and that have the resources to meet the basic needs of their citizens.

In any case, enumerating basic needs can't generate a complete picture of social welfare – but it does help us generate a more interpretable mapping from the welfare of the single individual to an aggregate conception of social welfare. In moving to *social* welfare we must make additional assumptions. After all, basic needs of citizens in any society are multidimensional, so we must compare the importance of the different dimensions. We also must make decisions regarding how to weight the number of individuals for whom the society is failing with the magnitude of those failures. So, we may wish to add an assumption about the relative value of failure across different dimensions. Doing so, we would have to take into account the percentage of the population left without basic needs being met and the level of their depravation. But even without satisfying all of these methodological requirements, we can develop a partial ordering of the need satisfaction component to social welfare. This gets us some distance beyond the Pareto criteria that has hobbled previous efforts to adequately characterize social welfare.

A PRELIMINARY INVENTORY OF NEEDS

There is an overlap in the needs of all people: things like food, shelter, clothing, and so on. But to complete the list we must be more specific and take into account what a person requires given his social context. Braybrooke (1987, p. 37) identifies two categories of needs: those associated with physical functioning, and those needed for social functioning. So, for example, in the latter category, democracies require that citizens participate in the political life of the society. And literacy and numeracy are prerequisites for considered participation. To identify these as basic needs of citizens in democracies is to be more inclusive and go beyond the most basic needs that we have as animals. Indeed, it acknowledges the social context of human existence. By specifying the essential roles of citizens of modern developed democracies we can understand needs requisite to social functioning. These social roles would normally include functioning in a market economy, a democratic polity, and a family structure.

"Basic needs" is a minimalist concept, and as such should not be padded. If in some societies the quality of basic housing, for example, is set above that of others, as it certainly is in the Scandinavian countries, this should not detain us. Quality beyond absolute minima is not relevant to the conceptualization of the meeting of basic needs for shelter unless it is such that it endangers the satisfying of other basic needs (e.g., security of person, raising one's children, etc.).

We still need some detail in order to approach an empirical task of evaluation. What, for example, constitute the specific needs that are under consideration? Although Braybrooke himself proposes a list of needs (and so do others, including the UN: UN, 2005) based on the functioning of the individual, the list is quite sparse and intuitive. For physical functioning he sets out (p. 39) a life-supporting relation to the environment, food and water, excretion, exercise, rest, sleep, and preservation of the intact body. Similarly, he identifies, for social functioning: companionship, education, social acceptance, sexual activity, recreation, and freedom from both harassment and constant fear. Clearly, not all of these are state responsibilities, although the state might be said to be required to ensure that others (e.g., violent gangs or mobsters) don't deprive individuals of these basic needs.

Gillian Brock (2005) is a bit more abstract in her approach when she says, "A need is basic if satisfying it is a necessary condition for human agency." Brock notes that by having agency on the list one "can circumvent concerns about how an account of such needs could be sufficiently 'objective' ... [to] ... enjoy widespread cross-cultural support .... For instance, by definition, to be an agent one must be able to deliberate and choose." She then identifies a number of necessities for performing these functions. To deliberate and choose doesn't tell one "about what." That would be determined by the specific nature of the society.

So we can see that enumeration is possible, and given that each society is different, there will be variations in what are the actual instantiations of basic needs. But food, shelter, health, education, medical care, work and other economic support when work is impossible, all are core needs that come into play along with the side constraints noted. Accordingly I propose that a first level evaluative criterion of how well democracies meet their promise should be the extent to which they meet these core basic needs of their citizens as measured by some empirical indicators.

PRELIMINARY COMPARATIVE PERFORMANCE
OF ADVANCED DEMOCRACIES

Numerous reports have been published to deal with these sorts of indicators, including the Millennia reports of the UN. To deal with the rather specific core items, I here utilize a rather preliminary measure of the extent to which basic needs are met in the developed democracies of the Organization of Economic Cooperation and Development (OECD). It focuses on on five dimensions: poverty, health, education, employment, and freedom (Oppenheimer, et al., 2010).[10] Roughly speaking, my measure of *poverty* captures both the absolute and relative depth and prevalence of poverty, which deprives individuals of the resources to adequately feed, shelter, and sustain themselves. *Health* reflects the effects of depravation of health-care resources that lead to avoidable and premature deaths. *Education* attempts to capture any failure to provide citizens with the secondary education deemed necessary to function adequately in a modern society. *Employment* reflects both short- and long-term failures in finding employment, especially for the insufficiently educated and most vulnerable on the labor market. *Freedom* measures the extent of incarceration of males in the society.

Each of these indicators can be criticized. As measures they are not overly sophisticated. The idea here is not to get a final measure, but to show that one can develop a useable measure of social welfare and make

---

[10] See details in the data appendix to that paper, available on my website as indicated in the bibliography.

useful comparisons. Rather than consider each of the five measures independently, for overall performance it is the aggregate that matters. But to aggregate performance on a disparate set of measures the scores need to be normalized. I normalized the scores and then sum them to form an overall performance index of meeting basic needs.

The scores are summed and reported as the total number of standard deviations above or below the mean that each country scores on the five statistical constructs. Results are shown in Figure 44. There is considerable variance among countries as to the extent to which they meet basic needs.

Recall, the notion that the peoples of different countries simply have different values regarding meeting basic needs flies in the face of the data from experiments about social justice and social welfare. There is widespread consensus in cross-national experiments regarding the importance of meeting basic needs. Then, an important question is, "Can these basic

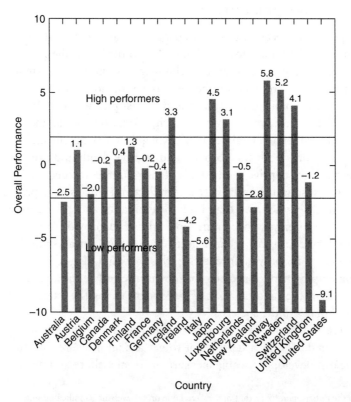

FIGURE 44. Performance of Countries on the Aggregate Index.

needs be met by public policy, or are these differences generated by social arrangements that go beyond politics?" After all, differences might not be due to failures of the political system, per se, but rather to alternative priorities or inherent inabilities. Consider a bit more data to develop a tentative response to this possibility.

If differences in these outcomes between countries is not determined by public policies, such a finding would absolve governments from having responsibility for outcomes regarding basic needs. If policy can't make a difference we ought neither to fault the political systems nor use unmet needs as a measure of democratic performance. One test of this possibility of political inefficacy might be the relationship between a country's poverty rate and social welfare spending.

Using 50 percent of the median income as a definition of poverty, the OECD, found that among its members, there is a very high correlation ($r = .824$) between spending on social welfare programs for working-aged people (excluding health) and ending poverty (see Figure 45). Apparently, effective policies do exist; political decisions make a substantial difference.

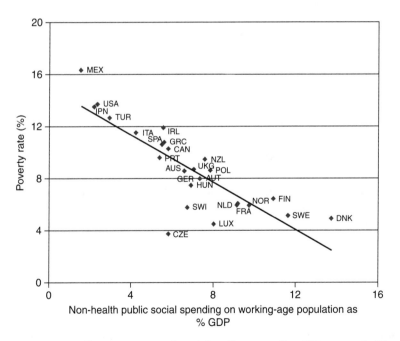

FIGURE 45. Poverty rates and social welfare spending [Förster and d'Ercole (2005)].

HOW TO EXPLAIN THE OBSERVED DIFFERENCES?

Recall the experimental finding: under conditions of impartial reasoning and moderate scarcity, humans have a universal desire for an effective social safety net. That doesn't help us explain the observed differences in social programs. The variation should lead us to ask why the differences exist if there is so much agreement. But identifying enormous variation in the obtaining of this universally held value among political systems ought not to surprise us. In all political systems, the outcomes are to be understood by the preferences of actors and rules of the game.

Circumstances can modify the pursuit of any universally held desire, including that of having citizens' needs met. The most obvious intervening variable would be cost. We all have desires, and even needs. But what we do about them has to do with their relative costliness. We can be very thirsty, and still, rather than purchase a drink, wait for a drinking fountain. For example, if in different societies, citizens believe an effective social safety net will generate differing levels of moral hazard, they will estimate the social costs of such policies to be different and will exhibit differing levels of enthusiasm for such a safety net.[11] Other factors can alter the direct valuation of a safety net, such as differing beliefs regarding self-reliance. So a universal valuation for a social safety net need not translate into equal support for policy in differing cultures.

This being said, institutional differences also are expected to play a substantial part in explaining the observed policy achievements. If the previous chapters are any guide, research should focus on issues of money in campaigns, checks and balances and veto players, party discipline as well as the availability of the vote to the needy and their capacity for political efficacy through political organization. Lijpart's extensive comparative institutional analysis identifies the consensual requirements imposed on governments with proportional representation as a factor.[12] The data clearly show a serious lack of equal performance, but the explanation remains a major subject for research as to why such variance exists.

---

[11] There are various possible causes for such differing beliefs: a variety of historical experiences, or differing levels of propaganda.

[12] On the other hand, Alesina and Glaeser's (2004) extensive study of the topic concludes that there is so much history, and hence "path dependency" in the build-up of policies that create a safety net, that a purely institutional explanation is not likely to generate much light.

CONCLUSIONS

It is perhaps obvious that without interpersonal comparisons of well-being we can't develop a sensible understanding of social welfare: from nothing one gets nothing. The same calculus lets us understand the comparative limitations of differing voting rules. That much of the incoherence in voting can be minimized by adopting improved rules gives hope. Further, the universal acceptance of a form of social justice, involving a floor guaranteeing basic needs in times of turmoil, helps us understand some of the content of social welfare.

These possibilities speak of potential improvement of our political institutions. They also argue for raising our sights beyond merely advocating democratic procedures and substantive freedom. It tells us to design procedures to achieve the substantive goals for individual and social well-being that have strong support. The track records of some countries demonstrate that these goals can be better approached through better architecture of our political institutions and social policies. Tools for complex institutional analysis should permit us to design more effective political systems.

From the basic premises of Arrow to the entire democratic and social welfare project, one can survey the central role and implications of individual well-being as a political goal. One would hope that this survey could serve as a basis for progress in normative political philosophy. Analyzing the desired properties of aggregated individual well-being can give us a sense of the potential of these normative arguments.

In any case, we must explore the justifiable basis for interpersonal comparisons of well-being. Without presumptions regarding this, it is fruitless to even try to define either social welfare or the basic goals of political structures. Arrow's findings show us that we will not easily find our way to a better society without thinking through the implications of the rules and institutions by which we organize ourselves and what the meaning of social welfare. Institutions give power to particular groups of individuals. They are then reluctant to allow others to change the rules that give them power (Michels, 1915). Those groups, or political elites, will argue against change. Hence, institutional structures are often very hard to alter. But rather than slavishly kowtowing to tradition and propaganda regarding one's institutions, the task is to investigate how those institutions can be improved so that the well-being of the citizens can achieve their potential.

FOR FURTHER READING

Social Welfare and Social Justice

Arrow, Kenneth J. (1951), *Social Choice and Individual Values* (2nd ed, 1963) New Haven: Yale University Press. Not only is this the original but it contains some side lights that are gems of reasoning. Examine his discussion of compensation and its role in making good policy choices. He also examines the possibility of unanimity and social choice. Here he puts considerable emphasis on the link to interpersonal comparisons.

Frohlich, Norman and Joe A. Oppenheimer (1992), *Choosing Justice: An Experimental Approach to Ethical Theory*, Berkeley: California University Press. We report the first experimental tests of theories of social justice and find the support for a floor of fundamental interest among all subjects.

Nozick, Robert (1974), *Anarchy, State and Utopia*, New York: Basic Books. This is a very readable classic attack on the impartial reasoning approach to justice and a basic argument for a minimalist state.

Rawls, John (1971), *A Theory Of Justice*, Cambridge: Harvard University Press. With some flaws, this revolutionary perspective redefined social justice for modernity. It is interesting, and fundamental. Also see John Rawls' (2001) *Justice as Fairness: A Restatement*, Cambridge: Harvard University Press. This is a shorter and final version of his thoughts on the matter of justice.

Sen, Amartya K. (1970), *Collective Choice and Social Welfare*, North Holland: New York. This is a great text for understanding Arrow's argument. It also deals wisely with numerous other issues and is an authorative introduction to the liberal paradox. Although overlooked by political scientists, as with Arrow, his fundamental interest is the analysis of social welfare and its relation to choice.

Sen, Amartya K. (1981), *Poverty and Famines: An Essay on Entitlement and Deprivation*, Oxford, Clarendon Press. This classic shows one of the surprising benefits of democracy: responsiveness to mass deprivation.

Sen, Amartya, "Capability and Well-Being" (1993), in Amartya Sen and Martha Nussbaum, ed. *The Quality of Life*, Oxford: Oxford University Press: 30–53. He develops what has become a very influential theory of social justice closely related, but not identical, to the needs satisfaction approach taken here. Sen prefers to focus on enabling the capabilities of the individual. This is an excellent place to explore the reasoning underlying his point of view.

Sen, Amartya (2002), "The Possibility of Social Choice," (Nobel acceptance speech) in *Freedom and Social Choice*, Cambridge, Mass: Harvard University Press: 65–118. Sen emphasizes that the classical interpretation of Arrow's impossibility theorem missed the point. He asserts that we must begin by asking what can be gained when we add limited interpersonal comparability.

Voting Rules

Mueller, Dennis C. (2003), *Public Choice III*, Cambridge: Cambridge University Press. This contains a very serious comparison and evaluation of voting rules.

Powell, G. Bingham (2000), *Elections As Instruments of Democracy: Majoritarian and Proportional Visions*, New Haven: Yale University Press. Powell discusses majoritarian and proportional ideas of democracy – then measures the degree to which different systems deliver the power of minorities to influence outcomes.

Conclusions: Questions and Lessons

Like medicine and pharmacology, political science is, by its very nature, an applied science. We value its study to improve the political processes of the world so that we might better meet the political challenges which face humanity. And in these early years of the twenty-first century we can easily identify some of these: economic injustice, global warming, wars and other forms of political violence, resource shortages, and regulation of markets to improve their functioning – just to name a few.

Social scientists have developed a set of propositions which appear to be justified and central to an understanding of politics. The foundations on which they rest must continue to be challenged: that is the way of scientific progress. So in these conclusions I briefly address, and partially respond to, three plausible arguments against the theoretical reasoning at the heart of the enterprise of this volume. My response will suggest a research frontier for political scientists who wish to further solidify the gains we have made in understanding politics using rational choice theory.

THE CHALLENGES

Anyone who has taught either political philosophy or rational choice theory in political science has heard three serious complaints.

The first complaint: people just do not behave in the manner predicted by the theory. They are neither simply rational nor self-interested. Human behavior is far more complex, and cannot be captured by such a simple theory. Often this is asserted on the basis of casual evidence. But these behavioral criticisms cannot be easily dismissed. And as the logic for many of the findings of the theory are built on the presumption of rational, self-interested behavior, we must ask for a more than casual response.

Second, some people are quick to notice that most political events and structures are far more complicated than our simple models. Why should we believe that the simple models are sufficient predictors of the "real-world" events to be of interest to us and motivate our study?

Finally, those who try to apply the normative reasoning of political philosophy to real-world politics have been criticized as dreamers. The very impartial point of view of such philosophical perspectives seems to violate the hyper-partial concerns of everyday politics. This is the third challenge that needs addressing.

Complex Human Behavior

Human behavior is not captured by the presumption of rational self-interest. Internally, we quietly celebrate our own acts of kindness and charity. And we all know people who have made large sacrifices for others. This is known to the rational choice theorists as well. It would seem time to discuss the evidence, and some possible answers being considered as to what we are to do about it.

Many experiments have been done that yield evidence challenging the simple notion of rational self-interest. The most straightforward experimental test of self-interest is the *dictator experiment*. In the experiment, two players (unknown to and unable to observe each other) are to divide up a sum of money. One player (the dictator) takes a share and leaves whatever he wishes for the other. If the dictator is purely self-interested she leaves nothing. But, although the most frequent, or modal, outcome in the early experiments, this is not what always happens.[1]

About 40 percent of the subjects leave something for their paired other. And if they do, the most frequent amount they leave is 50 percent. Further, when additional "values" are thrown in (such as when the amount of money that the dictator has to take or share comes from the joint work of the two anonymously paired persons) the outcome changes drastically. Depending upon details of the experiment only between 10 and 33 percent of the subjects then leave nothing. Since most real-world contexts involve more complicated situations with conflicting claims, this is strong evidence for the rejection of the self-interest assumption.

The situation gets much more interesting if we broaden the class of experiment we are looking at. Although less directly about self-interest,

---

[1] See Frohlich, Oppenheimer and Kurki, 2004 for a bibliography and criticism of previously run experiments. The results reported there also give one a sense of some of the power as well as the limitations of the presumption of self-interest. Also see Frohlich et al (2001) for why there was an over reporting of purely self-interested responses.

repeated n-person prisoner dilemma experiments have long been the most performed experiments in political science. The data from these experiments has been problematic and was discussed earlier (see page 55). Recall, people make their judgments (and hence choices) probabilistically, that people want to help each other and do their fair share, but that even more than that, they don't want to be taken advantage of.

So the critics are right: work must be done on the foundation of rational choice theory. But this means neither that the theory should be thrown out, nor that the theory isn't a good approximation for political modeling. The basis of rational choice theory can be, and is being, altered to take into account the findings that the traditional definition of rational choice and self-interest fall short. There is no inherent contradiction between rational choice and other-regarding preferences. And probabilistic behavior that stems from neurological properties of how we focus our attention also does no violence to the theory. Rather, what is needed is the further development of the implications of a revamped rational choice theory to discover new conjectures.

The applicability of the theory to politics is not seriously damaged by some of these anomalies. After all, experiments show that, at a more macro-level, groups behave much as predicted: over time contributions of a cooperative nature fall to a relatively low, and certainly suboptimal level. Further, many active political actors (think representatives, lobbyists, diplomats, etc.) act as fiduciaries for others and have little wiggle room to take into account the welfare of third parties in their decision making. Hence, political players may behave in a manner that partially blocks their other-regarding preferences. Such preferences may be sometimes filtered out by modern democratic systems. Thus, the assumption of self-interest may work quite well even though it is inaccurate.

Complex Political Systems

Not only do critics claim that behavior is more complex than presumed in our models but they also note that we model simplified situations that don't reflect complications found in the real world. And it is the real world that we must understand. Again, no doubt, this is so. Complexity is the bane of analysis when it comes to following the logical threads required by deductive modeling. To point out what one can expect to happen with a filibuster rule in a simple algebraic abstraction of a legislature does not do justice to the complexity of the U.S. Senate.

But, this does not mean that these simple models are to be given up. To understand the viability of a brick wall, one must understand the properties of bricks and mortar. So rather than give up the simple models, one must figure out how to understand complex systems that are made up of simpler pieces. Luckily, with modern computational power at one's desktop, one has such tools in simulation methods. Simulations allow the "building" of complex systems from a tool box of simple parts. From this, one can examine what sorts of interactions and complications need to be built into the models to account for the complexities of reality. Only then can one really explain the differential performance of political systems. Obviously such simulations of complexity would then need to be tested against fresh data reflecting the real world.

Impartial Reasoning in the Real World

While the political philosopher imagines a world where individuals engage in impartial reasoning, others argue that morals and ethics just aren't a major part of the brutal and hyper-competitive political world we know. This gives ground for criticism of some of the normative generalizations developed in this volume.

Although experimental research has shown that humans everywhere have very similar understanding of, and desires for, justice, everyday observations of social arrangements and policies don't seem to support conclusions of homogeneity. The variety of norms among societies stretches the imagination. While the Taliban requires that women remain uneducated, fully covered, and so on, other societies legalize abortions and make it illegal to discriminate against women. Indeed, looking at politics makes it clear that there are great manifest disagreements on values.

What is one to make of these vastly different empirical claims? Consensus regarding basic moral values is observed when one asks people to engage in impartial reasoning – with no consideration of where one is situated. Policy, on the other hand, is usually made in response to the very real political forces created by individuals who are situated in their particular worlds. Their views are often far from impartial and their judgements about politics specifically reflect their very particular circumstances.

This is one factor in the wide gulf that exists between the values expressed in experiments and politically expressed policy preferences. Two main questions arise from the gap between political outcomes and the human consensus on principles reached via reasoning from a moral point of view. First, what role *ought* these moral sentiments, these other-regarding preferences, to play in policy formation? After all, they are not an empirically strong element in the political mix that leads to public policy. Second, are there elements of institutional design that discourage or encourage impartial reasoning and the expression of these other-regarding preferences and hence change the quality of outcomes we arrive at from our political processes?

Experiments show that other-regarding values play a role in behavior that is similar to the role of other preferences (see Frohlich and Oppenheimer, et al. 1984; Frohlich, Oppenheimer and Kurki, 2004). People who want things for others, and that is most of us, carefully take into account the price they have to pay to achieve these outcomes. So the notion of a "moral imperative," so essential to much moral philosophy (as in Kant's Grounding for the Metaphysics of Morals) does not play a strong role in individual responses to these political values.[2] Rather issues like social justice and doing one's fair share are responded to as things that people will try to help along when it is not "too costly."

This implies that the design of political institutions can make these motivations more, or less, manifest. If institutions facilitate the taking of relatively noncostly actions on behalf of others and frame issues to favor such behavior, one can expect increased behavior reflecting such motives. If other-regarding policies and actions are framed primarily as costs, and effective support for them is seen as difficult and costly, behaviors will be less forthcoming to achieve such policies. In other words, thoughtful institutional design can decrease the gap between the moral and the public outcomes, but precisely how this can be achieved is beyond our current findings.

BETTER OUTCOMES, BETTER INSTITUTIONS

We all want a better world and, although it is clear that there are disagreements about details, there is a wide range of overlap in human aspirations. Some problems just seem to defy solution. You need not be a keen observer of politics to notice that many of these persistent problems stem from political failure. Politics makes it difficult for the Israeli-Palestinian conflict to reach solution. Politics makes it hard to reconcile budget and debt problems in the United States and throughout the Euro zone; to end wars; to stop global warming. The list is easy to formulate.

---

[2] Certainly, however, in some important contexts such imperatives *do* play a role for a many individuals. They even seem to spur the heroic actions that, though they remain rare, have enormous impact.

Taking to heart the many difficulties of collective action, responsible political leadership, social choice, and welfare aggregation, one must note the many traps of political and governmental failure lead to a sense that Malthus was wrong in targeting economics as the dismal science. Bad outcomes would seem to be avoidable only via a more responsive and responsible political system.

Note, however, that in spite of the failures of our economic and political systems, humanity has made enormous political and social progress over the centuries. Our systems, though faulty, have clearly been good enough to let humanity progress. It now seems that our problems are of sufficient scale that we must design better political institutions merely to ensure that we have a future and that our future enables continued progress. To match the escalating global problems we need to learn how to improve our political institutions quickly. With this pressure in mind, I present a few lessons for everyone concerned with the development of policies and systems that can maintain a sustainable planet, populated with an increasing number of humane, fair, and just societies. These lessons won't solve the problems we face, but ignoring them is extremely likely to lead to failure in our political efforts. First, perhaps we should identify the goals these institutions are designed to handle and achieve.

Political Goals

As before, I put the welfare of the citizenry as the fundamental goal of political institutions.[3] As many others have noted over the ages, the primary function of government is the security of the people. Our institutions must first and foremost be designed to keep politics a relatively safe and non-violent way of solving our problems: civil wars are catastrophes that bespeak of the failure of these institutions.

Non-Violent Succession

Domestically, non-violent succession means that the political structure must have rules of succession to which the citizenry and (especially) the powerful leaders can agree. Without such agreement, an agreement that is clearly part of what we call "legitimacy," the possibility of endless fighting and

---

[3] As the world becomes more interconnected (another way of saying that there are increasing spillover effects, or externalities) there must be some attention paid to the institutions above the sovereign nations. Unfortunately, that is beyond the scope of this volume.

degradation of civilization is severe.[4] To lead to a secure citizenry the major politicians and factions jostling for power must be able to agree upon the outcome of the competition and the transference of power without violence. Hence, the legitimacy of the government is a necessity.[5] Without that, political competition is likely to breed a deadly storm of civil strife.

On the surface, it would seem that democratic procedures are precisely the sort that would meet these needs. After all, electoral rules fully determine the winner, and loser, of elections. An electoral competition, with requisite liberties of speech, and so on, allows for rigorous discussion of policy alternatives. But such rules will not generate a consensus of legitimacy by themselves (see page XXX for the discussion of regime change and stability). We might hope that democratic procedures are to be an accepted mechanism to settle the issue of succession, and hence make such civil conflicts unnecessary. But such hopes are not easily translated into reality. One need only look at the violence that has attended electoral contests in Chile (the deposing of Allende), or more recently in Thailand, or elsewhere, to understand that establishing democratic rule is not a silver bullet. Indeed, as was pointed out by Boix (2003) there are predictable conditions when democratic rule will be too threatening to be accepted.

If there is no guarantee of legitimacy gleaned from democratic institutions, it follows that when a society has a benign and accepted established system of governance it would be the height of hubris to tear it down to *impose* democratic rule. Democracy as a goal must take a back seat to citizen security. Constitutional change is not usually on the agenda when everything is going smoothly.

Beyond Physical Security

Beyond simple physical security, the well-being of individuals requires good political outcomes. As discussed in the previous sections of the book, these include more than outcomes of acceptable efficiency: humans aspire to liberties, social justice, as well as responsiveness and responsible policy follow-through of our governments. To get such outcomes consistently requires considerable care in institutional design. Public policy,

---

[4] See Weingast (1997). But safety in politics also stems from the possibility of extraordinary individual material ambitions being able to be satisfied in spheres other than politics. Perhaps this is one of the reasons that economic wealth and enforced property rights are highly correlated with successful democracy. Those with strong material motivations are offered paths other than the political to gain their ambitions.

[5] See Nagel, 1991 for a good discussion of legitimacy.

which is the product of a political system, will reflect the incentives of that system: the elements that determine the tenure and rewards of the politicians. Foremost on the list must be the rules of elections, and associated rules determining the electoral districting, and rules determining how the status quo is changed. Rewards available to the politicians in all their decision-making capacities constitute their incentives. The variables that structure those rewards for behavior will usually determine, in great part, what the citizens get. Proper design of political institutions and processes requires a most careful analysis of the incentives that are implied by the arrangements. But there is more that we must keep in mind.

For the weak forces of electoral democracy to be able to reign in fawning governmental attention to the more privileged requires an ability of individuals to hold the government responsible.[6] When parties responsible for policy in the government are divided into myriad parts, none of which are coordinated by, say, party discipline, it can be almost impossible for the electorate to tether the government to generate responsible or responsive policy commitments.

Still, Riker's 1982 interpretation of the Arrow results (that there was no sense in preference aggregation or notions of collective interests) was too pessimistic. He argued the electorate can't make a substantive positive collective choice, but they can "kick the bums out." As we have shown, various factors argue against such a one-sided conclusion. And remarkably, democracies deliver what might be considered adequately good policies much of the time (Mackie, 2003).

So for example: two-party systems induce a one-dimensional political contest in which the median voter represents a sort of grand compromise; the uncovered set gives us a useful normatively attractive notion of how preference aggregation can work out; and with interpersonal comparability of needs and need deprivations, we can get quite an adequate understanding of some dimensions of social justice. The weak requirement of winning elections appears to be enough in some countries to keep things at least on track. With our analytic tools and our fledgling inventory of principles, it should be possible now to design institutions that do a better job than that. We should be able to improve our current institutions. The design of such improved institutions to help obtain adequate political results should be an important agenda item for all of us.

---

[6] One should not overemphasize the weakness of popular forces. As Powell (2000, pp. 48–49) has noted, a 5 percent decrease in electoral support given to an incumbent government nets a change in the government two-thirds of the time.

Bibliography

Ahn, T. K., Elinor Ostrom, and James M. Walker (2003), "Incorporating Motivational Heterogeneity into Game Theoretic Models of Collective Action" in *Public Choice*, 117, 3–4 (December): 295–315.

Aivazian, V. A. and Jeffrey L. Callen (1981), "The Coase Theorem and the Empty Core." *Journal of Law and Economics*, 24, 175–181.

Alesina, Alberto and Edward Glaeser (2004), *Fighting Poverty in the US and Europe: A World of Difference*. Oxford: Oxford University Press.

Arrow, Kenneth J. (1963), *Social Choice and Individual Values*, 2nd ed. New Haven: Yale University Press.

Arrow, Kenneth J. (1977), "Extended Sympathy and the Possibility of Social Choice." *American Economic Review*, 67 (December): 219–225. Reprinted in Collected Papers of Kenneth J. Arrow, 1, Social Choice and Justice. Cambridge: Belknap Press of Harvard.

Axelrod, Robert (1984), *The Evolution of Cooperation*. New York: Basic Books.

Baier, Annette (1981), "Frankena and Hume on Points of View." *The Monist*, 64, 3 (July): 342–358.

Barry, Brian M. (1970), *Sociologists, Economists, and Democracy*. London: Collier-McMillan Limited.

Baumol, William (1952), *Welfare Economics and the Theory of the State*. Cambridge, Mass: Harvard University Press.

Baumol, William J. and Wallace E. Oates (1979), *Economics Environmental Policy and the Quality of Life*. Englewood Cliffs, N.J.: Prentice Hall.

Bendor, Jonathan (1995), "A Model of Muddling Through," *American Political Science Review*, 89, 4 (December): 819–840.

Bendor, Jonathan and Piotr Swistak (1997), "The Evolutionary Stability of Cooperation," *American Political Science Review*, 91, 2 (June): 290–307.

Bergson, Abram (1938), "A Reformulation of Certain Aspects of Welfare Economics." *Quarterly Journal of Economics*, 52, 2 (February): 310–34.

Besedes, Tibor, Cary A. Deck, Sarah Marx Quintanar, Sudipta Sarangi and Mikhael Shor (2011), "Free-Riding and Performance in Collaborative and

Non-Collaborative Groups." Social Science Research Network. Working Paper Series. http://papers.ssrn.com/sol3/papers.cfm?abstract_id=1824524

Besley, Timothy (2006), Principled Agents? *The Political Economy of Good Government.* Oxford: Oxford University Press.

Bianco, William T., Ivan Jeliazkov, and Itai Sened (2004a), The Uncovered Set and the Limits of Legislative Action. *Political Analysis* 12: 256–276.

Bianco, William T., Michael S. Lynch, Gary J. Miller, and Itai Sened (2004b), "Retrodicting the Uncovered Set." Presented at the 2004 Meeting of the American Political Science Association.

Bianco, William T., Michael S. Lynch, Gary J. Miller, and Itai Sened (2006), "Constrained Instability: Experiments on the Robustness of the Uncovered Set." *Political Analysis* (2008) 16, 115–137.

Bickers, Kenneth N. and Robert M. Stein (1994), "Response to Barry Weingast's Reflections." *Political Research Quarterly* 47 (June): 329–333.

Binmore, Kenneth (1994), Game Theory & the Social contract. 1. *Playing Fair*, Cambridge, Mass.: MIT Press.

Birchfield, Vicki and Markus M. L. Crepaz (1998), The Impact of Constititutional Structures and Collective and Competitive Veto Points on Income Inequality in Industrialized Democracies, *European Journal of Political Research* 34, 175–200.

Black, Duncan (1958), *The Theory Of Committees And Elections.* Cambridge: Cambridge University Press.

Blake, Elizabeth L., John L. Guyton, and Steven Leventhal, (1994) "An Experimental Test of Coasian Bargaining in Games with Empty Cores." *mimeo. Revision of a paper of the same name presented at Public Choice Society Annual Meeting*, New Orleans, La. March 15–17, 1991. http://www.bsos.umd.edu/gvpt/oppenheimer/831/blake.pdf

Boix, Carles (2003), *Democracy and Redistribution*, New York: Cambridge University Press.

Brams, Steven and Fishburn, Peter (1978), "Approval Voting." *American Political Science Review* 72, 3, 831–847.

Braybrooke, David (1987), *Meeting Needs.* Princeton, N.J.: Princeton University Press.

Brock, Gillian (1994), "Braybrooke on Needs" in *Ethics* 104 (July): 811–813.

Brock, Gillian (2005), "Needs and Global Justice" in *The Philosophy of Need*, ed. Soran Reader. Philosophy, Supplement 57: Cambridge: Cambridge University Press, 51–72.

Brock, Gillian (2005a), Egalitarianism, Ideals, and Cosmopolitan Justice, *The Philosophical Forum.* V. XXXVI, 1 (Spring): 1–30.

Brock, Gillian (2009), *Global Justice: A Cosmopolitan Account.* Oxford: Oxford University Press.

Buchanan, James (1965), "An Economic Theory of Clubs," *Economica* 32, 1 (February): 1–14.

Buchanan, James and Gordon Tullock (1962), *The Calculus of Consent.* Ann Arbor: University of Michigan Press.

Cervone, Davide P., William V. Gehrlein, and William S. Zwicker (2002), "Which scoring rule maximizes Condorcet Efficiency?" Union College Department of

Mathematics, web publication: http://www.math.union.edu/~dpvc/papers/2001-01.DC-BG-BZ/DC-BG-BZ.pdf

Chong, Dennis (1991), *Collective Action and the Civil Rights Movement*. Chicago: The University of Chicago Press.

Coase, Ronald (1960), "The Problem of Social Cost." *Journal of Law and Economics* 3, 1–44.

Coughlin, Peter (1984), "Probabilistic Voting Models," in *Encyclopedia of the Statistical Sciences*, ed. Sam. Kotz, Norman Johnson, and Campbell Read, 6, New York: Wiley.

Coughlin, Peter (1988), "Expectations about Voter Choices." *Public Choice*, 44, 1, 49–59.

Cox, Gary W. and Mathew D. McCubbins (2001), "The Institutional Determinants of Economic Policy Outcomes," in Stephan Haggard, ed., *Presidents, Parliaments, and Policy*, Cambridge: Cambridge University Press: 21–63.

Camerer, Colin F. (2003), *Behavioral Game Theory: Experiments in Strategic Interaction (The Roundtable Series in Behavioral Economics.)* Princeton, N.J.: Princeton University Press.

Caplin, Andrew and Barry Nalebuff (1988), "On 64% Majority Rule." *Econometrica*, 56 (July): 787–814.

Collier, Kenneth E., Richard D. McKelvey, Peter C. Ordeshook, and Kenneth C. Williams (1987), "Retrospective Voting: an Experimental Study." *Public Choice*. 53: 101–130.

Dawes, Robyn M. (1980), "Social Dilemmas." *Annual Review of Psychology*. 31: 169–193.

de Waal, Frans (1982), *Chimpanzee Politics: Power and Sex among Apes*. New York: Harper & Row.

de Waal, Frans (1991), "Social Regularity in Chimpanzees and its Relation to the Human Sense of Justice." *American Behavioral Scientist*. 34, 3 (January/February): 335–349. Special Issue, ed. Margaret Gruter, Behavior, Evolution, and the Sense of Justice.

de Waal, Frans (1996), *Good Natured: the origins of right and wrong in humans and other animals*. Cambridge, Mass: Harvard University Press.

Dixit, Avinash (2003), "Some Lessons from Transaction-Cost Politics for Less-Developed Countries," in Joe A. Oppenheimer, Piotr Swistak, and John Wallis, eds., "On the Shoulders of a Giant: Essays in Honor of Mancur Olson." *Special volume of Journal of Economics and Politics* 15, 3 (July): 107–135

Dixit, Avinash and Susuan Skeath (2004), *Games of Strategy*, Second edition. New York: Norton.

Dougherty, Keith L., and Julian Edward (2005), A Nonequilibrium Analysis of Unanimity Rule, Majority Rule, and Pareto. *Economic Inquiry* 43, 4, 855–864.

Dougherty, Keith L. and Julian Edward (2004), "The Pareto Efficiency and Expected Costs of k-Majority Rules- Politics." *Philosophy & Economics* 3, 2 (May): 161–189.

Downs, Anthony (1957), *An Economic Theory Of Democracy*. New York: Harper and Row.

256   *Bibliography*

Doyle, Len and Ian Gough (1991), *A Theory of Human Need*. Basingstoke: MacMillan Education Ltd.

Dryzek, John S. and Christian List (2002), "Social Choice Theory and Deliberative Democracy: A Reconciliation," forthcoming in British Journal of Political Science.

Eavey, C. and G. Miller (1984),"Bureaucratic Agenda Control: Imposition or Bargaining?" *American Political Science Review*, 78, (September): 719–733.

Ellickson, Bryan (1973), "A Generalization of the Pure Theory of Public Goods." *American Economic Review* 63 (June): 417–32.

Enelow, James and Melvin Hinich (1984), *The Spatial Theory of Voting*. Cambridge: Cambridge University Press.

Epley, Nicholas and Eugene M. Caruso (2004), Egocentric Ethics. *Social Justice Research*, 17, 2 (June): 171–187.

Epstein, David (1999), "Legislating from Both Sides of the Aisle: Information and the Value of Bipartisan Consensus." *Public Choice*, 101, 1–22.

Falaschetti, Dino and Gary Miller (2001), "Constitutional Design Constraining Leviathan: Moral Hazard and Credible Commitment in Constitutional Design." *Journal of Theoretical Politics*, 13, 4, 389–411.

Farquharson, Robin (1969), *Theory of Voting*. New Haven: Yale University Press.

Fearon, J. D. (1998), "Bargaining, enforcement, and international cooperation." *International Organization* 52, 2, 269–305.

Fearon, J. D. (1995), "Rationalist explanations for war." *International Organization* 49, 3, 379–414.

Fehr, Ernst and Klaus M. Schmidt (1999), "A Theory of Fairness, Competition, and Cooperation." *Quarterly Journal of Economics*, 114, (August): 817–868.

Flood, Merrill M. (1952), "Some Experimental Games," *Rand Corporation Research Monograph*, RM 789–1, June 20. Published in 1958 in Management Science, 5, 1 (October): 5–26.

Flood, Merrill M. (1958), "Some Experimental Games." *Management Science*, 5, 1 (October): 5–26.

Förster, Michael and Marco Mira d'Ercole (2005), "Income Distribution and Poverty in OECD Countries in the Second Half of the 1990s." (OECD Social, Employment and Migration Working Paper 22). www.oecd.org/els/workingpapers

Frankena, William K. (1983), "Moral-Point-of-View Theories," in *Ethical Theory in the Last Quarter of the Twentieth Century*, Charles L. Stevenson, William K. Frankena, R. B. Brandt, and A. I. Melden, eds. Indianapolis: Hackett Publishing Company.

Frohlich, Norman (1974), "Self-Interest or Altruism: What Difference?" *Journal of Conflict Resolution*, 18, (March): 55–73.

Frohlich, Norman (1992), "An Impartial Reasoning Solution to the Prisoner's Dilemma." *Public Choice*, 74, 447–460.

Frohlich, Norman and Joe A. Oppenheimer (1970), "I Get By with a Little Help from My Friends," *World Politics*, 23 (October): 104–121.

Frohlich, Norman and Joe A. Oppenheimer (1974), "The Carrot and the Stick," *Public Choice*. 19 (Fall): 43–61.

Frohlich, Norman and Joe A. Oppenheimer (1978), *Modern Political Economy*. Englewood Cliffs, N.J.: Prentice Hall.

Frohlich, Norman and Joe A. Oppenheimer (1990), "Choosing Justice in Experimental Democracies with Production." *American Political Science Review*, 84, 2 (June): 461–477.

Frohlich, Norman and Joe A. Oppenheimer (1992), *CHOOSING JUSTICE: An Experimental Approach to Ethical Theory*. Berkeley: University of California Press.

Frohlich, Norman and Joe A. Oppenheimer (1994), "Alienable Privatization Policies Inefficiency or Injustice – Between a Rock and a Hard Place," in *Resolution of Water Quantity and Quality Conflicts*, Ariel Dinar and Edna Loehman, eds., 131–142,

Frohlich, Norman and Joe A. Oppenheimer (1996), When Is Universal Contribution Best for the Group? Characterizing Optimality in the Prisoners' Dilemma. *Journal of Conflict Resolution*, 3 40, (September): 502–516.

Frohlich, Norman and Joe A. Oppenheimer (1996a), "Experiencing Impartiality to Invoke Fairness in the n-PD: Some Experimental Results." *Public Choice*, 86, 117–135.

Frohlich, Norman and Joe A. Oppenheimer (1996b), "Ethical Problems when Moving to Markets: Gaining Efficiency While Keeping an Eye on Distributive Justice." Arieh Ullmann and Alfred Lewis, eds. *Privatization and Entrepreneurship: The Managerial Challenge in Central and Eastern Europe, in the International Management Series published by Haworth Press, Erdener Kaynak, Senior Editor*. (International Business Press, New York: International Business Press: 11–26.

Frohlich, Norman and Joe A. Oppenheimer (1997), A Role for Structured Observation in Ethics, *Social Justice Research*. 10, 1 (March): 1–21.

Frohlich, Norman and Joe A. Oppenheimer (1998), Examining the Consequences of E-Mail v. Face to Face Communications in Experiments. *Journal of Economic Behavior and Organization*, 35, 389–403.

Frohlich, Norman and Joe Oppenheimer (1999) "Kenneth Arrow, Welfare Aggregation and Progress in Political Theory." In James Alt, Elinor Ostrom, and Margaret Levi, (eds.) *Taking Economics Seriously: Conversations with Nobelists about Economics and Political Science*. New York: Russell Sage Foundation: 4–33.

Frohlich, Norman and Joe Oppenheimer (2001), "Choosing from a Moral Point of View." *Interdisciplinary Economics*, (February) 12, 89–115.

Frohlich, Norman and Joe Oppenheimer (2004), "Self-Interest," in Rowley, Charles K. and Fritz Schneider, eds., *Encyclopedia of Public Choice Kluwer* Academic Publishers.

Frohlich, Norman and Joe A. Oppenheimer (2006), "Skating on Thin Ice: Cracks in the Public Choice Foundation." *Journal of Theoretical Politics* 18, 3, 235–266.

Frohlich, Norman and Joe A. Oppenheimer (2007). "Justice Preferences and the Arrow Problem." *Journal of Theoretical Politics*. 19, 4, 363–390.

Frohlich, Norman, Joe Oppenheimer, and Anja Kurki (2004), "Problems in Modeling Social Preferences: Insights from Modified Dictator Experiments." *Public Choice* 119, 1–2, 91–117.

Frohlich, Norman, Joe Oppenheimer, and Bernard Moore (2001), "Some Doubts About Measuring Self-Interest Using Dictator Experiments: The Costs of

Anonymity." *Journal of Economic Behavior and Organization* **46**, 3 (November): 271–290.

Frohlich, Norman and J. Oppenheimer, w Pat Bond and Irvin Boschman (1984), "Beyond Economic Man." *Journal of Conflict Resolution* **28**, 1, (March, 1984): 3–24.

Frohlich, Norman, Joe A. Oppenheimer, and Oran R. Young (1971), *Political Leadership and the Supply of Collective Goods.* Princeton, New Jersey: Princeton University Press.

Gage, Nicholas (1983), *Eleni.* New York: Random House.

Giere, Ronald N. (1988), *Explaining Science: A Cognitive Approach.* Chicago: University of Chicago Press.

Goldfarb, Robert S., and Lee Sigelman (2010), "Does 'Civic Duty' 'Solve' the RationalChoice Voter Turnout Puzzle?" *Journal of Theoretical Politics*, **22**, 3 (July): 275–300.

Goodin, Robert E., Bruce Headey, Ruud Muffels, Henk-Jan Dirven (1999), *The Real Worlds of Welfare Capitalism.* Cambridge: Cambridge University Press.

Gopnik, Alison (2010), *The Philosophical Baby.* Farrar, Straus, Giroux.

Green, Donald P., and Ian Shapiro (1994), *Pathologies of Rational Choice Theory: A Critique of Applications in Political Science.* New Haven: Yale University Press.

Greenberg, Joseph (1979), "Consistent Majority Rule over Compact Sets of Alternatives." *Econometrica*, **47**, 627–636.

Grether, David M., and Charles R. Plott (1979), "Economic Theory of Choice and the Preference Reversal Phenomenon." *American Economic Review*, **69** (September): 623–638.

Grosskopf, Brit (1998), "Competition, Aspiration and Learning in the Ultimatum Game: An Experimental Investigation." Universitat Pompeu Fabra. Discussion Paper presented at the 1999 European Economics Association Meetings.

Grosskopf, Brit (2003), Reinforcement and Directional Learning in the Ultimatum Game with Responder Competition. *Experimental Economics*, **6** (October): 141–158.

Habermas, Jurgen (1996), *The Inclusion of the Other: Studies in Political Theory.* Ciaran Cronin and Pablo De Greiff, eds., Cambridge: MIT Press.

Halperin, Morton H., Joseph T. Siegle, and Michael M. Weinstein (2004), *The Democracy Advantage: How Democracies Promote Prosperity and Peace.* New York: Routledge.

Hamada, Koichi (1973), "A Simple Majority Rule on the Distribution of Income." *Journal of Economic Theory*, **6**, (June): 243–76.

Hammond, Thomas H., and Gary J. Miller, "A Social Choice Perspective on Expertise and Authority in Bureaucracy." *American Journal of Political Science*, **29**, 1 (February): 1985: 1–28.

Hammond, Thomas H. and Gary J. Millers (1987), "The Core of the Constitution," *American Political Science Review.* **81**, 1156–1174.

Hardin, Garrett (1968), The Tragedy of the Commons. *Science*, **162**, 1243–1248.

Hardin, Russell (1971), "Collective Action as an Agreeable N-Prisoners' Dilemma." *Behavioral Science* **16**, 5, 472–479.

Hardin, Russell (1982), *Collective Action*. Baltimore: Johns Hopkins University Press. (RFF)

Hardin, Russell (1999), *Liberalism, Constitutionalism, and Democracy*. Oxford: Oxford University Press.

Hardin, Russell (2004), "Rational Choice Political Philosophy," in *From Anarchy to Democracy*, Irwin Morris, Joe Oppenheimer, Karol Soltan, eds., Palo Alto: Stanford University Press: 95–109.

Harrison, Glenn W. and Michael McKee, Experimental Evaluation of the Coase Theorem. *Journal of Law & Economics*, 28 (1985): 653–670.

Harsanyi, John C. (1953), Cardinal Utility in Welfare Economics and in the Theory of Risk-Taking. *Journal of Political Economy*, 61, 434–435.

Hausman, Daniel M. (1989), "Economic Methodology in a Nutshell." *The Journal of Economic Perspectives*, 3, 2 (Spring): 115–127.

Hausman, Daniel M. (1995), "Rational Choice and Social Theory: A Comment." *The Journal of Philosophy*, 91, 2 (February): 96–102.

Hausman, Daniel M. (2008), "Philosophy of Economics." The Stanford Encyclopedia of Philosophy, ed. Edward N. Zalta, http://plato.stanford.edu/entries/economics/

Hayek, Frederick A. (1960), *The Constitution of Liberty*. Chicago: University of Chicago Press.

Hempel, Carl G. (1965), *Aspects of Scientific Explanation*. New York: Macmillan Free Press.

Hinton, William (1966), *Fanshen: A Documentary of Revolution in a Chinese Village*. New York: Random House.

Hirschman, Albert O. (1970), *Exit Voice and Loyalty*. Cambridge, Mass: Harvard University Press.

Hobbes, Thomas (1651), Leviathan or The Matter, Forme and Power of a Common Wealth Ecclesiasticall and Civil.

Hoffman, Elizabeth and Matthew Spitzer (1982), "The Coase Theorem: Some Experimental Tests." *Journal of Law and Economics*, 25, 73–98.

Hoffman, Elizabeth and Matthew Spitzer (1986), "Experimental Tests of the Coase Theorem with Large Bargaining Groups." *Journal of Legal Studies*, 15, 149–171.

Hotelling, Harold (1929) "Stability in Competition," *Economic Journal* 39, 1, 41–57.

Immergut, Ellen M. (1992), *Health politics: interests and institutions in Western Europe*. Cambridge: Cambridge University Press.

Immergut, Ellen M. (1998), The Theoretical Core of the New Institutionalism. *Politics & Society*, 26, 1 (March), 5–34.

Johnson, Chalmers (1962), Peasant Nationalism and Communist Power: *The Emergence of Revolutionary China, 1937–1945*. Stanford: Stanford University Press.

Kahneman Daniel and Amos Tversky (1982), "The Psychology of Preference." *Scientific American*, 246 (January): 160–173.

Kahneman Daniel and Amos Tversky (1979), "Prospect Theory: an Analysis of Decision Making Under Risk." *Econometrica* 47 (March): 263–291.

Kahneman, Daniel, Jack L. Knetsch, and Richard H. Thaler (1986), Fairness and the Assumptions of Economics, in a specially edited volume (by Robin

M. Hogarth and Melvin W. Reder) of *The Journal of Business*, 59, 4, Part 2 (October): S285–S301.

Kagel, John H. and Alvin E. Roth, eds. (1995), *The Handbook of Experimental Economics*. Princeton: Princeton University Press.

Kant, Immanuel (1785), *Grounding for the Metaphysics of Morals*, translated by James W. Ellington, 1993, 3rd ed. Indianapolis: Hackett.

Knack, Stephen (1992), "Civic Norms, Social Sanctions, and Voter Turnout." *Rationality and Society* 4, 2 (April): 133–156.

Knetsch, Jack, Richard Thaler, and Daniel Kahneman (1987), Reluctance to Trade: An Experimental Refutation of the Coase Theorem. Public Choice, *Tucson, Ariz.* 3/27–30.

Knight, Jack and James Johnson (1994), "Aggregation and Deliberation: On the Possibility of Democratic Legitimacy." *Political Theory*, 22, 2 (May): 277–96.

Konow, James (1996), "A Positive Theory of Economic Fairness." *Journal of Economic Behavior and Organization*, 31, 1 (October): 15–35.

Konow, James (1997), *Fair and Square: Four Tenets of Distributive Justice*. LMU Working paper. Dept. of Economics, Loyola Marymount University, Los Angeles.

Konow, James (2003), Which is the Fairest of All? A Positive Analysis of Justice Theories. *Journal of Economic Literature* 61, 4, 1188–1239.

Krehbiel, Kenneth (1998), *Pivotal Politics*. Chicago: University of Chicago Press.

Kreps, David M. (1990), Game Theory and Economic Modelling. *Clarendon Lectures in Economics*, Oxford: Oxford University Press.

Kuhn, Steven T. (1996), Agreement Keeping and Indirect Moral Theory. *The Journal of Philosophy*, 93, 3 (March): 105–128.

Kuhn, Steven T. and Serge Moresi (1995), Pure and Utilitarian Prisoner's Dilemmas. *Economics and Philosophy*, 11 (October 1995): 123–33.

Laing, James D. and Benjamin Slotznick (1990), "The Pits and the Core: Simple Collective Decision Problems with Concave Preferences." *Public Choice*, 66, 3, 229–242.

Lakatos, I. (1970), "Falsification and the Methodology of Scientific Research Programmes," *in Criticism and the Growth of Knowledge*, I. Lakatos and A. Musgrave,eds., 91–97. Cambridge: Cambridge University Press.

Lambert, Karel and Gordon G. Brittan, Jr. (1970), An Introduction to the Philosophy of Science. Englewood Cliffs, New Jersey: Prentice Hall.

Lasswell Harold Dwight (1935), Politics, Who Gets What, When, and How. New York: New York: McGraw-Hill.

Ledyard, John O. (1995), "Public Goods: A Survey of Experimental Research," in *The Handbook of Experimental Economics*, John H. Kagel and Alvin E. Roth, eds., Princeton, New Jersey: Princeton University Press, 111–194.

Lijphart, Arend (1999), *Patterns of Democracy: Government Forms and Performance in Thirty-Six Countries*. New Haven: Yale University Press.

Lohmann, Susanne (1994), "The Dynamics of Informational Cascades: The Monday Demonstrations in Leipzig, East Germany, 1989–91." *World Politics*, 47, 1 (October): 42–101.

Lohmann, Susanne (2000), "Collective Action Cascades: An Informational Rationale for the Power in Numbers." *Journal of Economic Surveys*, **14**, 5, 655–84.

Luce, Duncan and Howard Raiffa (1957), *Games and Decisions*. New York: Wiley. (Reprinted: NY: Dover, 1985.)

Mackie, Gerry (2003), *Democracy Defended*. Cambridge: Cambridge University Press.

Maioni, Antonia (1998), *Parting at the Crossroads: The Emergence of Health Insurance in the United States and Canada*. Princeton: Princeton University Press.

Maxwell, Nicholas (1972), "A Critique of Popper's Views on Scientific Method." *Philosophy of Science* (June): 131–152.

May, K.O. (1952), "A Set of Independent, Necessary, and Sufficient Conditions for Simple Majority Decision." *Econometrica*, **20**, 4 (October): 680–4.

May, Kenneth O. (1954), "Intransitivity, Utility, and the Aggregation of Preference Patterns." *Econometrica*, **22**, 1, (January): 1–13.

McGuire, Martin and Olson, Mancur (1996), "The Economics of Autocracy and Majority Rule: The Invisible Hand and the Use of Force." *Journal of Economic Literature*, March, **34**, 72–96.

McKelvey, Richard D. (1976), "Intransitivities in Multidimensional Voting Models and Some Implications for Agenda Control." *Journal of Economic Theory*, **12**, 472–82.

McKelvey, Richard D. (1986), "Covering, Dominance, and Institution Free Properties of Social Choice." *American Journal of Political Science* **30** (May): 283–314.

Michels, Robert. (1915). *Political Parties*. Hearst's International Library. Republished in 1959 by Dover Publications: New York.

Miller, David (1975), "The Accuracy of Predictions." *Synthese* **30**, 159–191.

Miller, David (1991), "Deliberative Democracy and Social Choice." *Political Studies*, **40** (special issue), 54–67. Also reprinted (2002) in Democracy, ed. David Estlund, Oxford, Eng.: Blackwell: 289–307.

Miller, Gary J. (1981), *Cities By Contract: The Politics of Municipal Incorporation*. Cambridge, Mass: MIT Press.

Miller, Gary, (1992), *Managerial Dilemmas: The Political Economy of Hierarchy*. New York: Cambridge University Press.

Miller, Gary J., and Joe A. Oppenheimer (1982), "Universalism in Experimental Committees." *American Political Science Review*, **76** (2, June): 561–574.

Miller, Gary J. and Thomas Hammond (1994), Why Politics is More Fundamental Than Economics: Incentive-Compatible Mechanisms are Not Credible. *Journal of Theoretical Politics* **6**, 1, (January): 5–26.

Miller, Gary J. and T. H. Hammond (1990), "Committees and the Core of the Constitution." *Public Choice*. **66**, 3, 201–228.

Miller, Nicholas R. (1983), "Pluralism and Social Choice." *American Political Science Review*, **77**, 734–747.

Miller, Nicholas R. (1980), "A New Solution Set for Tournaments and Majority Voting: Further Graph-Theoretical Approaches to the Theory of Voting." *American Journal of Political Science*, **24**, 1, (February): 68–96.

Miller, Nicholas R. (2007), "In Search of the Uncovered Set." *Political Analysis*, **15**, 1, 21–45.

Mueller, Dennis (1978), "Voting by Veto." *Journal of Public Economics*, 57–75.

Mueller, Dennis C. (2003), *Public Choice III*. Cambridge: Cambridge University Press.

Moore, Don A., and George Lowenstein (2004), Self-Interest, Automaticity, and the Psychology of Conflict of Interest. *Social Justice Research*, **17**, 2 (June): 189–202.

Morris, Irwin (2000), *Congress, the President, and the Federal Reserve: The Politics of American Monetary Policymaking*. Ann Arbor: University of Michigan Press.

Nagel, Thomas (1991), "Legitimacy and Unanimity," in *Equality and Partiality*. Chap **4**, 33–40. New York: Oxford University Press.

Ng, Yew-Kwang (1983). "Individualistic social welfare functions under ordinalis a reply to Mayston." *Mathematical Social Sciences*, **4**, 3, 305–307.

Niskanen, William A. Jr. (1971), *Bureaucracy and Representative Government*. Chicago: Aldine.

Nola, Robert (2004), "Pendula, Models, Constructivism and Reality." *Science and Education*, **13**, 349–377.

Nola, Robert and Howard Sankey (2000), "A selective survey of theories of scientific method." In Robert Nola and Howard Sankey, (eds.) *After Popper, Kuhn and Feyerabend*. London: Kluwer Academic Press: 1–65.

North, Douglass C. and Barry R. Weingast (1989), "Constitutions and Commitment: The Evolution of Institutional Governing Public Choice in Seventeenth-Century England." *Journal of Economic History*, **49**, 4 (December): 803–32.

Nozick, Robert (1974), *Anarchy, State and Utopia*. New York: Basic Books.

Olson, Mancur (1965), *The Logic of Collective Action*. Cambridge, Mass: Harvard University Press.

Olson, Mancur (1993), "Dictatorship, Democracy, and Development." *American Political Science Review*. **87**, 3 (September): 567–576.

Olson, Mancur (1969), "The Principle of Fiscal Equivalence." *AER* **59**, 479–487.

Olson, Mancur and Richard Zeckhauser (1966), "An Economic Theory of Alliances." *Review of Economics and Statistics*, **48**, 266–279.

Oppenheimer, Joe A. (1985), "Public Choice and Three Ethical Properties of Politics." *Public Choice* **45**, 241–255.

Oppenheimer, Joe A. (2002), "Considering Social Justice: A Review of David Miller's Principles of Social Justice." *Social Justice Research*. **15**, 3 (September): 295–311.

Oppenheimer, Joe and Norman Frohlich (2007), "Demystifying Social Welfare: Foundations for Constitutional Design." *Maryland Law Review*, **67**, 1, 85–122.

Oppenheimer, Joe Stephen Wendel, Norman Frohlich (2011), Paradox Lost: Explaining and Modeling Individual Behavior in Social Dilemmas. *Journal of Theoretical Politics* **23** (June): 1–23.

Oppenheimer, Joe A., Norman Frohlich, Cyrus Aghamolla, and Maria Dimitriu (2010), *Some Democracies Are More Equal than Others: Using Social Welfare as a Metric for Political Evaluation*. (Mimeo: College Park, University of Maryland.) Originally presented at 2008 American Political Science Association annual meeting, Boston, 2008. http://www.bsos.umd.edu/gvpt/oppenheimer/research/somedemos.pdf

Ostrom, Elinor (1994), "Constituting Social Capital and Collective Action" in Local Commons and Global Interdependence: Heteorgeneity and Cooperation in Two Domains, R. O. Keohane and E. Ostrom, eds. A special issue of the *Journal of Theoretical Politics.* 6, 4, 527–562.

Ostrom, Elinor (1998), "A Behavioral Approach to the Rational-choice Theory of Collective Action: Presidential Address, APSA 1997." *American Political Science Review*, 92, 1 (March): 1–22.

Ostrom, Elinor (2003), "How Types of Goods and Property Rights Jointly Affect Collective Action." *Journal of Theoretical Politics*, 15, 3, 239–270.

Ostrom, Elinor (1990), "*Governing the Commons: The Evolution of Institutions for Collective Action.*" Cambridge: Cambridge University Press.

Ostrom, Elinor and James Walker (1991), "Communication in a Commons, Cooperation without external Enforcement," in *Laboratory Research in Political Economy*, ed. Thomas R. Palfrey, 287–322. Ann Arbor: University of Michigan Press.

Ostrom, Elinor, James Walker, and Roy Gardner (1992), "Covenants with and without a Sword: Self-Governance is Possible." *American Political Science Review*, 86, 2, (June): 404–417.

Ostrom, Elinor, Roy Gardner, and James Walker (1994), *Rules, Games, and Common-Pool Resources.* Ann Arbor: University of Michigan Press. 1994.

Palast, Greg (2002), *The Best Democracy Money Can Buy.* London: Pluto Press.

Pigou, Arthur Cecil (1912), *Wealth and Welfare* London: Macmillan and Co.

Piven, Frances Fox and Richard A. Cloward (1977), *Poor People's Movements.* New York: Vintage.

Plott, Charles (1967), "A Notion of Equilibrium and its Possibility Under Majority Rule." *American Economic Review*, 57 (September): 787–806.

Plott, Charles (1976), "Axiomatic Social Choice Theory: An Overview and Interpretation." *American Journal of Political Science*, 20, 3 (August): 511–594.

Plott, Charles R. (1983), "Externalities and Corrective Policies in Experimental Markets." *The Economic Journal*, 93 (March): 106–127.

Popper, Karl (1959), *The Logic of Scientific Discovery.* New York: Harper and Row. [First Edition, 1934.]

Powell, G. Bingham (2000), *Elections As Instruments of Democracy: Majoritarian and Proportional Visions.* New Haven: Yale University Press.

Preston, Lee E. (1961), "Utility Interactions in a Two-Person World." *Journal of Conflict Resolution.* 5, 4, 354–365.

Quine, Willard Van Orman (1951), "Two Dogmas of Empiricism." *Canadian Journal of Philosophy* 21, 265–274.

Prior, A. N. (1970), "Correspondence Theory of Truth." *Encyclopedia of Philosophy.* 2. New York: Macmillan, 223–232.

Przeworski, Adam (1999), "Minimalist Conception of Democracy: A Defense" in Ian Shapiro and Casiano Hacker-Cordon, eds., *Democracy's Value.* Cambridge: Cambridge University Press: 23–55.

Rasmusen, Eric (1989), "Games and Information: An Introduction to Game Theory." Oxford: Blackwell Publishers.

Rawls, John (1958), "Justice as Fairness." *Philosophical Review.* 67.

Rawls, John (1971), *A Theory Of Justice*. Cambridge, Mass: Harvard University Press.

Rawls, John (1985), "Justice and Fairness: Political not Metaphysical." *Philosophy and Public Affairs*. **14**, 3 (Summer): 223–251.

Rawls, John (1993), *Political Liberalism*. New York: Columbia University Press.

Rawls, John (2001), *Justice as Fairness: A Restatement*. Cambridge, Mass: Harvard University Press.

Regenwetter, Michel, Jason Dana, and Clintin P. Davis-Stober (2008), "Testing Transitivity of Preferences on Two-alternative Forced Choice Data." *Frontiers in Quantitative Psychology and Measurement*, Jan 2011.

Riker, William H. (1982), *Liberalism Against Populism: A Confrontation Between the Theory of Democracy and the Theory of Social Choice*. Prospect Heights, IL.: Waveland Press.

Riker, William (1962), *The Theory of Political Coalitions*. New Haven: Yale University Press.

Riker, William H. (1982), *Liberalism Against Populism: A Confrontation Between the Theory of Democracy and the Theory of Social Choice*. Prospect Heights, IL.: Waveland Press.

Riker, William H. and Ordeshook, Peter C. (1968), "A Theory of the Calculus of Voting," *American Political Science Review* **62**, 25–42.

Riordon, William L. (1994), *Plunkitt of Tammany Hall*. Boston: Bedford Books of St. Martin's Press.

Rogowski, Ronald (1999), "Institutions as Constraints on Strategic Choice" in David A. Lake, and Robert Powell, eds., *Strategic Choice and International Relations*. Princeton, N.J.: Princeton University Press: 115–135.

Romer, Thomas and Howard Rosenthal (1978), "Political Resource Allocation, Controlled Agendas and the Status Quo." *Public Choice* **33**, 4, 27–43.

Roth, Alvin, E. (1995), "Bargaining Experiments" in Kagel, John H. and Alvin E. Roth, eds. (1995) *The Handbook of Experimental Economics*. Princeton: Princeton University Press: 253–342.

Samuelson, Paul (1955), "A Diagrammatic Exposition of a Theory of Public Expenditure. *Review of Economics and Statistics*, **35** (November): 350–6.

Samuelson, Paul (1954), "The Pure Theory of Public Expenditure." *Review of Economics and Statistics*, **36** (November): 387–89.

Sayre-McCord, Geoffrey (1988), "Introduction: The Many Moral Realisms" in *Essays on Moral Realism*, ed. Geoffrey Sayre-McCord. Ithaca, NY: Cornell University Press, 1–26.

Schapera, Isaac (1956), *Government and Politics in Tribal Societies*. New York: Schoken Books.

Schelling, Thomas C. (1973), "Hockey Helmets, Concealed Weapons, and Daylight Savings: A Study of Binary Choices with Externalities." *Journal of Conflict Resolution*, **17**, 3 (September): 381–428.

Shepsle, Kenneth A. and Mark S. Bonchek (1997), *Analyzing Politics: Rationality, Behavior, and Institutions*. New York: W.W. Norton Publishers.

Shepsle, Kenneth A. and Barry R. Weingast (1984), "Uncovered Sets and Sophisticated Voting Outcomes with Implications for Agenda Institutions." *American Journal of Political Science*, **28**, 1 (February): 49–74.

Shepsle, Kenneth A. and Barry R. Weingast (1981), "Political Preferences for the Pork Barrel: A Generalization." *American Journal of Political Science*, 25, 1 (February): 96–111.

Schofield, Norman (1978), "Instability of Simple Dynamic Games." *Review of Economic Studies*. 45, 575–594.

Schotter, Andrew (1990), *Free Market Economics: A Critical Appraisal*, 2nd Edition. Chapter 7: "Blame Free Justice." Cambridge, Mass: Basil Blackwell, Inc., 121–32.

Schultz, Kenneth A. (2001), *Democracy and Coercive Diplomacy*. Cambridge: Cambridge University Press.

Schumpeter, Joseph (1909), "On the Concept of Social Value." *Quarterly Journal of Economics*, 23, 2 (February): 213–32.

Schwartz, Thomas (1981), "The Universal Instability Theorem." *Public Choice*, 37, 3, 487–502.

Sen, Amartya K. (1966). "A Possibility Theorem on Majority Decision." *Econometrica*. 34, 491–499.

Sen, Amartya K. (1970), *Collective Choice and Social Welfare*. New York: North Holland Publishing.

Sen, Amartya K. (1970b), "The Impossibility of a Paretian Liberal." *Journal of Political Economy*. 78, (January/February): 152–7.

Sen, Amartya K. (1973), *On Economic Inequality*. New York: Norton.

Sen, Amartya K. (1977), "Rational Fools: A Critique of the Behavioral Foundations of Economic Theory." *Philosophy and Public Affairs* 6, 4 (Summer): 317–344. Reprinted in Jane J. Mansbridge, ed., Beyond Self-interest. Chicago: University of Chicago Press.

Sen, Amartya K. (1981), *Poverty and Famines: An Essay on Entitlement and Deprivation*. Oxford: Clarendon Press.

Sen, Amartya (1992), *Inequality Reexamined*. Cambridge, Mass: Harvard University Press.

Sen, Amartya (1993), "Capability and Well-Being" in Amartya Sen and Martha Nussbaum, eds. *The Quality of Life*. Oxford: Oxford University Press: 30–53.

Sen, Amartya (1999a), *Development as Freedom*. New York: Random House.

Sen, Amartya (1999b), "Democracy as a Universal Value." *Journal of Democracy* 10, 3, 3–17.

Sen, Amartya (2002), "The Possibility of Social Choice" in *Freedom and Social Choice*. Cambridge, Mass: Harvard University Press: 65–118.

Sen, Amartya (2009), *The Idea of Justice*. Cambridge, Mass: Harvard University Press.

Sened, Itai (1997), *The Political Institution of Individual Rights*. Cambridge: Cambridge University Press.

Shepsle, Kenneth A. and Mark S. Bonchek (1997), *Analyzing Politics: Rationality, Behavior, and Institutions*. New York: W.W. Norton Publishers.

Shepsle, K. and Barry Weingast (1981), "Structure Induced Equilibrium and Legislative Choice." *Public Choice*, 37, 3, 503–520.

Shepsle K. (1979), "Institutional Arrangements and Equilibrium in Multidimensional Voting Models." *American Journal of Political Science*, 23, 1 (February): 27–59.

Simon, Herbert (1992), Bounded Rationality: Discussion, in: *Bounded Rationality and the Cognitive Revolution*; Massimo Egidi and Robin Marris, eds. Brookfield, VT: Edward Elgar.

Skitka, L. J. and D. Houston (2001), When due process is of no consequence: Moral mandates and presumed defendant guilt or innocence. *Social Justice Research*, **14**, 305–326.

Smith, Adam (1759), The Theory of Moral Sentiments.

Smithies, Arthur (1941) "Optimum Location in Spatial Competition." *Journal of Political Economyy* **49**, 423–439.

Snow, Edgar (1968), *Red Star over China*. New York: Random House. (Grove Press First revised and enlarged Edition.)

Standage, Dominic I., Thomas P. Trappenberga, and Raymond M. Klein (2005), Modelling divided visual attention with a winner-take-all network, *Neural Networks* **18**, 620–627.

Strang, Colin (1960), "What if Everyone Did That?" *Durham University Journal*, **53** (1960), 5–10. Reprinted in Baruch A. Brody, ed., *Moral Rules and Particular Circumstances*, 135–144. Englewood Cliffs, New Jersey: Prentice Hall, 1970.

Tenbrunsel, Ann E. and David M. Messick (2004), Ethical Fading: The Role of Self-Deception in Unethical Behavior, *Social Justice Research*, **17**, 2 (June): 223–236.

Thaler, Richard H. (1986). "The Psychology and Economics Conference Handbook: Comments on Simon, on Einhorn and Hogarth, and on Tversky and Kahneman." *Journal of Business*, **59**, 4, Pt. 2, S279–S284.

Thomson, David (1992), "Generations, Justice, and the Future of Collective Action" in Peter Laslett and James S. Fishkin, eds., *Justice Between Age Groups and Generations Groups and Generations* 206–235. New Haven: Yale University Press.

Thurow, Lester (1971), "The Income Distribution as a Pure Public Good." *Quarterly Journal of Economics*, **85** (May): 327–336.

Tiebout, Charles (1956), "A Pure Theory of Local Expenditures." *Journal of Political Economy*, **64** (October): 416–24.

Tsebelis, George (2002), *Veto Players: How Political Institutions Work*. Princeton: Princeton University Press.

Tullock, Gordon (1977), The Demand Revealing Process Coaltions, and Public Goods" in *Public Choice*, XXIX-2, Special Supplement to Spring 1977: 103–106.

Tullock, Gordon (1981), "Why so much stability?" *Public Choice*. **37**, 2 (January): 189–204.

Tversky, Amos and D. Kahneman (1981), "The Framing of Decisions and the Psychology of Choice." *Science* **221** (January): 453–458.

Tversky, Amos and Daniel Kahneman (1986), "Rational Choice and the Framing of Decisions." *Journal of Business*, **59**, 4, Pt. 2, s251–s278. Reprinted in Karen Schweers Cook and Margaret Levi, eds., The Limits of Rationality. Chicago, Ill.: University of Chicago Press.

Tversky, Amos and Daniel Kahneman (1992), "Advances in Prospect Theory: Cumulative Representation of Uncertainty." *Journal of Risk and Uncertainty*, **5**, 4, (October): 297–323.

Tversky, Amos and Daniel Kahneman (1973), "Availability: A Heuristic for Judging Frequency and Probability." *Cognitive Psychology*, 5, 2, 207–232.

UN (2005). UN Millennium Development Goals: http://www.un.org/millennium goals/index.htm.

Valavanis, Stefan (1958), "The Resolution of Conflict When Utilities Interact." *The Journal of Conflict Resolution*, 2, 156–69.

Veenhoven, Ruut (2009), World Database of Happiness: Tool for Dealing with the 'Data-deluge.' *Psychological Topics* (special issue on Positive Psychology), 18, 221–246.

von Neumann, John and Oskar Morgenstern (1944), *Theory of Games and Economic Behavior*. Princeton: Princeton University Press.

Wagner, Richard (1966), "Pressure Groups and Political Entrepreneurs: A Review Article." Papers on Non-Market Decision Making: 161–170.

Weingast, Barry R. (1979), "A Rational Choice Perspective on Congressional Norms." *American Journal of Political Science*, 23 (May): 245–262.

Weingast, Barry R. (1994), "Reflections on Distributive Politics and Universalism." *Political Research Quarterly* 47 (June): 319–327.

Weingast, Barry R. (1997), "The Political Foundations of Democracy and the Rule of Law." *American Political Science Review*, 91, 2 (June): 245–263.

Weingast, Barry R. (2002), "Rational Choice Institutionalism" in *Political Science: The State of the Discipline*, Ira Katznelson and Helen Milner, eds. New York: W.W. Norton & Co., 660–692.

Wendel, Stephen and Joe Oppenheimer (2010), "An Analysis of Context-Dependent Preferences in Voluntary Contribution Games with Agent-Based Modeling." *Journal of Economic Psychology* 31, 3 (June): 269–284.

White, Alan R. (1967), "Coherence Theory of Truth." *Encyclopedia of Philosophy*, 2, New York: Macmillan, 130–132.

White, Alan R. (1970), *Truth*. Garden City, NY: Doubleday Anchor.

Wilson, Rick K., Jörn P. Scharlemann, Catherine C. Eckel, and Alex Kacelnik (2001), "The Value of a Smile: Game Theory with a Human Face." *Journal of Economic Psychology*, 22, 617–640.

Young, Peyton H. (1974), "An Axiomatization of Borda's Rule." *Journal of Economic Theory*, 9 (September): 43–52.

Zeckhauser, Richard and Elmer Shaefer (1968), "Public Policy and Normative Economic Theory" in Raymond A. Bauer and Kenneth J. Gergen, eds., *The Study of Policy Formation*. New York: Macmillan, The Free Press, 27–101.

Name Index

Subject Index